The Modern Station

Brian Edwards

The Modern Station

New approaches to railway architecture

E & FN SPON
An Imprint of Chapman & Hall

London · Weinheim · New York · Tokyo · Melbourne · Madras

Published by E & FN Spon, an imprint of Chapman & Hall, 2–6 Boundary Row, London SE1 8HN, UK

Chapman & Hall, 2–6 Boundary Row, London SE1 8HN, UK

Chapman & Hall GmbH, Pappelallee 3, 69469 Weinheim, Germany

Chapman & Hall USA, 115 Fifth Avenue, New York, NY 10003, USA

Chapman & Hall Japan, ITP-Japan, Kyowa Building, 3F, 2-2-1 Hirakawacho, Chiyoda-ku, Tokyo 102, Japan

Chapman & Hall Australia, 102 Dodds Street, South Melbourne, Victoria 3205, Australia

Chapman & Hall India, R. Seshadri, 32 Second Main Road, CIT East, Madras 600 035, India

First edition 1997

©1997 Brian Edwards

Typeset in 9.5/12pt Helvetica 45 by Fox Design, Guildford

Printed in Great Britain by the Alden Press, Oxford

ISBN 0 419 19680 3

A catalogue record for this book is available from the British Library

Contents

Contents

Preface

Stations are one of the most important modern building types. They perform a variety of functions, besides giving access to trains: they are shopping malls, meeting places and urban landmarks. Like airports, stations are distinctive and complex places – helping to shape and define the cities they serve by their social, cultural and functional interactions. Stations are also where the architecture of space and the engineering of structures meet. The nature of this meeting is the essence of railway architecture.

Stations are more relevant today than at any time since the nineteenth century. The 'green' age has ushered in a new generation of different types of trains – from Eurostar and TGV to the quiet unassuming electric tram. Trains transport people with only a fraction of the greenhouse gases produced by planes, cars and buses, and move them from city centre to city centre, not city edge to city edge. Trains and their stations are part of the essential infrastructure of the environmental age, and one of the means by which we can renew the inner city.

Railway architecture is about space, light and structure. All three are necessary components if customer satisfac-

tions are to be met. These three elements provide a framework of legibility and of sensual uplift. The new breed of stations illustrated in this book bring these elements to new heights of architectural expression.

The perception of route and space made manifest through natural light and bold, dynamic structure is one of the prime objectives of station design. At a more detailed level, the play of materials, transparency, textures and construction joints provides further richness and expressive opportunities, and helps to give the traveller a sense of order in complex places.

This book is a guide and hopefully an inspiration to those who design, commission and manage stations. It is an attempt to set out the principles of good railway architecture, drawing upon examples recently built in Europe and further afield, others still on the drawing board, and yet others that have become classic examples from the past. The book is a balance between technical and functional dictates on the one hand and traveller perceptions of safety and comfort on the other.

Acknowledgements

No author can write a reliable guide to the design of modern railway stations without considerable help from those actively engaged in the many aspects of the process.

Both individual architects and architectural practices have provided indispensable assistance in the development of the theory, knowledge and case studies contained within these pages. Of the former I should particularly like to acknowledge the helpful guidance of Jane Priestman, Nick Derbyshire, Ian Hurst, Roland Paoletti, Alan Brookes, Michael Edwards, Alec Colbeck, Robert Evans and Tony McGuirk at various stages in the production of the book. Of the latter, many practices in the UK and abroad have furnished me with answers to queries, plans and photographs for publication. Without mentioning them all, I acknowledge my particular gratitude to Sir Norman Foster and Partners, Santiago Calatrava, Jourda and Perraudin, Austin-Smith: Lord, Building Design Partnership, Troughton McAslan, Nicholas Grimshaw and Partners, Michael Wilford and Partners, Ahrends Burton and Koralek, Terry Farrell and Partners, Richard Rogers Partnership, Renzo Piano Building Workshop, Arup Associates, Michael Hopkins and Partners, Aéroport de Paris, and Holland Railconsult.

Mention should also be made of public or quasi-public bodies who have provided information and critical commentary – notably South Yorkshire Passenger Transport Executive, Greater Manchester Passenger Transport Executive, London Underground, British Rail and Eurostar.

I acknowledge a debt also to the University of Huddersfield for providing the support needed to travel, research and write this book.

Finally, I wish to record my debt to Linda Stanley for combing newspapers for articles of relevance to ensure that the technical perspectives were well balanced by social, political and cultural ones.

Introduction

1 King's Cross Station, London: proposed new transport interchange designed by Sir Norman Foster and Partners. The triangular glass facade is designed to reflect the listed facades of the two adjacent stations. Although unlikely to go ahead in this form, the design captures well the spirit of the new railway age.

The design of railway stations is one of the more challenging and rewarding fields of practice today. The opportunity to enhance the public realm and to balance engineering with more practical considerations results in a building type of particular relevance and visual complexity. As a typology the railway station employs a distinctive architectural language of large-span roofs, grand entrance halls, interior concourses and wide public entrances. The great passenger stations of the nineteenth century were one of the engineering miracles of their age, and a high point of urban design. St Pancras Station in London, Penn Central in New York and Gare de l'Est in Paris were all celebrations of a powerful social, economic and cultural force, and a visible manifestation of the fusion of architecture and engineering. Today, after half a century of neglect of the railway infrastructure when public investment was directed worldwide to road construction, the ecological benefit of rail travel combined with technical breakthroughs in high-speed trains has resulted in a renaissance of interest in railways.

The great passenger station was one of the most important new building types of the nineteenth century. There were no parallels in terms of feats of engineering, scale of human movement, or complexity of function. Designers generated highly inventive design solutions, which exploited the potential of the new materials of iron and glass, new methods of site construction and prefabrication, and new professional organizations. It is no coincidence that the granting of the Royal Charter to the Institute of British Architects in 1837 occurred at the peak of railway exploration and construction in the capital. Architecture and railways benefited from each other's development, and look to do so again as governments return, on environmental and social grounds, to travel by train.

The UK, which led other nations in the development of a comprehensive railway network, has been one of the last nations to signal a return to the train. France, the Netherlands, Japan and even the USA have, for ecological and energy reasons, begun to invest more of their capital expenditure on railways than on road building. The UK, too, has started to realize that the quality of life, especially in cities, continues to deteriorate under the impact of cars and ever more road construction. In 1994, the UK joined with much of Europe in re-addressing the balance in public investment between road and railway building, partly under pressure from the influential Royal Commission on Environmental Pollution. After undermining the rail system for much of the twentieth century, the UK and most of Europe is now embarking upon ambitious plans to have an integrated transport system where travel by air, rail, bus and car are part of a smoothly functioning and publicly regulated system.

Ecological concerns are one of the justifications for this change in emphasis. Car travel threatens the health of the global environment and that of our children. It is now widely recognized that car use at present levels is not sustainable. Even if the roads could be created for predicted increases in car use the resulting destruction to the communities and fabric of cities would no longer be tolerated. Railways represent a better long-term investment, especially in technically advanced, highly congested areas such as Europe and the Pacific Rim. With air travel reserved for intercontinental journeys, the railways are ideally placed to serve internal communications between such places as London and

2 King's Cross Station, London: view of model of proposed concourse linking rail and underground system designed by Sir Norman Foster and Partners.

3 The well-being of cities depends upon integrated transportation systems. Here in Genoa new underground railway stations such as San Giorgio are being constructed to designs by Renzo Piano to relieve traffic congestion.

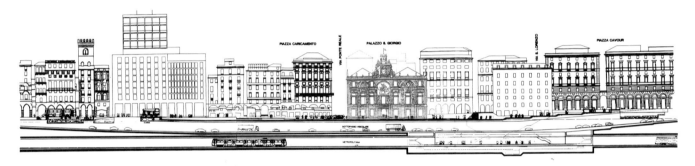

Paris, Washington and New York, Barcelona and Madrid, Tokyo and Osaka.

For journeys up to 3 hours' duration the train is currently competitive in time, comfort and price with air travel. With technical innovations, such as the French TGV system, the railways could in the future usurp aircraft for journeys that today take 5 hours. The advantages of rail travel are obvious: one usually journeys from city centre to city centre; there is space and peace enough on the train to work or even hold business meetings; and the journey is more relaxing and less interrupted than by air. With the skies becoming more crowded and airports more costly to build, high-speed intercity travel by rail is rapidly proving more popular for governments and customers alike.

The past decade has seen three particular areas of development for railways. The first is the introduction of technically sophisticated high-speed rail systems crossing national boundaries. A good example is the TGV network extending across much of Western Europe, which by the year 2000 will have 14 000 kilometres of high-speed lines.[1] A second distinctive field of development has been the linking of airports to city centres by new railway routes. Governments have begun to realize that in developing transport systems the linkages between the parts are important: hence Santiago Calatrava's airport station at Lyon-

Satolas, Paul Andreu's station at Paris-Charles de Gaulle airport and Austin-Smith: Lord's station at Manchester Airport. The third area of growth in railway investment has been in the development of metro or light rail systems. These have the benefit of reducing congestion, especially that caused by car commuting. In the UK the extension of the Jubilee Line to London Docklands with Canary Wharf Station by Sir Norman Foster, in Los Angeles a revived Metro system with stations by Ellerbe Becket, and in Berlin the upgraded and extended Bahnhof line with stations by Sir Richard Rogers, all promise to bring fresh new architecture to inner city areas.

Recent Dutch stations are further evidence, in Europe at least, that railway architecture has entered a new age. There is a geometric simplicity in Dutch architecture that finds particular expression in the railway architecture of the state railway designers Holland Railconsult, led mainly by Harry Reijnders and Peter Kilsdonk. Their approach to design is based upon an understanding of traveller needs (comfort and light) and passenger concerns (safety and security) balanced by good proportion and skilful handling of open interior volumes. Brightly lit at night, the sun-drenched atrium-like station spaces during the day ensure that public concourses and waiting rooms in recent Dutch stations feel safe and friendly to use. The large glazed spaces are

4 A new generation of railway architecture has emerged to serve new high-speed trains. In these the structural engineer and architect have collaborated to produce adventurous and poetic stations, such as Lyon-Satolas by Santiago Calatrava.

5 New tunnelling techniques have opened up a fresh generation of underground railway stations. Underground railways (unlike urban motorways) also allow new forms of mass transportation to be constructed in cities without destroying the urban fabric. Architects: Renzo Piano Building Workshop.

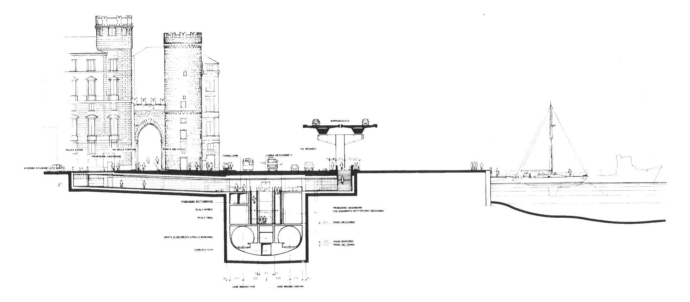

warm during the day and glow at night. Overheating is effectively dealt with by a combination of fixed external shading on the south and west sides and the air currents of passing trains, which provide effective and regular cooling. Added to this, Reijnders' stations (at Sloterdijk, Amsterdam and Rotterdam Blaak, for example) are a sophisticated play of cubes, cylinders and circles, some tilted in daring fashion. With the addition of colour, often in bold primaries, the compositions begin to approach the abstraction of a de Stijl painting. This is particularly true of major urban stations, where daring modern design is used to express their role as landmark buildings.

Passenger stations are the architectural manifestation of the railway system. They are both the gateway to the rail network and the point of entry for passengers entering the city. The interface between the two worlds – the railway system and the urban backcloth – gives the railway station particular significance as architecture. Many great passenger stations are essential elements in the life and culture of cities. They form handsome cliffs of masonry to the outer edge, great cavernous spaces inside, and teaming centres of social and economic exchange. Both London and Paris would be unthinkable as urban experiences without the fine passenger terminals that serve them.

At the smaller scale, railways both serve and shape their communities. The outward growth of suburban rail systems led to the establishment of thriving suburbs in many cities earlier in the century. Even today the building of new railways, many based upon light rail, gives shape to new communities, or helps – as in London Docklands – in reshaping old ones. Railways have led to the growth of edge-cities in the past, and as generators of economic activity can do much to revitalize depressed urban neighbourhoods today.

It is now realized that railways and the architecture that serves them are 'cultural and social as much as an economic force'.[2] As such, the passenger stations and great termini

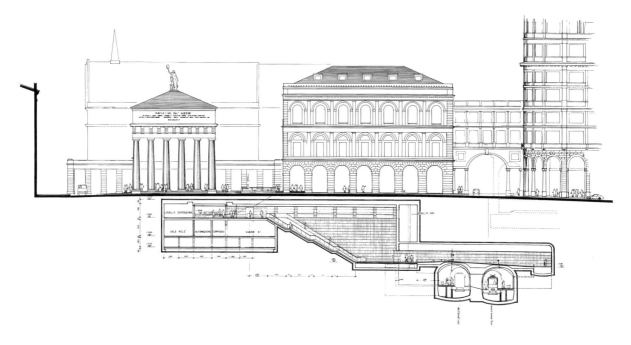

6 Efficient public transport allows cities to be given over to civilized values based upon pedestrian and cycle movement. Architects: Renzo Piano Building Workshop.

7 Stations have traditionally provided city centres and suburbs alike with distinctive public buildings. This recent station at Redhill in Surrey, England, by architects Troughton McAslan won the Brunel Award for the best small European station in 1992.

have a distinctive railway typology. Not all recent railway station design has recognized the distinctiveness of the traditions of railway architecture. The redevelopment of London's Euston Station in the 1960s led not only to the ignominious removal of the handsome neoclassical Euston Arch (symbolic of the urban gateway) but replaced a distinctive Victorian railway station by one that recalled a second-rate airport. What is interesting about the current renaissance in railway architecture is the way designers from Calatrava to Grimshaw have recognized the need to celebrate the new railway age with eye-catching designs. Their buildings are heroic in spirit, and give a sense of drama to movement and arrival. Technology is not hidden

but expressed; space is not disguised by timid detailing but highlighted by bold lighting effects and exaggerated scale. This book is an attempt to give shape and meaning to the architecture of contemporary railways, to highlight issues facing designers, and to suggest through exemplar case studies the direction that railway stations will be taking in the future.

References

1. Kenneth Powell, 'New directions in railway architecture', *Architecture Design Profile* No. 109, 1994, p. 17.
2. *Ibid.*

Part one

Perspectives
on station
architecture

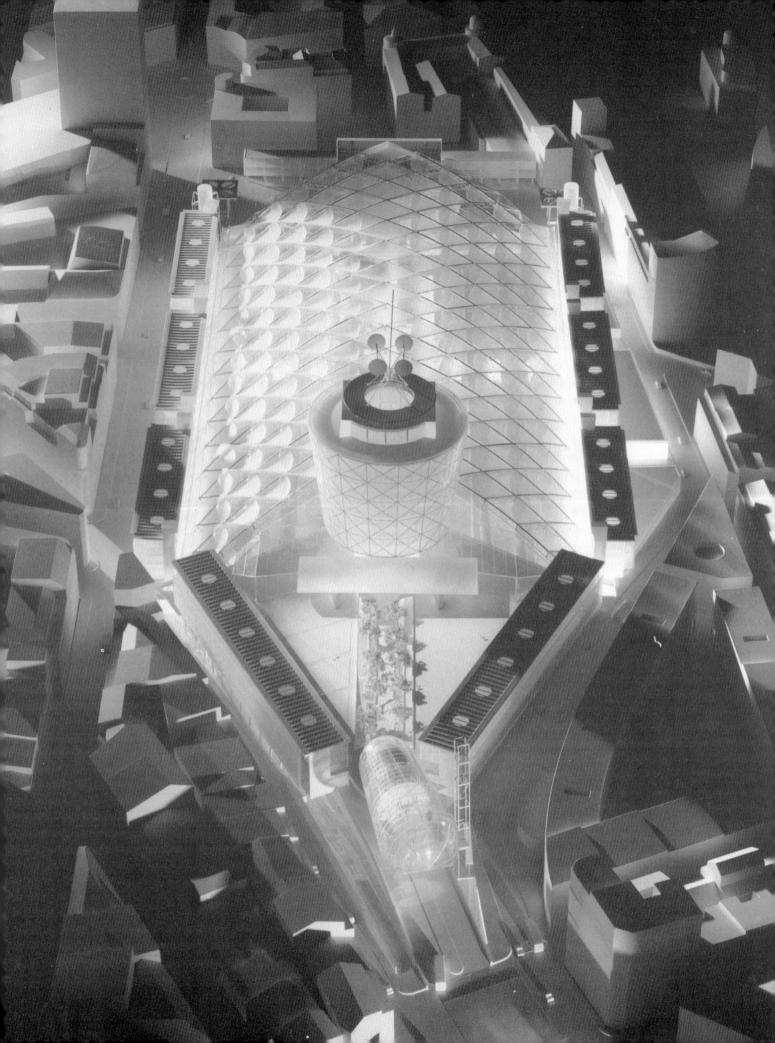

The politics of railways

Railways and economic well-being

The future of railways looks good. International environmental agreements such as those made by many world governments at the Rio Summit of 1992, and the increasing imperative to move towards more sustainable patterns of urbanization, have fuelled a return to rail investment. The reasons are obvious: railways provide transport of goods and people at less energy cost than most other forms; new technology is making rail movement cheaper, faster and smoother; and roads take more land, cause greater pollution and are more dangerous than travel by train. Added to these advantages is the fact that people can work or eat while taking the train (of benefit to many business travellers). Richard Rogers has described modern, intercity trains as moving piazzas where you meet people, eat, and watch contemporary life roll by.[1] Also, as people travel from city centre to city centre by train, rather than from suburb to suburb, the effect is to reinforce town centres as hubs of culture and commerce, as against city edges, which car travel tends to support.

As demand for travel grows, road congestion is forcing a realignment from motorway to railway construction. Because of greenhouse gas generation (mainly CO_2), such investment is justified in global warming terms alone. The wider case for rail, embracing a broader range of environmental and social factors, is also increasingly accepted by governments from Japan to the USA. One aspect of the UK Conservative government's justification for the privatization of the railways is that private capital will be attracted to help create a more sustainable transport framework, where road and rail are not so much competing but complementing each other. In other countries (in Germany and France for instance) more direct state investment is on the basis that railways are more efficient, safer and less environmentally damaging than other modes of transport.

Transport is not a luxury but a product of economic growth. The movement of people and goods is essential for national prosperity. As motorways become more congested and air travel is restricted by community safeguards, rail emerges as the most benign of alternatives. Railways are not without their environmental and community impacts,

1.1 Major stations are great economic magnets, which draw investment to their hinterland. Unlike airports, railway stations promote the regeneration of town centres not city edges. This design by Michael Wilford and Partners is for the Abando Interchange in Bilbao.

1.2 Urban regeneration and the upgrading of transportation systems need to go hand-in-hand. Here at La Défense new metro stations and a TGV link ensure that an office community of nearly 100 000 is well integrated with the remainder of Paris.

1.3 (left) Stations direct the flow of huge numbers of people. The station entrance is the point where transportation and the economic and social dimension of cities interface. This design for the new Canary Wharf Station on London's Jubilee Line by Sir Norman Foster and Partners expresses in its curved glazed carapace the sense of urban arrival.

1.4 (above) Light rail systems can help to upgrade the economy of cities and improve their image. Here the Manchester Metrolink, using street space at the expense of cars, enhances tourist and visitor potential.

but relatively speaking these are less than with competing systems.

Heavy rail on the surface and light rail underground or in the streets is the pattern in many cities. For inter-urban transport, surface rail serving centrally located termini or main-line stations is the usual pattern. Such stations then give direct access to metro-type services, which frequently run underground (as in London or Paris) or overground (as in Manchester or Sheffield). As speeds increase on heavy rail, the distance between stations also increases. With the French TGV train able to travel at around 300 mi/h (480 km/h) and the Japanese Bullet trains at about 250 mi/h (400 km/h), they are able to compete in time with travel by air. With stops about once per hour, stations can be as far as 200 miles (320 km) apart. Where journeys require frequent intermediate stops, these tend to be served not by electrically powered units but by diesel, which readily achieves speeds of 130 mi/h (200 km/h), yet has the acceleration to make frequent stops.

A hierarchy of rail provision from international, national, regional and local services seems set to become established in the more populous regions of the world. Europe has set an example with the TGV service linking France to Germany, Spain, Holland and soon also to the UK. Below this level,

national services such as the UK's InterCity and then regional railways (such as Network SouthEast) provide the next level of provision down. At the city level, services such as London's expanded Jubilee Line to Docklands and Barcelona's excellent modernized underground provide the level of provision between regional railways and buses.

The various levels tend to be funded separately and served by different types of stations and designs of rolling stock. Though one may talk of a railway system, in reality it consists of a network of companies serving quite distinct transport needs. This is reflected at the level of design, where trains, stations and ticketing systems have quite distinctive characteristics depending upon the type of provision being used.

As railways expand, national characteristics will gradually disappear. Train technology and carriage design in one country will appear in many others, just as they did in the nineteenth century, when steam locomotives built on the Clyde were exported to India and China, and Scottish engineers built railways in Burma. The high-speed railway system of Europe takes French trains into the heart of London and Seville. The architecture of stations will also break down national boundaries. A well-designed station in one region will be taken as a model in another. Just as motorways and

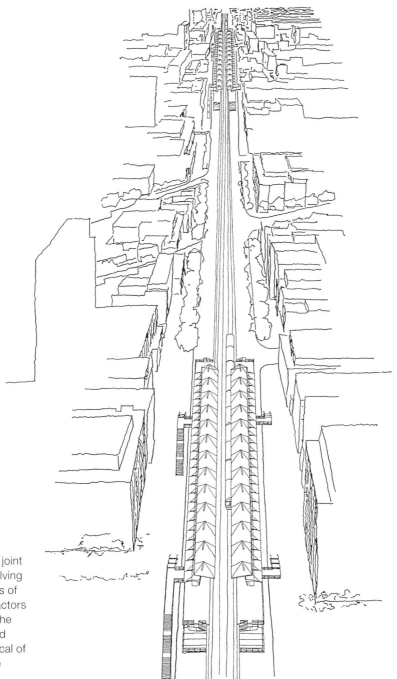

1.5 Many new railway schemes are the result of joint investment initiatives involving public and private sources of funding, often with contractors taking a financial stake. The new street-based elevated railway in Bangkok is typical of partnership funding in the Pacific Rim.

their service areas look much the same in different countries, railways will gradually lose their regional characteristics. If distinctiveness is to survive in rolling stock and station design, it will be found in local systems not international ones. Here the stamp of indigenous design and engineering may leave its mark, just as the Paris Metro did at the end of the last century.

Relaxing political control of railways

Political parties worldwide are relaxing their grip upon the running of national railways. The trend, most marked in the UK, USA and Japan, is to invite private corporations to take on the complicated business of operating the railway system. This entails not only the sale to different companies of the track, but also the trains and stations. Without a single unifying vision for the railways, as had been adopted successfully by British Rail (BR) since nationalization in 1948, the railway system is set upon a path of fragmentation of estate, of diversification of operation, and the franchising-out of services. In terms of design, what was once a coherent aesthetic system of signs, rolling stock and station architecture seems likely to separate into a host of different design ambitions. With some 25 new operating

1.6 Grand older stations such as Union Station, Washington, lend themselves to a variety of retail and commercial uses while still providing access to trains.

companies, each possibly employing its own architectural, industrial or graphic designer, the visual landscape of stations and trains will quickly diversify. Where unity and control was exercised until recently by BR's Design Director Jane Priestman, the future holds the prospect of a range of corporate images, a variety of architectural styles, and a wide spectrum of interior designs.

The shift from aesthetic purity to pluralism of design will inevitably follow the UK government's decision of 1994 to privatize British Rail. Instead of BR's Architecture and Design team being responsible, either directly or through its briefing of private architectural consultants, for the design of stations, signal boxes and the like across the BR empire, now the separate companies will appoint their own designers. Where once a spirit of public service reigned, the privatized railways in the UK and elsewhere appoint their architects through competitive fee tendering for design services. A lowering of standards is a possible consequence; a loss of expertise built up over decades is inevitable without effective design guidance. What is also likely is the emergence of railway architecture fashioned by competing designers working for companies set in competition with each other. Here 'design' may no longer be serving the wider commu-

nity, but helping franchisers to improve their market penetration.

In the UK the infrastructure of 10 000 miles of railway track and most of the 2500 stations will be owned by Railtrack Group Plc after 1996. Railtrack, which remains at the time of writing a nationalized company subject to UK Treasury control, will be responsible for the track, signalling and maintenance (but not operation) of the stations. These, excluding 14 of the mainline stations and termini in London and other major cities, will be owned and operated by the major train companies using the stations. Stations and track are therefore being separated in ownership management and in terms of design delivery. Twenty-five new operating companies will run the stations on a leasehold arrangement with three different companies, which will own the rolling stock. A similar arrangement of three regional freight companies will run the non-passenger services. These 25 franchise companies will operate in different geographical areas and will be appointed on the basis of competitive bidding. They have, under the Railways Act passed by the British Parliament in 1993, power to set train timetables in collaboration with the Franchising Director. BR Infrastructure Services remains to carry out maintenance

1.7 Waterloo International Station is typical of the division between the station as real estate and Eurostar as the main operating company using the station. The orchestration of different interests at the station requires the architect to be a design coordinator, using design briefs and guides to regulate the station environment. Architect: Nicholas Grimshaw and Partners.

of the track system for a two-year period while Railtrack is being established.

The system may have the benefit of a single political vision, but it is complex at an operational level. Travellers at mainline stations may find that more than one operating company has a franchise: hence there may be a choice of tickets with different fare structures. There may also be a collection of ticket booths (each with a different design) selling tickets and operating services. Stations will begin to approach the character of a covered market, with not only railway companies selling a variety of services but retailers and restaurateurs competing for the passengers' attention. The importance of good building design cannot be underestimated in maintaining an intelligible environment in such circumstances.

At present the UK government subsidizes BR with an operating grant of £1.8 billion per year. The intention of the changes in ownership and management is gradually to remove this over a 15-year period. A 'rail regulator' appointed by government to protect the interest of consumers provides one, rather thin, safeguard to such radical plans. The implications for the management of railway stations is quite clear: they will increasingly come under pressure to maximize earnings, not just from the sale of tickets but from other things such as soft drinks, food and commodities. Where the great railway termini were once part of the public realm of grand enclosed urban spaces, they will gradually shift their emphasis towards semi-private shopping malls. Free access may be controlled; 'dwell time' for those with money to spare may be exploited by 'creative' timetabling.

Designers and managers of the railway estate have a role to play in providing an open, democratic railway architecture available to all classes and for a variety of uses besides the maximizing of profits. Privatization of the railways may well bring efficiency gains, but should not diminish choice or undermine the station as a great and largely unique building type.

Privatization of bus services in the UK in 1982 led to the loss of 20% of passengers over a ten-year period. Bus passengers were deterred by the fragmentation of local services and increase in fares. Although the rail regulator has powers to require 'minimum passenger services', this

may not provide the guarantee of quality and cost that travellers require. In France and the Netherlands, railways are viewed more as social services than in the UK, where the present government (in 1995) maintains that only private investment and private control of former public assets can deliver a modern railway infrastructure. As with other public utilities, architecture is at the mercy of political ambition.

From road to rail investment: changing governmental priorities

Many European governments are reviewing their planning and development processes to encourage a change from

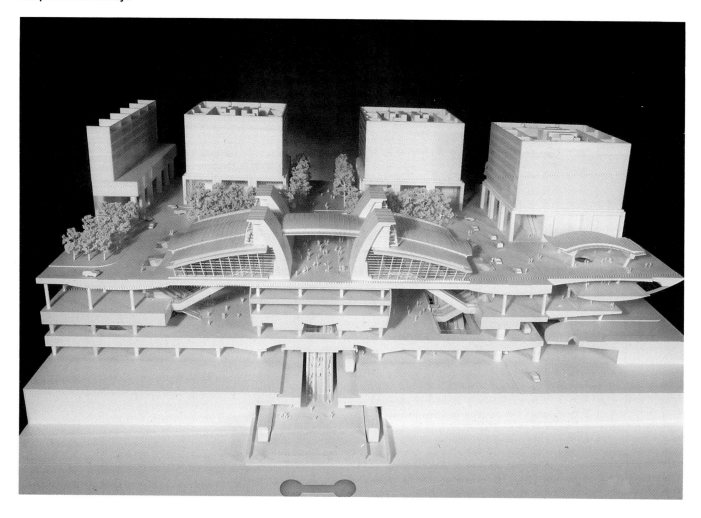

1.8 New stations are often multiple interchanges where heavy rail, light rail, bus and taxi facilities meet. Here at Kowloon Station, designed by Terry Farrell and Partners, commercial and public interests overlap, making the station a new node of Hong Kong's economy.

car to rail use. In the UK, Planning Policy Guidance (PPG) note 13 on transport suggests that the shift from private to public means of transport has wider community as well as environmental benefits. Such benefits range from the social and economic integrity of towns to the recent realization that funding for public transport represents better value for money for the taxpayer than does road construction. Two important principles embodied in EU law are undermining car usage: the concept that the 'polluter pays' is beginning to impact upon a fuller assessment of the environmental costs of private transport, and the notion that Europe's cities are an essential part of a region's cultural inheritance is discouraging the construction of urban roads and motorways. Without further roadbuilding, the growth in car ownership is likely to lead either to 'grid-lock' levels of congestion or to road pricing. Both are effective constraints, and the latter is increasingly mooted as desirable policy for governments seeking to implement their responsibilities entered into at the Rio Summit.

Transport is an essential prerequisite for modern life. The question is how to gain access to the benefits of contemporary civilization (employment, recreation, attractive housing, education) without destroying the environment of the planet, the health of city dwellers and the fabric of towns in the process. Much current policymaking at governmental level is concerned with establishing the right balance between public and private means of transport, between inter-urban and local journeys, between freedom of movement for the rich and the poor, and between able-bodied and disabled people. In urban areas, congestion is economically inefficient and environmentally damaging. Managing demand and use for road space (through pricing and traffic calming) coupled with improvement to public transport is the preferred strategy of many Western governments. Improvements to public transport entail, besides investment in various types of rail provision, support for connecting bus and tram services, and the notion of compact corridors of development along rail routes. As the switch to public transport gathers momentum, land-use planning and urban design policies will need to follow suit. Widespread low-density development will no longer be permitted or sustainable.

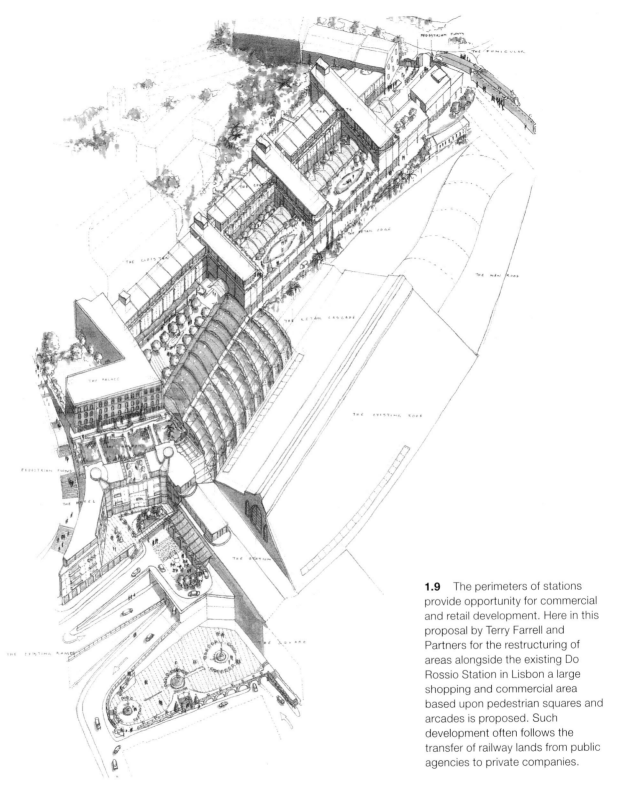

1.9 The perimeters of stations provide opportunity for commercial and retail development. Here in this proposal by Terry Farrell and Partners for the restructuring of areas alongside the existing Do Rossio Station in Lisbon a large shopping and commercial area based upon pedestrian squares and arcades is proposed. Such development often follows the transfer of railway lands from public agencies to private companies.

Where existing rail provision exists, one can predict a revival of economic activity around the stations, both for housing and for industrial uses. Where new development is under consideration this will only be viable in the long term (20–50 years) if it has access to public transport. Urban development and public transport will increasingly be under-taken in parallel (as the Dutch case studies illustrate; see Chapter 7). To facilitate this change in emphasis, existing rail track must be maintained; new road and building construction should not, for instance, cut across a redundant railway route (thereby preventing its reopening later). In its report *This Common Inheritance*, the UK government

1.10 A new generation of high-speed trains has led to the construction of a fresh generation of stations throughout much of Europe. Here a TGV train sits incongruously beneath the nineteenth-century platform roof at Gare de Lyon Station, Paris.

1.11 Urban railways can do much to relieve congestion, reduce greenhouse gas production, and revive inner city areas. Architects: Renzo Piano Building Workshop.

in 1990 signalled the desirability of examining the integration of land-use policy, environmental policy and transport investment. The balancing of road and rail investment in the mid-1990s heralds the cultural change that has followed this examination.

The settlement structure in most Western countries is already in place. What may not fit so smoothly is the relationship between development and access. Recent rail investments (such as TGV in France, Metro line extensions in Berlin and London, light rail in Lyon and Manchester) all seek to achieve a better balance between population, employment and economic viability. Adjustments to the settlement pattern are slow and expensive. With more homeworking and part-time employment, the relationship between house and factory is changing. Not only does this reduce the demand for transport, it also generates new patterns of movement and fresh methods of communication (such as telecommuting). The provision of light rail and metro systems, which have seen significant growth in Europe, Pacific Rim countries and North America, are driven by these broader social changes. Rather than change the pattern of development (though this is desirable with low densities in the long term), it is easier to connect suburbs and local towns by new rail systems.

In theory, as the car loses its cultural and social superiority, there begins to emerge a new urban order based upon public and individual non-car transportation. The three scales of rail provision (heavy rail, light rail and underground), buses, cycles and walking will constitute the main means of journeying within and between towns into the next century. The environmental, health and community benefits will lead to restraint upon car and lorry usage. The importance of design, safety and security with public transport should not be underestimated. Design has 'sold' cars throughout much of the twentieth century; design needs to do the same for the railway system and its stations.

A few simple principles help to smooth the transition from private to public means of transport within urban areas:

- intensification of land-uses and levels of activity around existing stations;
- development along public transport corridors;
- integration of land uses to discourage the need for car-based journeys;
- provision of secure cycle storage at railway stations and in new commercial development;
- incentives to encourage movement of goods by rail rather than road through pricing and fiscal policy.

At a practical level, the UK government in 1992 removed a parliamentary obstacle to the construction of new rail

1.12 Airport stations are a relatively new phenomenon. At Manchester Airport the station stands guard over the usual means of travel to airports – the car. Planners are increasingly conscious of the social and economic benefits of integrating air, rail and car transportation systems. Architects: Austin-Smith: Lord.

lines. Until then, light rail schemes and metro extensions required a private Act of Parliament, which had to compete for legislative time with government business. Under the Transport and Works Act 1992 such consent is deemed to be granted as long as the proposal was embedded within an adopted development plan (under Town and Country Planning Acts). This allows local authorities to move more speedily towards the construction of public transport systems. In place of Private Bills, the law now requires no more than an order made by the appropriate minister. Generally, the order will be granted subject to a local public inquiry but without reference to Parliament (unless it is deemed to be of national importance). As a safeguard, the 1992 Act requires that an 'environmental statement' is provided. The statement will normally evaluate and describe the impacts – including design. Such a provision provides for the employment of architects at the beginning rather than at the end of the design and engineering process.

Reduced car use, coupled with a railway system that is reliable, safe and attractive, is the cornerstone of policy throughout much of Europe (though at the time of writing less conspicuously of the UK than of her EU partners). A single European market with a single European currency and freedom of movement across national borders harbingers a new railway age. The need to achieve sustainable patterns of development has led to a reappraisal of different modes of transport. The railways have proved to be the most environmentally acceptable way of moving people and goods. The lesson of Birmingham and Los Angeles is that, without railways of one form or another, traffic congestion will under-

mine the economic and to some extent social viability of large urban areas. It is no surprise to find that those cities that advocated private means of transport with the greatest vehemence are the ones that in the 1990s are moving most speedily towards public transport.

Integrating rail and car use

The report in November 1994 of the Royal Commission on Environmental Pollution heralded a significant change in contemporary transport philosophy. Its proposals, which included doubling petrol tax, abandoning a policy of out-of-town development, and the halving of government spending on roads, are seen by many as a watershed in quasi-official thinking. Implicit in the report is a shift from private to public means of transport, and particularly a political and cultural move from an almost iconic regard for the car to an acceptance of the environmental benefits of mass transit.

In parallel, a report of the House of Commons Environment Select Committee (also of November 1994) recommended, amongst a raft of 40 policy changes, a correspondence between transport and planning policy in the UK. What particularly concerned the MPs on the Committee was the continuing development of suburban retail and business parks, whose survival depends upon ready access by car. As both reports highlight, the indiscriminate and unregulated use of the private car is no longer sustainable from three important points of view – global warming, urban air quality and public health.

1.13 Investment in new railway technology by the French government has allowed France to export its engineering and design expertise around the world. Eurostar has helped to take this know-how to England and Belgium. This view is of the French terminal of Eurotunnel near Calais, designed by Paul Andreu.

1.14 European rail investment over the past decade has led to dramatic railway architecture. This station, to link the French TGV rail system to Lyon Airport, is a notable example. Architect: Santiago Calatrava.

1.15 Mainline stations need also to provide an element of integration with the car. Here at Waterloo International car, bus and taxi access is provided at various points. Architects: Nicholas Grimshaw and Partners.

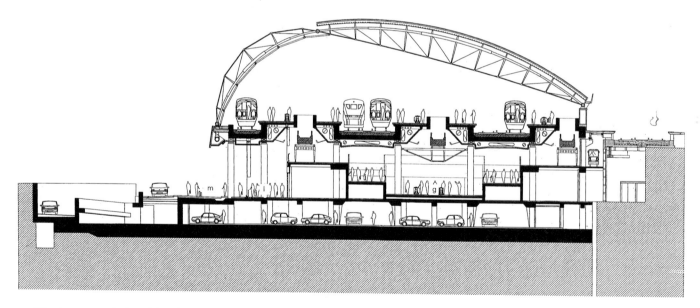

The two reports herald a significant change in direction, and one that will be to the benefit of railways. If, as the Environment Select Committee wants, future retail and office growth is located near to town centres, then urban rail systems will benefit. Not only will this increase rail usage and revenue, it will also encourage the kind of integration of station and development already evident at London's Liverpool Street Station and at EuroLille.

There are no plans to ban the car; merely to encourage alternative means of transport by establishing a better fit between development trends and public transport infrastructure. The car has its place in the rail system by providing access to stations. The combination of local trips by car and regional journeys by rail has many benefits from environmental, social and business points of view (workers can be productive on trains but hardly while driving along

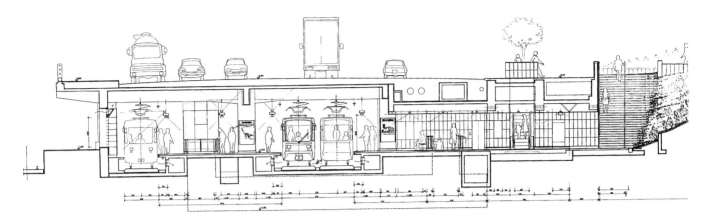

1.16   Road and rail systems work most effectively when they are physically integrated. Here at Dinegro Station in Genoa, designed by Renzo Piano Building Workshop, direct car access and casual parking allow travellers to interchange readily between systems.

1.17   Suburban stations need in particular to cater for travellers arriving by various means: cycle, taxi, bus, car and on foot. All five means are represented in this design by Alan Brookes Associates for a new station near Watford, north of London.

motorways). To date, in the UK the 'company car' and business mileage tax thresholds have been to the rail system's disadvantage. Both the Royal Commission and Select Committee's reports have pointed to the incentives in taxation that discourage business travellers (who make up 40% of long-distance motorway journeys) from using the railways. In order to promote greater rail use by this section of the community, InterCity has developed 'park and ride' tickets whereby a secure parking space at a station is provided in conjunction with a rail ticket.

There are implications in these wider policy changes. If stations and urban development are to be closely combined in dense pedestrian prioritized packages, then the nature of the station and the city will change. We shall in effect see a return to the nineteenth-century pattern of diversified land uses focused upon a great bustling railway station. This compares with the somewhat sanitized model represented by London's Euston Station or Birmingham's New Street Station, where open plazas and largely single patterns of activity prevail. Another, and arguably more worrying, trend will be towards the 'station as car park' concept. If 'park and ride' is to be expanded, then suburban and country stations will need to be surrounded by secure, well-lit parking areas. This makes physical integration between station and town difficult to achieve in terms of social aspects of urban design, and has the effect of isolating the station as a landmark. If ready access by road to stations is to be given greater priority, then stations threaten to be cut off from their urban hinterland by large-scale road construction along their frontage (Sheffield Station is a good

example). The resolution of these problems through case studies is discussed later.

Funding urban railways

Few urban railway schemes (as against inter-urban), whether light or heavy rail, are cost-effective in terms of the revenue generated by passengers' fares. Most are justified because of the reduction in air pollution or congestion, or because of the economic benefits that flow to adjoining land. These wider benefits allow government (national, regional or local) to subsidize investment in new railway projects, or to prop up existing lines. As such, railways have advantages beyond normal cost–benefit analysis, and this gives them value over and above more orthodox laws of accountancy.

Those who design and promote railway schemes are well aware that most projects are not profitable by fares alone, and seek to involve all those who will benefit in helping to fund their schemes. It is well known that railways are efficient movers of people; that air pollution is greatly reduced by persuading people to travel by train rather than by car; that railways are good for the image of a town (Sheffield Supertram for example); and that property developers reap windfall profits from railway investment. For these reasons, those who promote railway schemes look to a wide range of government subsidies (in the UK often involving the EU) and support from property developers and building owners along the line. Those with property near stations benefit particularly; not only does the value of the land increase but also that of the property on it, and

1.18 Providing parking spaces and access for buses at station entrances encourages the smooth transition between transport systems. Duivendrecht Station, the Netherlands. Architect: Peter Kilsdonk, Holland Railconsult.

1.19 Railways are expensive undertakings, and often require the support of adjoining landowners, property developers or direct stakeholding by the private sector. The extension eastwards into London Docklands of the Jubilee Line depended upon a significant investment in its construction from Olympia and York, the developers of Canary Wharf. This view shows a model of the Canary Wharf Station as designed by Sir Norman Foster and Partners.

1.20 A new generation of double-decker trains promises to improve rail efficiency, reduce passenger congestion and revive many marginal routes. This Siemens-designed train is being operated by NS, the Dutch national railway company.

hence rents rise. The increase in land values often leads to redevelopment of land near to stations, thereby allowing developers to further exploit the economic benefits of railway construction. These windfall gains allow promoters of railway projects legitimately to expect a contribution from major property developers. This was precisely the argument that persuaded Olympia and York to pay £400 million towards the Jubilee Line extension to Canary Wharf in London Docklands.

John Kellett has shown that in Victorian Britain the railways brought wide economic advantages to urban areas.[2] Warehousing initially and later commercial development flowed from investment in railways, the economic benefits spreading outwards from main to secondary stations. As new termini were often built on the edge of central business areas, or on land cleared from insanitary slums, Victorian railways were perceived as aiding the commercial growth of cities. Such growth led to new business centres being established, which not only had economic advantages but, in the eyes of many city councils, aesthetic ones as well. Much of the argument used in support of railway schemes in the nineteenth century centred upon the commercial and social benefits of railway construction to inner city neighbourhoods.

It is the economic benefit of railway construction that has led to the renewal of Lille in northern France. Here, as in Victorian England, a large new interchange to serve the TGV and Eurostar network has encouraged the development of new offices, shopping and cultural facilities on the station's doorstep. The marriage of mutual advantage between railway and property development leads inevitably to a situation where the station is merely part of a large tract of urban development. This is precisely what Canary Wharf and Lille represent: in both cases quality is determined not by questions of station design alone but by urban design and economic benefit.

Success or failure of railway schemes is, in the public's eye at least, determined by their effect upon the quality of urban life. Social, economic and aesthetic benefit are today as mutually supportive as they were in the railway expansions of the nineteenth century. Stations that are well connected to buildings, that are well used, and which are valued by the communities they serve, are worthwhile investments. Railway schemes that enhance the quality of life for people in towns will be valued, irrespective of how they are funded. If the public value railways as civic assets, those who stand to gain financially are increasingly willing to invest in them. In Los Angeles a new metro system was subsidized by a tax

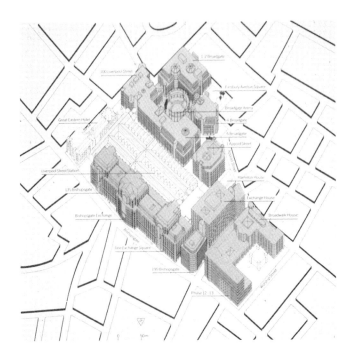

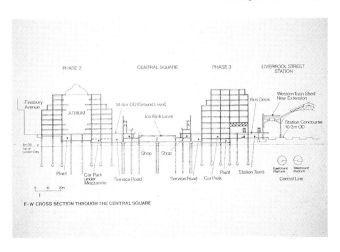

1.21 Investment in new or upgraded railways can be offset by integrating adjoining development with the railway estate. At London's Liverpool Street Station the commercial area of Broadgate was effectively linked to the refurbishment of the nineteenth-century station, with new shopping malls formed as connecting routes. Architects: Arup Associates.

on all business properties within half a mile of the proposed stations. The scheme for local taxation was advocated by local businessmen themselves, who recognized the commercial advantages that the metro line would bring.[3]

Railways bring broad advantages to corridors of towns and also more immediate benefits to those nearby. The redirecting of pedestrian flows at a station entrance, for example, to take people past new shopping arcades (as at Kensington High Street Station on the London Underground or at Liverpool Street Station by British Rail) can enhance shop rentals. The opportunities to exploit urban design by a coalition of railway and property-owning interest, to the commercial advantage of both parties, has been a growing feature of recent railway development across the world. The economic consequences of increasing pedestrian flows around stations have led to promoters of railway schemes deliberately arranging joint funding of projects with adjacent property owners. The logical conclusion of this approach is to design the station as a gateway to a large urban development, with the property owner becoming the lead investor, simply leasing space within the complex for the railway station, as at EuroLille. Although such projects are easier to fund than standalone stations, the identity of the station tends to be lost, and the management of it shifts from those with railway experience to general property managers.

Exploiting the commercial benefits of station building has aesthetic and urban design advantages. The trend towards joint funding of railway schemes and property development brings clear advantage to each party. Mixed-use development of a community nature adjacent to or above stations is, however, less easy to fund, as housing sits less happily alongside railway stations than do offices or shops. On the whole, partnership funding for railway schemes is supported by commercial developers with strong retail and office interests. Such developers can include local authorities anxious to ensure that social facilities such as sports halls or even whole new towns are an economic success. In the Netherlands, railway construction and the infilling of polders for large-scale housing development have been undertaken by a partnership of the state and private railways with similar economic interests in mind. In Paris, a new railway station at La Défense was paid for by the French government to help with the relocation of offices out of the centre of the city. La Défense, nearly the size of the Isle of Dogs Enterprise Zone in London, was not considered viable without adequate state investment in railway links.

The question of funding railway schemes is a complex one, and it is equally difficult to determine who benefits. As railways have broad social, environmental and economic advantages, the lead is often taken by a public-spirited city council or regional government. However, as land and property rise in value along the route of railway schemes, it is reasonable to assume that private developers should be financial stakeholders. Not only are there increases in building value (especially near proposed stations), but railway schemes can open up land for development that would have remained unattractive without the railway investment. Railways improve accessibility, and good access is a prerequisite for sustainable development – and, for that matter, for successful urban regeneration. The question is not so much who benefits from railway schemes but what is the scale of advantage for the different parties? Once the relative weight of advantage has been determined, it is easier to allocate a share of capital and revenue funding – particularly for projects, for example, that exploit air rights.

Where disputes occur over sharing the costs of railway schemes, local authorities can use their planning powers to insist that a developer makes a contribution. By withholding planning permission for development, the authority can force property developers wishing to build on land adjacent to stations to pay their share of the railway infrastructure which services their land. At Port Greenwich in the East Thames Corridor, British Gas paid £25 million towards the Jubilee Line extension to allow this large tract of derelict inner-city land to be developed, the contribution being a condition of planning consent.[4]

Working with developers at an early stage of designing railway schemes ensures not only that property development is well integrated with stations, but also that there is a sharing of financial risk between the parties. Well-knitted development is to everybody's advantage – government, users, communities and investors. The engineer's task, and that of architects, is to ensure that joint ventures (such as Terry Farrell's redesigned Charing Cross Station and the adjoining Embankment Place office scheme in London) do not compromise railway architecture by giving over-due weight to commercial interests. This is a particular problem when individual stations on a railway line are designed by different architects working for separate developers. Consistency of general design and detail, which the corporate imagery of railway companies such as SNCF or British Rail once imposed (and NS still do in the Netherlands) upon a network of stations, may become lost. Commercial developers have a natural concern to ensure that their contributions are reflected in an approach to design that corresponds with their (not the railway company's) architectural aspirations. Referring to Canary Wharf Station on the Docklands Light Railway, this station does not carry the colours and details elsewhere of the line but Olympia and York's grander language of design, evident in the nearby commercial development. Where other stations on the DLR have stridently painted red and blue steelwork and curved glass canopies, I.M. Pei's station employs white, grey and marble finishes reminiscent rather more of the Moscow Metro. The same is true of Waterloo International Station, which departs from the colour palette of the rest of the British Rail estate.

For a railway scheme to reach fruition, the promoter often has to win the support of a number of potential

1.22 Light rail or tram systems are relatively inexpensive, but their construction can greatly disrupt the economic life of streets chosen for their path.

developers along the line. They may already hold land and property, or may simply have indicated (as with the Toronto Subway in the 1960s and Vancouver Skyline in the 1980s) a willingness to act as commercial developers at different suburban railway stations. With a number of potential construction companies seeking to act as joint-venture developers of stations and adjacent land, the problem becomes one of maintaining the aesthetic coherence of the railway line as a designed system.

Developers can frequently subsidize railway schemes by exploiting the air rights over stations (as was common in the 1970s in the USA and more recently in Hong Kong) or by being given the option to redevelop surplus railway land (such as goods yards) alongside stations. Such land transfers to private developers from public or private railway companies may be sufficient to make an urban railway project viable. However, these partnerships tend to be undermined by different perceptions of value, cost and return on investment. Promoters of railway schemes are not usually motivated by profit but by public and environmental benefit. As such they take a long-term view of profit and loss. Commercial developers, on the other hand, seek to break even in ten years, after which they expect a regular return. Mixed-source investment, though it is increasingly a prerequisite for successful implementation of railway schemes, carries implications for the phasing and design of railway projects. It also has consequences for the make-

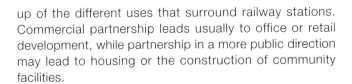

1.23 View of Lille-Europe station in the context of EuroLille, whose main tower helps to landmark the station. Architect: Rem Koolhaas.

1.24 Lille-Europe Station entrance and square. Architect: Rem Koolhaas, with Jean-Marie Duthilleul.

up of the different uses that surround railway stations. Commercial partnership leads usually to office or retail development, while partnership in a more public direction may lead to housing or the construction of community facilities.

The station as economic magnet: the example of EuroLille

Railway stations are important economic catalysts. They have in the past led to massive urban development, initially of warehousing and in the twentieth century of offices and retailing, and promise to do the same into the millennium. EuroLille, a massive edge-of-town development on the periphery of Lille in northern France, takes advantage of the social, cultural and economic advantages of an international rail junction. With cross-European railway systems focused upon Lille, the town has proved attractive to a collection of retail, leisure, conference and office developers. Just as motorway junctions in the 1970s and 1980s led to car-based edge cities, rail junctions in the 1990s are

proving major economic centres. The main difference is not one of scale or type of architecture, but of means of transport. EuroLille is reached by rail, not car, and as a consequence is a development that operates and feels as if it is part of the public rather than private realm.

As nations curb the car and reduce their expenditure upon road-building, the railways have taken on greater economic significance, with the station the centre of attention. This bodes well for architecture, which feeds off complexity of function, daring feats of engineering, and notions of community well-being. The advent of rapid-rail transport fuelled by the development in France of TGV has been to Lille's advantage. The town is now the centre of an ambitious rail network linking Paris, London and Brussels, and has a population of 70 million within two hours' travel time by train.[5] Such a powerful magnet has led to dramatic new architecture, both at the station and in the immediate hinterland.

The development, of 8 million ft² (740 000 m²) and costing £750 million, was masterplanned by the Dutch architect Rem Koolhaas. It consists of a large triangular

1.25 The integration of bus and rail services is needed if people are to be encouraged to abandon their cars. Here at Leiden Station in the Netherlands a new square at the station entrance has been formed, where interchange between bus, cycle and train systems has priority over private cars. The advantages to air quality and convenience are obvious. Architect: Harry Reijnders of Holland Railconsult.

1.26 Rail-based public transport reduces greenhouse gas emissions per passenger mile to about 20% of that of car use. The sustainable city is dependent upon the integration of transportation systems, with railways at their centre. Such integration need not be as visually damaging as this late nineteenth-century overhead railway in Paris.

three-storey shopping centre, through which a collection of towers of different uses (residential, office, conference, hotel) sprout in undisguised modern fashion. To one side stands a new city park; to the other an elevated roadway leading to the convention centre. Alongside the retail centre stands the new TGV station, not buried but visible, and engineered with the panache of Victorian ancestors. It is marked in the cityscape by a public square to the front, a finely detailed glass canopy over the platforms, and a pair of office towers directly above the station. In urban design terms, station and city fabric are well integrated; from an economic and social point of view both benefit from each other's presence. Nothing is banal about the architecture; technology is exploited and expressed on a superhuman scale.

At Lille the involvement of the city council, under its *major* Pierre Mauroy, encouraged a joint funding partnership of council, railway company and private developers. The explicit objective was to produce a model development of mixed-use urban architecture for an area that was once a desert of underutilized land and derelict buildings. Most shops were pre-let; different buildings have been

designed and constructed by different companies, with the result that EuroLille has the 'rich and dense mix of commercial and social activities that makes a successful metropolis buzz'.[6] Compared with Canary Wharf in London Docklands (the nearest development in the UK in scale of ambition), EuroLille demonstrates the business and aesthetic benefits of integrating large-scale commercial development with modern railway stations.

Environmental benefits of railways

The main environmental advantages of rail travel are the reduction in energy use and pollution over travel by road. Low-level air pollution caused mainly by vehicle exhausts is thought to account for 10 000 deaths a year in Britain alone. Intercity rail uses only 15% of the energy needed to move people by car, and suburban rail about 20%. There are obvious benefits from a global warming point of view for nations that invest in their railways. These wider advantages need to be balanced by local adverse environmental and community impacts (noise, air pollution, vibration), which occur with the construction and operation of new and

1.27 Stations provide the opportunity to civilize town centres by creating new squares and pedestrian routes. This unrealized design by Terry Farrell for a station in London shows the importance of railway architecture to the life of cities into the next century.

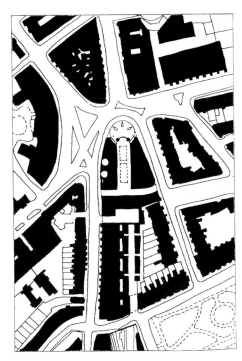

existing railway services. Too often the broader benefits that follow movement by rail rather than road (passengers and freight) are obscured by middle-class opposition along the route of proposed new lines or upgrading. Both in Kent, with the Channel Tunnel rail link, and in Provence with the extension of the TGV, local opposition has slowed down the construction of railways whose national benefits in environmental and economic terms are overwhelming.

The wider advantages of rail movement in reduced energy use (and hence less global warming gas production) are well catalogued. A shift from car or plane to rail brings significant environmental and climatic advantages. Taken worldwide, the change could be an important brake upon planetary temperature rise. These broader benefits are, however, too rarely perceived by those landowners and professional people who argue against the construction of new railway lines near their property. Under EU legislation, new railway infrastructure requires an environmental impact statement (EIS) to be prepared. The EIS then becomes a yardstick with which to compare one infrastructure project with another, and to balance local or regional impacts with wider environmental advantages. This means that the relative impacts of motorways, regional airports and railways can be compared for the first time.

Most EISs seek to quantify noise, air pollution, visual intrusion, vibration, ecological effects, impacts on resources of various kinds (agricultural land, minerals), heritage, severance and community disturbance. This list is by no means exhaustive, and with a railway line proposed through an area of natural beauty or along the coast, the balance of weight attached to various impacts would change.

It has to be remembered that per passenger carried, the scale of infrastructure for railways is less than for roads. A motorway has a far larger range of impacts (such as greater land loss, pollution, and severance) than a high-speed rail link. Only noise is significantly higher with railways, but here the noise is intermittent and can be effectively reduced by barriers, and by placing the tracks beneath ground in urban areas. There is little doubt that the movement towards sustainable development will help greatly to underpin the advantages of railways over other forms of transport, not only for local trips but for inter-urban and, in the future, international journeys.

References

1. The remarks were made by Sir Richard Rogers in his 'Future of cities' lecture at Manchester Town Hall, 21 June 1995.
2. John Kellett, *The Impact of Railways on Victorian Cities*, Routledge & Kegan Paul, London, 1969, pp. 115–116
3. Michael Schabas, 'Involving property developers', in N.G. Harris and E.W. Godward (Eds), *Planning Passenger Railways*, Transport Publishing Company Limited, Glossop, 1992, p. 217
4. *Ibid*, p. 225.
5. Martin Spring, 'Lille's on the fast track', *The Independent*, 26 October 1994, p. 26
6. *Ibid*.

Design types

What is a railway station?

Railway termini are a vital part of what makes places into great cities. The magnificent passenger stations in Tokyo, Washington, Helsinki, Milan and Bombay were built in response to economic and political ambitions in the nineteenth or early twentieth centuries, and gave their cities symbolic presence. The great masonry and glass railway stations converted otherwise worthless urban land (often slum-ridden, derelict areas) into highly desirable locations. They were external magnets drawing enterprise to their doorsteps, and internal commercial centres with shops, hotels and bars grouped around a grand civic space. Like a modern airport, the Victorian terminus was a small city controlled by the powerful industrialists of the railway age, set within a larger urban whole. This railway mini-city was enclosed by a protective wall, marked by grand entrances, and often landmarked with a clocktower, and fronted by a handsome hotel.

The modern railway station is a place where tourists, commuters, salesmen, retailers, train spotters and the homeless converge. The station is a microcosm of the city – it has the strengths and weaknesses of the urban whole neatly packaged beneath its roof. Just as the nineteenth-century termini attracted shoppers and political activists, today's big railway stations recall retail malls and hotel foyers. They are the point in the city where the greatest variety of land uses coalesce in the smallest most intense enclosed area. London's Liverpool Street Station after its refit in 1992 could easily pass for a conference centre, superstore or craft fair. Such complexity is good for the city, though many regret the infilling of massive station foyers with the bric-à-brac of retailing and fast food stores. 'Dwell time' is what station managers call the deliberate exploitation of the natural desire to stand, wait and gaze upon the spectacle of movement. Though stations express the manipulation of dwell time with particular finesse, the concept is common enough in art galleries and museums, where foyer shops are as attractive to visitors as the works of art on display.

If modern railway stations are beginning to look inside like shopping centres, it is simply because designers have learned to exploit the time that passengers wait around for

2.1 The traditional railway terminus was marked by a grand hotel and ostentatious office of the railway company. The legacy of this approach to design can be seen throughout the world, as here at St Pancras Station in London. What a modern station should look like is less readily prescribed.

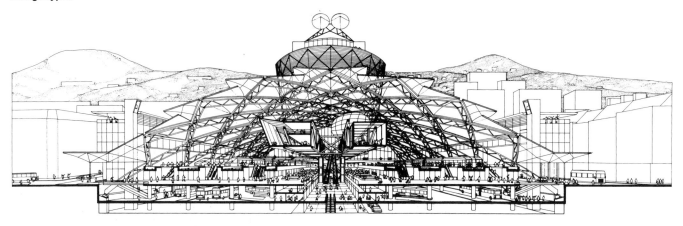

2.2 This complex interchange at Bilbao, which integrates under a single roof international, suburban and metro railways with regional bus services, is typical of the new generation of mainline railway stations. Architects: Michael Wilford and Partners.

2.3 The public concourses of stations, as here at Waterloo, are increasingly places of exchange – banks, currency dealers and fruit stalls all vie for the attention of travellers.

Unlike airports, railway stations do not have segregated arrival and departure levels. Passengers are not separated vertically, but intermix in great cross-currents of movement. Railway termini are usually at one level, diverse activities spreading beneath a magnificent glazed roof. Though Waterloo International Station departs from the norm (because of customs control), the most profound but brief experience of the station is that of the curving glazed shed above the platforms. It is this quality – the use of wide-span engineering technologies – that sets the modern station apart from the modern airport. Even where, as at Stansted Airport, the architecture exploits light and openness, it has little to compare with the spectacular column-free engineering of some Victorian railway stations. This is because stations generally twist in plan to reflect the configuration of railway tracks and allow the trains right into the centre. The graceful rippling curves of steel and glass that follow are quite unlike the straight-edged rectilinear airport buildings.

their trains. Small shops, burger bars and tourist information offices have grown up on the approach to ticket offices, feeding off the passengers arriving and leaving by train. As in the retail mall, one accepts higher prices in the small shops because they are convenient, have short queues, and offer just what a hungry traveller needs – neat packaged sandwiches, drinks of reliable quality, and flowers that keep their petals for the duration of a train journey. Those who cannot afford the goods beg for the small change at counters or sing for their living along exit routes. Taken together, the whole environment adds up to a powerful source of wealth and employment creation. What was once seen as part of railway infrastructure has become an essential element of a city's economic structure, begging the question of what exactly is a railway station.

Modern railway termini are an important expression of national and corporate prestige. Bilbao Station by Stirling Wilford and Hong Kong Station by Arup Associates make manifest the use of architecture to assert civic pride. At a more local level, town and suburban stations such as that at Woolwich in southeast London (by BR's Architecture and Design Group), Canary Wharf DLR Station (by I.M. Pei), Wood's Back Bay Station in Boston (by Kallman McKinnell) and Sloterdijk in the Netherlands (by Harry Reijnders of Holland Railconsult) proclaim an interest in using good design for wider social benefit. Without the multiplicity of uses that characterize bigger stations, the smaller town station can quietly serve community needs by attaching

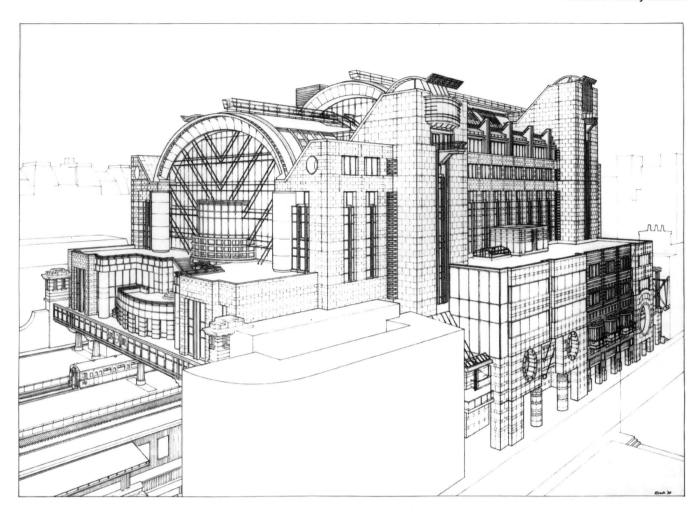

2.4 The physical distinction between station and commercial development has been eroded as air rights over platform areas have been exploited. Here at Embankment Place in London the lines into Charing Cross Station are now bridged by a new landmark building facing the Thames. Architects: Terry Farrell and Partners.

2.5 As here at Gare de Lyon in Paris, stations are plays of structure, light and volume. This quality, distinctive of few other building types, makes them immediately recognizable and memorable.

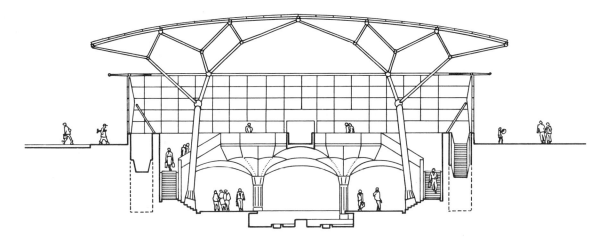

2.6 The key elements that help to define the station as a building type are canopy, column, stair and trackside. Each is skilfully expressed in this design by Jourda and Perraudin for Metro upgrading at Parilly Station in Lyon.

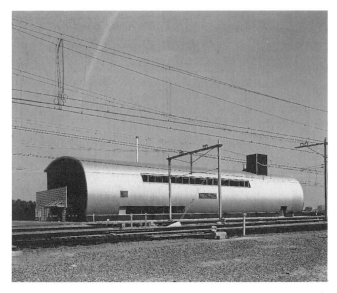

2.7 Engineering prowess is one of the defining elements of railway architecture. Architect: Wienke Scheltens of Holland Railconsult.

particular value to a kind of responsive design where safety, security and architectural dignity prevail (the model of Charles Holden's stations of the 1930s for London Underground is an obvious precedent).

The big international railway station consists of four separate domains, each serving a distinct functional or programmatic need. The most obvious and usually most ambitious space (in an architectural sense) is the main station concourse, where passengers, visitors and shoppers congregate. The second domain or functional zone is the booking halls, which are often designed as rooms within the larger space. The third consists of the platforms, where passengers board and alight from trains. This area may be divided by ticket barriers or left as part of the open public space. The fourth and final domain is the zone that the passenger rarely enters – the offices, stores, maintenance yards and railway tracks. Here the management of the station is undertaken, and the trains are shunted, serviced and prepared for their journeys.

Architecture and management respond in a direct fashion to these four separate domains. Traditionally the dis-

tinction between the first, second and third was marked by the transition from a great stone or brick enclosure to one of glass, with screens and islands of booking halls subtly hinting at the degree of preparedness for the journey. The sense of a landside and trackside environment is best seen from the air, where the different hand of architect or engineer is clearly distinguishable. Many of today's designers use these zonal divisions to articulate their buildings. Calatrava, in particular, strives to express the different functions at various parts of the station through the modification of his expressive structure, as at Zurich Station.

Under commercial pressure, railway stations are taking on the wider characteristics of the city. They are now shopping centres, locations of tourist attraction, places where security has grown in visibility, and points of destination separate from the need to journey. Railway stations are also gateways, where the first taste of national or civic pride can be asserted. For the less fortunate, they are places of shelter and sometimes comfort. When the question is asked what is a railway station, the answer is by no means as simple as it was a century ago. Stations have grown in

2.8 Huddersfield Station consists of two unrelated parts: a fine classical facade (which could be a court house), and a train shed behind. Modern railway architecture has, on the whole, integrated the two elements.

2.9 Enormous structural portals provide the means to signal the presence of Kowloon Station in Hong Kong. Architects: Terry Farrell and Partners.

economic complexity; have responded to wider shifts in social and cultural policy. The modern station is a contradictory and diverse creature, a place where architecture and technology come together in close and dramatic association with large numbers of people. It is these qualities that make the railway station almost unique as a building type, certainly a great challenge to designers, and one of the best symbols of civilized nationhood.

The station as urban gateway and landmark

Mass, long-distance travel is a phenomenon of the twentieth century. Only in the present century have large sections of the world population enjoyed as commonplace experiences continental and intercontinental journeys. Rapid transport by air or rail is one of the enduring characteristics of a mature industrial economy. Although sophisticated new forms of electronic communication make the movement of information a flicker of a computer screen, there remains much evidence that the actual movement of people is essential for conducting business, engaging in social contact, and contributing towards cultural well-being.[1]

Travel is an expression of a civilized society. The more people move, the greater the sense of personal freedom,

and the greater the degree of access to the pleasures and riches of the modern world. Transport is not a luxury, as it was in much of the eighteenth and early nineteenth centuries, but an essential component of the modern age. Railways, the first mass means of rapid transport, are returning to the centre of national transport investment throughout much of the world. The reason is not difficult to see: railways carry ecological and social advantages over their rivals. Travel by air is more costly in pollution, energy use and disturbance, and the same is true of travel by car, which in addition lacks the speed and civilizing values of rail. In terms of land take for infrastructure, fossil fuel use and community disturbance, rail wins over air, bus and car transport.

Railways have one further advantage: trains connect city centre to city centre. As cities are revalued, culturally and socially, the advantage of travel to the core rather than the edge of towns has obvious advantages. The facilities that make cities are in the centre, not the suburbs. Railways usually run to termini and mainline stations located near the city centre. The effect is to make railways part of the fabric of cities, not appendages at the edge. This quality makes stations great gathering places, urban gateways for floods of arriving and departing passengers, who do not usually stay long in stations but experience them in passing. Unlike an art gallery or shopping mall that people travel to, stations

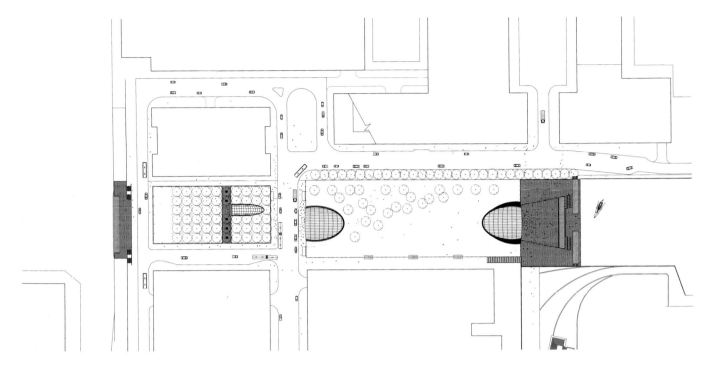

2.10 Stations act as landmarks if they are set apart from other buildings, employ memorable forms, and have public gathering space around the entrance. This site plan for Canary Wharf Station by Sir Norman Foster and Partners uses a similar motif to Bilbao.

are places that people travel through. Movement of people, many in a hurry, is a characteristic of railway stations. As a social focus, the station has the task of humanizing mass trans-port – of giving journeys a dignified beginning and end.

Unlike the airport, the station is part of city life, locked into its dense network of central facilities. The station is both a city square and part of what should be a smooth transition from public street to a seat on a train. As the station is part of the compact central infrastructure of most large towns, it has to be seen and recognized for what it is, and it has to be readily accessible. Stations are one of the most public of functions in cities that are increasingly witnessing the loss of public realm. Except for the streets themselves, the great railway station concourse represents one of the last public enclosed spaces in the modern city. Civilized life depends upon the existence of public gathering places where people can meet friends and enjoy a drink. As the pendulum of investment returns to the railways, stations will again become part of urban life, with the quality of their external architecture and the magnificence of their internal spaces shaping perceptions of cities as in the past.

The drama of modern life is acted out in transport buildings – airports, railway and bus stations, ferry termini. There is no denying the intensity of human activity at busy ports, airports or stations. It is here that people move from one mode of transport to another, where 'rites of passage' are celebrated in new forms of structure, new arrangements of interior space, and new methods of handling large flows of people. With their noble pedigree, modern railway stations are again experimenting with bold construction, grand inter-

nal volumes and dramatic roof lighting. The return to the railways at the end of the twentieth century has revitalized a fine tradition, and taken the expressive opportunities of the stations' sense of social purpose a few steps forward. With this perspective, modern stations carry the legitimacy of public landmarks with greater authority than many contemporary building types.

Form, function and meaning in station design

The station as a functional label carries clear connotations in our mind of spatial and structural patterns. Of all building types the station has predictable formal consequences that allow us to anticipate the essential elements that define it – entrance, booking hall, glazed canopy, platform etc. The name 'station' allows us to construe a particular type of building whose meaning and form are closely tied to function. The station has a distinctive typology related to but different from that of the airport or bus station. It is a typology easy to recognize, recall and recreate. Stations such as Waterloo International exploit this typological distinctiveness, creating in the process notable new landmarks, which are clearly railway stations as against airports.

Purpose in station design is usually expressed in unambiguous and elementary form (as in Abando Station, Bilbao). The contract between form, function and purpose cannot be compromised without confusing the public. However, as the function of stations has changed, a new ambiguity has crept in. The single transportation function of the traditional

2.11 For many people the platform canopy signals the presence of the station.

station has given way to multi-functionalism, which in turn has led to complex and diverse station forms. Implicit in the diversification of station functions is the need for architects to ensure that stations still carry the visual and formal codes of railway architecture in spite of the expanded range of activities increasingly housed in them or built at their periphery.

In many towns the station, like the courthouse, library and stadium, has an immediately recognizable typology. This makes it a public monument, even if in reality it is owned by a private company. As Markus points out, its architecture is a kind of text that allows the civic dimension to be read.[2] The 'style' of the station is irrelevant: what matters are the cues that direct public consciousness to the presence of the station. The obvious cues are the station roof, the platform canopy, the bridge over the tracks and the public gathering space at the station entrance. The medium is the plan and the section, and the key elements are structural rhythm and articulation. The geometry of space and light are the internal means by which functional patterns are communicated. Questions of civic order and the hierarchy of patterns in the station are matters that the designer addresses using the means above. The mutual interdependence of form, meaning and function makes the design of stations, with their complex and erratic patterns of movement, a particular challenge.

International termini, mainline and airport stations

The scale of international and national stations sets them apart from much of the urban fabric of cities. Unlike airports,

which they resemble in size and complexity, railway stations are in towns, not at their edge. Stations are not isolated landmarks surrounded by a sea of parking, taxiing and service areas, but structures that stand in streets and form continuous frontages with housing, offices, shops and warehouses. This sense of urban juxtaposition is distinctive to railway stations: it provides the sharp contrasts of scale, activity and civic content. It also adds to the difficulty of providing access for rescue services (fire and ambulance particularly), deliveries of various kinds, car and pedestrian links, and the integration of different types of public transport (light rail, metro, etc.). Yet putting aside these difficulties, the modern railway station is a dramatic and powerful statement of transport provision – more ambitious and with greater potential for celebrating the public realm than most building types.

In the international station the size of concourses, the diversity of main and secondary spaces (many on different floors), the loftiness of ceilings recalls the majesty of medieval cathedrals. No wonder the stations in Montreal, Delhi, Paris and London looked like chateaux or cathedrals. Today the big international station, such as Lille-Europe, Bilbao or Waterloo, has the character of a modern cathedral, with emphasis placed by its designers upon structural rhythm, space and light. In these buildings structure plays an important role, which goes beyond the support of roofs. Beams and columns are used to give meaning to interior public spaces, to help in directing people towards booking offices and platforms, and to give one station a character different from another. Just as medieval cathedrals use the masonry column to direct movement along the nave, and

2.12 At Bilbao's new Abando Station, the design presents a grandly conceived entrance front and over-sailing canopy to a newly formed square. Architects: Michael Wilford and Partners.

2.13 An inviting canopy provides both shelter and land-marking qualities for smaller stations. Architects: Jourda and Perraudin.

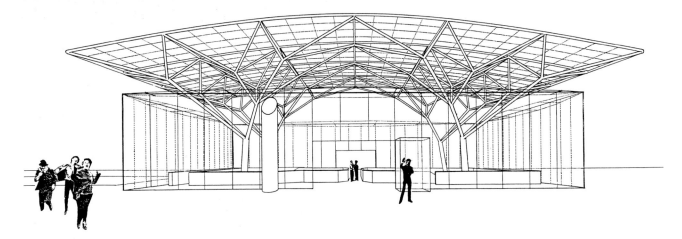

to assert the unity of interior volume, so too in modern railway stations structure has symbolic content. Columns, trusses and framing are, therefore, aesthetic as well as practical elements. The same is true of lighting, which has the capacity to guide passengers through complex stations. Natural light, with its associated moods and colours, is an effective means by which legibility can be introduced. Where natural light and structural expression are used in unison (as for instance by Calatrava at Lyon-Satolas Station and Grimshaw at Waterloo International), the effect is both uplifting and helpful at a practical level.

Spaces inside modern railway stations are vast, fluid and disorientating. The proliferation of shops and stalls add to the confusion at an architectural level. Architects have the task of designing stations that accommodate various needs – those of passengers, station managers, franchisers of different kinds, and rescue services. It is important

that light and structure are designed to aid the intelligibility of space and route. This places a responsibility on both building designer and structural engineer to ensure that space, which is the medium of the architectural experience, is articulated and expressed for the benefit of passengers.

There are various ways in which this can be achieved. A spine of natural light through the centre of a railway station concourse aids navigation even when signs are poorly displayed. Light flooding a wall, or views through to trains waiting by platforms and bathed in natural light (as at Leiden Station in the Netherlands), guide the passenger more effectively than internal signs. Where view and light are exploited in collaboration with structural expression there begins to emerge a strategy that gives legibility and aesthetic pleasure to complex building programmes. The exploitation of light and structural arrangement, coupled with the deliberate manipulation of internal volume, results in an interior

2.14 The route from station to town centre should be a processional corridor marked by public space and civic events. Amsterdam Central Station.

2.15 The mainline terminus has great impact upon the physical, social and economic structure of the city. Good design (as here at Abando Station, Bilbao) consists of achieving effective integration between railway interests and those of metropolitan areas. Architects: Michael Wilford and Partners.

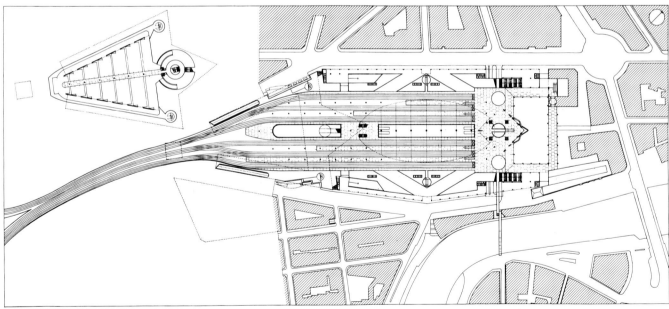

that is pleasant and safe to use. It is no coincidence that recent railway disasters (such as the King's Cross fire of 1987) occurred in stations with little structural legibility or natural light. Observers who complain that modern structural expression is becoming too sculptural fail to realize that the role of the column is more than merely to hold up the roof.

The most important quality to be provided in the design of large railway stations is that of clarity of orientation. As stations have a linear progression from city to platform edge this is an obvious point of departure for the designer. The concept of land- and trainsides (similar to land- and airsides in airports) is well established. It is essential that transparency, structural logic, the flow of spaces, and the

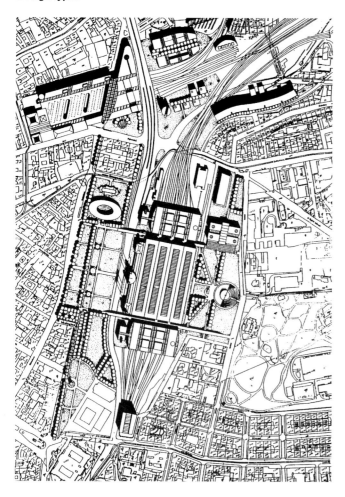

2.16 This scheme, a successful competition entry by UK architects Weston Williamson, seeks to integrate Prague Station with adjoining urban areas. The site owners, Czech Railways, wished to realize the development potential of redundant railway land. The masterplan is based upon axially connected packages of mixed-use development and new urban parks, with the existing station at the centre.

2.17 From the station the view out is usually through a great portal, which frames the prospect of the city. Handling the transition in scale at the station edge is often a problem for designers.

manipulation of light are collectively used to allow passengers to find their way from taxi rank to train door. Without this legibility imposed by architectural and structural means, the cross-currents of movement will overwhelm many passengers. Given that stations are on many levels, and travellers move freely between transport systems (underground, suburban, mainline and international as at Waterloo), the role of the architect is not to add unnecessary complexity or to sanitize the parts aesthetically, but to use spatial richness, light and constructional elements to guide movement.

Airport stations

The air industry is one of the fastest-growing sectors of the world economy, and linking airports to cities via railway lines is one of the fastest-expanding sectors of public transport infrastructure. It is not only more convenient for passengers to travel by rail rather than by bus, taxis or car, but generally cheaper. Connection by rail is also greener in terms of energy consumption per passenger mile.

Today it has become the norm to build direct rail links between urban areas and new airports and, where railway lines were missing at the time of construction, to extend them to existing airports. Airport railway stations have become

a distinctive new station type, often combining elements of traditional airports with station architecture. Generally speaking they come in two types – either integrated structures containing airports and stations within the same building envelope (horizontally integrated at Kansai or vertically integrated at Stansted) or standalone stations that exist as independent, though linked, buildings within the airport environment (as at Manchester Airport or Lyon-Satolas).

The predicted growth in air travel and the consequent effect upon the global economy (the economic impact of airports is expected to rise from US$700 billion in 1989 to US$1500 billion in 2010 and jobs from 21 million to 30 million over the same period[3]) is the reason for the emergence of the airport station as a new classification of railway architecture. Airports are only successful in the long term if the growth in air traffic and airport facilities (hotels, shopping, etc.) is matched by a growth in surface transportation (rail and road). The experience of Heathrow is that limitations in road and rail access are more likely to reduce growth potential than are restrictions in airport facilities.

Rail can carry a high proportion of airport users when the following conditions are met:[4]

- Stations need to provide easy transfer of baggage between train and airport check-in facilities. Ideally,

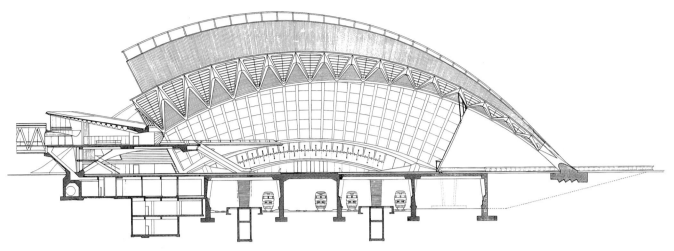

2.18 Airport stations consist of expansive public circulation areas connected by staircases and escalators. Here, in this plan and section of Lyon-Satolas Station, angles and curves are used to direct passenger movement through the termini. Architect: Santiago Calatrava.

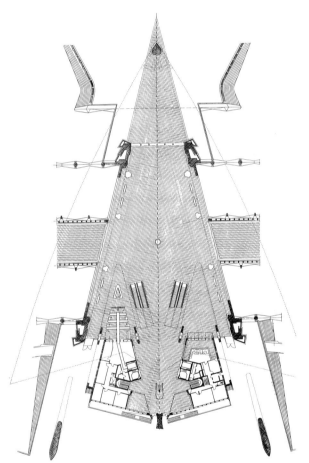

baggage transfer and security will be provided at the city centre check-in station rather than at the airport station.
- Stations are designed for the needs of airport travel: that is, extra facilities for baggage, greater widths for travel by groups, signs in a variety of languages.
- Routes between airport stations and airport facilities (especially termini) are legible, convenient and assisted (by use of travellators or monorail).

In operational terms, greater use of rail airport links will be achieved if:

- Rail operators and airlines offer combined rail and air tickets.
- Dedicated services (as at London's Gatwick) are provided between city centre stations and airport.
- Rail services are frequent, and connect with other transport facilities (underground, bus, car parking).

The railway station as interchange

The distinction between railway station, airport, bus station, and even motorway is becoming eroded as railways are connected to other transport facilities. Where once separate systems of mass transportation existed in an unconnected fashion, today the trend is towards an integrated public transport system. One characteristic of this is the linking of railways to a variety of other forms of transport, particularly airports. Twenty years ago airports were seen as large independent transport centres joined to cities by motorways, along which travelled taxis for the wealthy and airport buses for the remainder. Now it is commonplace to connect airports to their geographical hinterland by a variety of means, including overground and underground railways. As airports become more effectively integrated into other forms of transportation their sense of isolation and distinctiveness as building types becomes eroded. This same is true of railway stations at airports, which combine the characteristics of airports, bus stations and traditional railway stations rolled into one.

As a type of station the airport station has to face particular conditions and constraints. Unlike other stations,

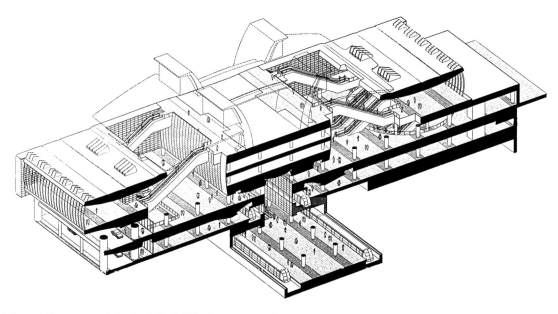

2.19 Mainline stations present the logistical difficulty of integrating different types of railways – from intercity to suburban and under-ground metro. Strong three-dimensional design both helps to solve the engineering problems and provides a spatial framework that enhances travellers' perceptions of movement and destination. Architects: Terry Farrell and Partners.

2.20 Daringly wide-spanned roofs with bands of glazing are one of the characteristics of great railway stations. Amsterdam Central Station.

2.21 Airport stations are an expanding new station type, built either as free-standing structures (as here at Manchester Airport) or integrated within airport termini (as at Stansted). Architects: Austin-Smith: Lord.

2.22 Section through Manchester Airport Station. The change in level from platforms (on right) to connecting bridge (on left) is handled with particular skill.

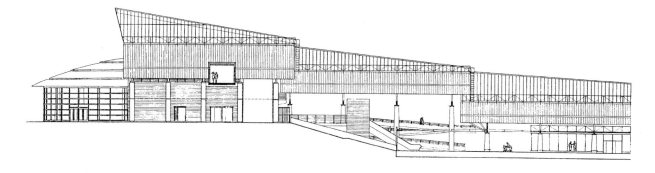

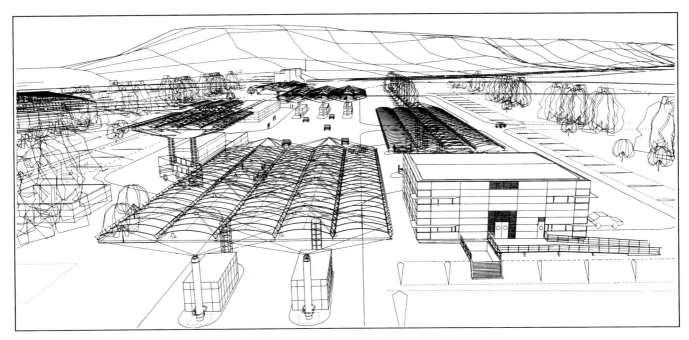

2.23   The Channel Tunnel rail terminus at Folkestone, Kent, represents a new kind of integrated rail, car, lorry and bus interchange. This computer simulation shows the various elements that make up the terminus. Architects: Building Design Partnership.

those at airports carry large numbers of foreign travellers, many of whom are business travellers used to high-quality transport environments. The airport station also has to cater for passengers carrying a greater volume of baggage than is usual, and passengers travelling in large family groups. As the airport station is a means of reaching the airport terminal as directly as possible, it is often constructed (as at Stansted in London and Kansai in Japan) as part of the airport itself. Elsewhere (as at Manchester) the airport station is an independent but closely related structure.

As airport stations become a common type of station their particular characteristics can be identified. Generally speaking they differ from other stations in the following ways:

- Circulation spaces are wider.
- Lifts and escalators, rather than stairs, are provided at changes in level.
- Finishes more appropriate to airports are used (such as carpets, or stone veneers).
- They are frequently built as part of the airport buildings.
- They are built partly or wholly beneath ground in order for the railway tracks not to interfere with the path of runways.
- They are able to share the facilities (such as shops, restaurants and toilets) of their parent building.
- Signs are usually in a variety of languages.
- Architectural means (daylight, internal volume and structure) are used to indicate routes and functional hierarchies.

Although some of the above points are to be found in other types of modern railway station, it is at the airport station

that these characteristics are most frequently encountered.

Other types of railway interchange, such as the road/rail link at the Channel Tunnel, display a similar blurring of the differences between building types. Where once ferry terminal, motorway service station, bus station, airport and railway station were readily identifiable building types, the trend of combining elements of each in a new integrated transport centre has meant that a fresh generation of buildings dedicated to transportation has emerged. A station absorbed into a ferry terminal or airport takes on the functional and aesthetic characteristics of each. For the designer or engineer the task is to ensure that the complexity of integration does not prejudice clarity of use. Finding a station buried beneath an airport or tucked to the side of a busy ferry port can pose a considerable frustration to a tired traveller. Where the station is absorbed within a large transport megastructure one cannot rely upon signs alone to guide passengers who may be quite unfamiliar with the building.

Having a separate railway station as an independent but linked structure provides a more readily identified facility for those approaching from either direction: that is, arriving or departing. Where a standalone station is provided, the task of connection in the form of elevated travellators (as at Manchester Airport) or monorail (as is planned at Liverpool Airport) may be needed. Here the links themselves can add to the drama of travel by adding a further layer of structures to the openness of airports, ferry ports or bus stations. Rather than play down these structures, the designer or engineer should ensure that their distinctiveness allows travellers to easily recognize their function and find their way to access points.

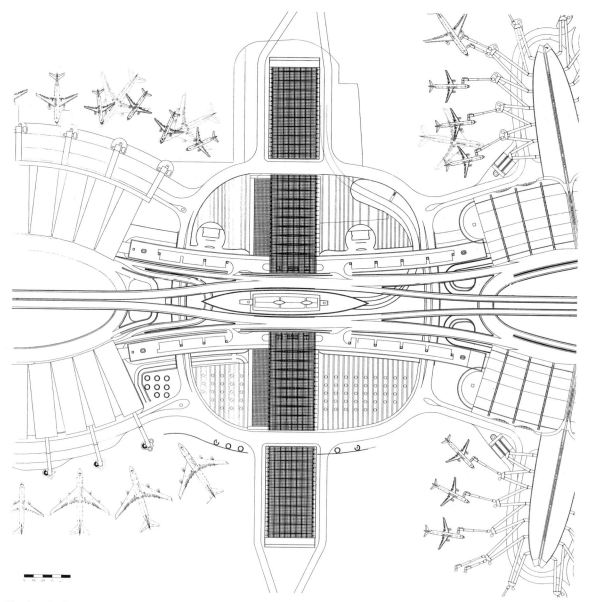

2.24   At Charles de Gaulle Airport in Paris the new railway station has been well integrated. Bold sweeping geometries allow rail, road and airport to be effectively combined. The station roof is the shaded area. Architect: Paul Andreu.

Roissy interchange: the integration of rail and air transport

The TGV station at Roissy-Charles de Gaulle Airport comprises what the French authorities call an 'interchange module'. The station connects directly into the Terminal 2 building, thereby sharing road accesses and facilities (shops, restaurants, duty-free, etc.) with the airport. By taking the TGV line to the airport in 1992 the state railway company has effectively linked Paris's principal airport to major French cities. In so doing, the traditional opposition between rail and air has been replaced by what its architects Paul Andreu and Jean-Marie Duthilleul call 'complementarity' of services.[5]

It took nearly 20 years for the French high-speed rail network to be extended to the airport. When Terminal 2 was

under consideration in the 1980s, the decision was made to construct an integrated terminal and high-speed railway station. This had the advantage of connecting the TGV system with the French regional railway (RER), which already served outlying facilities at the airport such as parking areas. The new station (known simply as Roissy Station) has now become the centre of local airport movement. The extended railway, with stops at the main two terminals and peripheral airport sites, provides an efficient means of transport within the great expanse of Charles de Gaulle airport, and quick connection to the national railway infrastructure.

Roissy Station, built at a cost of £150 million, is placed at the intersection of the TGV line and the axis of Terminal 2 building. Being at a functional crossroads it commands other movement systems – road, pedestrian, taxiing aircraft.

The station is organized on four main levels: road at the top level (slightly elevated above the ground), air terminal facilities on the floor below, next the train station proper, and finally on the lowest floor the platforms. The latter form a trench between the aircraft taxiways. By avoiding the use of a central tunnel to enclose the tracks (as happened at Stansted) and using instead an open channel roofed in glass, the station remains visible within the whole complex.

The integration of station and terminal within a building of great openness and light allows the moving objects (trains, aircraft, taxis, cars and buses) to be seen as the elements that link the separate architectural masses. This, the designers contend, allows the station environment to be easily readable.[6]

Whereas other large transportation megastructures have a functional air, here the rationality is tempered by what the architects call 'a poetic concern for light'.[7] Andreu and Duthilleul have sought to use different types of light to create areas of calm, to help define time and distance, and to light the structure in such a fashion that travellers are guided through the building. Materials, particularly those of internal walls, were selected to help create 'a serene and luminous space', where the logic of movement was not compromised by posturing technology. To help maintain this purity of conception, walls, floors and structural members are all finished in white, either as painted surfaces (as with the steelwork) or light natural materials such as white marble on the floors.

Suburban stations

Intermediate in size and function between mainline stations and rural unmanned stations, the suburban station is a particularly important type. This is because the suburbs it serves are usually faceless places devoid of good architecture, and the railway tracks great divisive features. The suburban station has therefore to bridge areas of urban land in a meaningful and distinguished fashion. As road crossings over railways are often widely spaced, the suburban station is a place shared by people who are not always railway travellers. In this sense the station has to address the symmetry of the division imposed by railway tracks and the asymmetry of the function of a station. The

2.25 Crossing the tracks via underground routes is less inviting than via bridges. Here, at Stadelhofen Station, Zurich, Santiago Calatrava has used elemental concrete structure to provide interest in the concourse beneath the tracks.

asymmetry is one of scale, between pedestrian movement and the speed of trains, and of organization – the linear flow from car park to ticket office and platform, and from one side of the town to another.

Exploiting the ambivalent forces of symmetry and asymmetry allows suburban stations to become landmark buildings in neighbourhoods usually starved of good public buildings. As suburban stations need to be approached from both sides of the track, bridges and tunnels are essential ingredients. These are needed at two scales: to join the areas of town divided by the parallel railway lines at the very point where transition from road to rail travel occurs, and to link the 'up and down' platforms together. Combining the two flows of movement (cross-town movement and access to platforms) into a single structure is a common feature of suburban station design, though it can pose difficulties with ticket control and conflicts of pedestrian routes. It has the advantage, however, of exploiting the functional symmetries rather than the asymmetries. When the station is not incorporated into a public bridge, the pedestrian flows create an emphasis architecturally upon one side of the station. Where this occurs, the balance

Design types

2.26 The platform canopy is a key feature of suburban stations, exploited here to provide a rhythm of light and structure. Stadelhofen Station, Zurich. Architect: Santiago Calatrava.

2.27 Plan of Vasteras Station, Sweden (below, left), with concept diagrams (below, right) explaining how the station links the town to the waterfront across the railway tracks. The station is an elegant bridge, anchored at the town side by the ticket office. Architects: Weston Williamson.

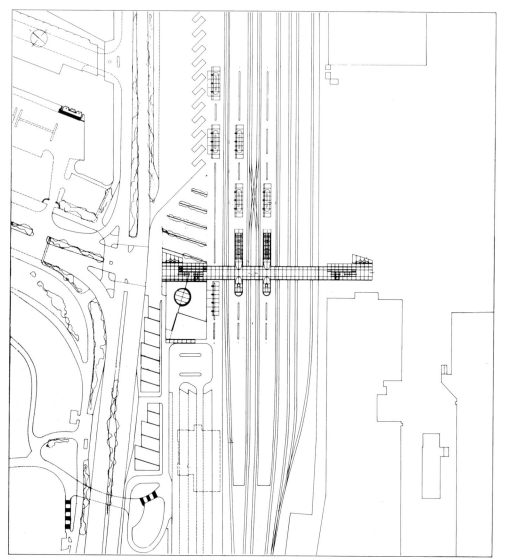

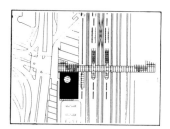

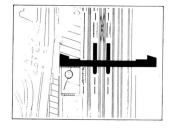

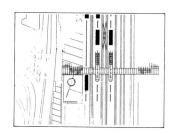

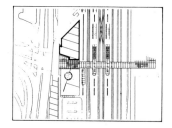

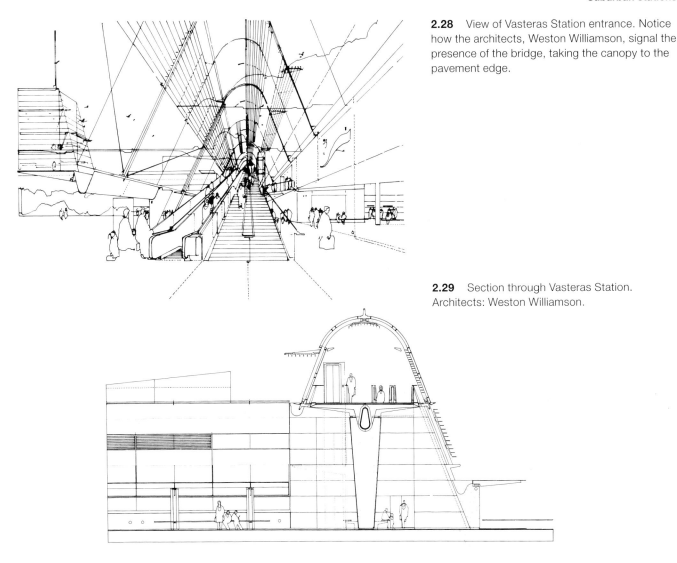

2.28 View of Vasteras Station entrance. Notice how the architects, Weston Williamson, signal the presence of the bridge, taking the canopy to the pavement edge.

2.29 Section through Vasteras Station. Architects: Weston Williamson.

and counterbalance of forms need to direct people to the pertinent parts; to signal the entrance and ticket areas; and to direct travellers to the platforms. Clearly the asymmetry of the station needs also to address the asymmetry of the neighbourhood, with the station forecourt facing the major roads and whatever civic realm may exist.

Suburban stations can be seen as decks bridging the railway tracks and uniting two suburban districts. As Kevin Lynch noted in *The Image of the City*, tracks are one of the major 'edges' encountered in urban areas.[8] People perceive railway lines as boundaries between neighbourhoods. Spanning the tracks with a broad deck on which various public facilities are built, and gestures towards social space (such as a paved square) are provided, helps to heal the divisions caused by railways in suburban areas. In this the design of the station is a crucial element. It needs to recognize that the station is a crossing point, an urban interchange, and a valuable social or meeting place. Thinking about the secondary functions of a suburban station allows the designer to add complexity and richness to a form that otherwise can be rather singular in nature.

The balancing of primary and secondary functions provides the means to resolve the potential conflict between symmetry and asymmetry in station design. Three types of suburban station frequently occur: first, the *bridge station*, where the private function of the railway station and the public territory of a road bridge are combined; second, the *square station*, where a public space combines as peripheral buildings railway activities with civic ones; and third, the *island station*, where railway functions exist as an isolated structure separate from the neighbourhood it serves. The main advantage of the first is that of maintaining urban continuity, of the second that of creating a civic realm, of the third that of making a landmark.

Bridge stations

An example of the bridge station is East Croydon Station on Network SouthEast, designed by Alan Brookes Associates. Serving 10 million passengers a year, East Croydon Station is conceived as a bridge spanning six railway lines that for years have parted the urban fabric of this

2.30 East Croydon Station (the hatched area) in South London is designed as a bridge linking two quarters of the town. The divisive nature of suburban railways is well illustrated in this plan. Architects: Alan Brookes Associates.

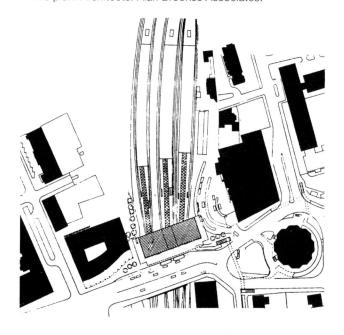

busy town in southern England. The station is used mainly as a commuter station, with direct links to central London, Gatwick Airport and Channel ports. Its redevelopment emphasizes the bridge as an element of the public realm. It effectively provides access to railway facilities (such as ticket offices) and thence via ramps to platforms, and stitches together two divided sections of Croydon. As a consequence, the station is experienced by two distinct groups of people: those intent upon rail travel and those crossing the railway tracks as pedestrians escaping nearby congested roads beneath the station's canopy. A similar example is Leiden Station in the Netherlands (see Chapter 7).

The ambiguity of purpose enhances the meaning and complexity of the station. A generous canopy of pressed metal and glass suspended from boldly engineered frames unites a collection of different functions at bridge level. For the railway traveller there are booking offices, waiting areas and timetable information screens; for the footbridge user there is shelter and protection from surrounding traffic. Both flows of people intermingle contentedly, adding a sense that this station belongs to the town of Croydon

rather than to Network SouthEast, which runs it. A small station forecourt provides space for buses and taxis as a widening of the main access road.

The station sits upon a wide-span superstructure extending across six railway tracks with dividing platforms. The main structural abutments for this structure provide the support for a lighter steel canopy (55 m × 19 m), which forms the roof for the station. Beneath the roof canopy stand islands of railway accommodation, which order movement at pedestrian level. As an architectural experience the station consists of three clearly defined vertical zones: the track and superstructure level, the pedestrian level (the bridge), and the roof level. It is the roof that gives the station its landmarking qualities: large steel masts extend upwards to provide cable supports for the lightweight roof. Each level is designed differently, providing legibility to the station both within its rather disjointed urban context and for the casual user. For example, at platform level the engineering is heavy, based mainly upon solid concrete construction; at bridge level the character is one of pavilions in an urban square; at roof level all is light, transparent and airy.

The design of the station, with its high-tech overtones, reflects British Rail's thinking on an appropriate image for modern railways. Alan Brookes Associates were encouraged to pursue the language of engineering design partly as a gateway to the railway system and as a foil to the dour office blocks immediately nearby. The generous canopy that is the station's principal element unites complex activities in a pleasant fashion. Not only does it landmark the station externally; the steel structure of the masts and trusses gives meaning and a sense of direction to interior spaces.

Modern glazing technology and assemblies (some developed by the architect) allow the different expansion needs of curtain walling and steel structure to be tolerated without fracture. Sophisticated detailing of the engineering of the station extends to ticket office and many of the details, thereby providing a sense of unity of purpose. That it will in future extend to the design of rolling stock provided part of the justification for BR's endorsement of such a bold design.

Being largely glazed, the station exploits passive solar gain to provide casual heat in public areas. Summer-time

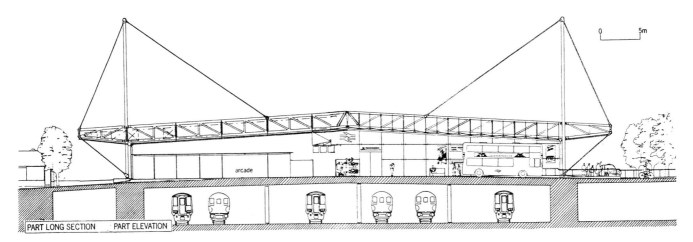

2.31   Section through East Croydon Station.

cooling is provided by vents in the roof, which double up as smoke extracts in the case of fire.[9] These are activated by thermal and rain sensors, with other sensors switching on concourse lights, which are placed outside the canopy and shine through the glass, thereby enhancing the station as an external landmark at night. As the station is highly glazed, very little daytime lighting is needed.

East Croydon Station exploits many of the tenets of modern architecture: transparency, structural daring and openness. In its constructional refinement it alludes to the nineteenth-century railway station, yet it borrows imagery also from modern airport design (such as Stansted). Structural refinement is not used as false gesturing but to guide passengers to the parts of the station that are functionally important. For example, the glass of the canopy is carried as a single large sheet over the ticket hall to help mark its position.

The square station

An example of the square station is Sandvika Station in Norway, designed by Arne Henriksen in 1994.[10] The civic space is small, bounded by shops that deflect passengers into the station concourse, and enclosed on the other sides by blank walls or existing buildings. The effect of the square is to give dignity to the station, to provide a gathering space sheltered by trees, and to mark the station entrance. The sequence of public square, station concourse, ticket point and platform represents a smooth transition from town to train.

Unlike the usual arrangement, where shops are within the station itself, at Sandvika they face outwards, looking across a wide space to nearby apartment buildings. The station entrance reads like the last of four shops, with the route to the ticket office defined by a circular timber canopy and an open framework of columns. The platforms are reached by a broad, low-level concrete vaulted walkway, which bisects the railway tracks at right angles and opens out on the opposite side upon a secondary square. This contains a bus station and car park. The effect of the two squares

– one civic in character, the other mainly functional – is to establish the station as a monument within this suburb of Oslo. The squares are linked into the existing pattern of civic routes, using the straight edges of the elevated railway tracks as justification for the formal geometry of the spaces. By keeping the squares and station concourse at road level, the station is effectively stitched into the fabric of the suburb. The high-level railway embankment, rather than forming a barrier, is used to define the boundaries of the two squares and to maintain an appropriate scale. The squares effectively link back into the suburbs they serve and herald inwards the station entrances.

A more ambitious application of the same idea is found in Santiago Calatrava's competition-winning design for Spandau Station in Berlin and also at St Pierre des Corps Station on the French TGV system. In Berlin the idea was one of creating a square, into which the station sits, formed by two large but low office blocks placed at right-angles to the four lanes of railway track. The station is placed asymmetrically in the square, with a high-level glazed canopy, supported directly over the platforms, reflecting in its structural arrangement the trees planted in the remainder of the square. The proximity of the office buildings and railway station exploits the commercial potential of this suburban station, with the new square helping to define the main entrances. The railway tracks, being high level at this point, pass through the office blocks in a cutting four storeys high.

In Calatrava's design the architect has formed 'a complex, yet delicately homogenous whole'.[11] The square that defines the station also leads to an underground car park via another distinctive glass and steel canopy. The architecture of the different elements is not combined into an enormous, brutal whole (as happened for instance in the redevelopment of London's Euston Station in the 1960s), but kept as separate elements. This allows the station canopy to be read as a distinctive element, different in form and style from that serving the car park, and also clearly different from the architecture of the office blocks.

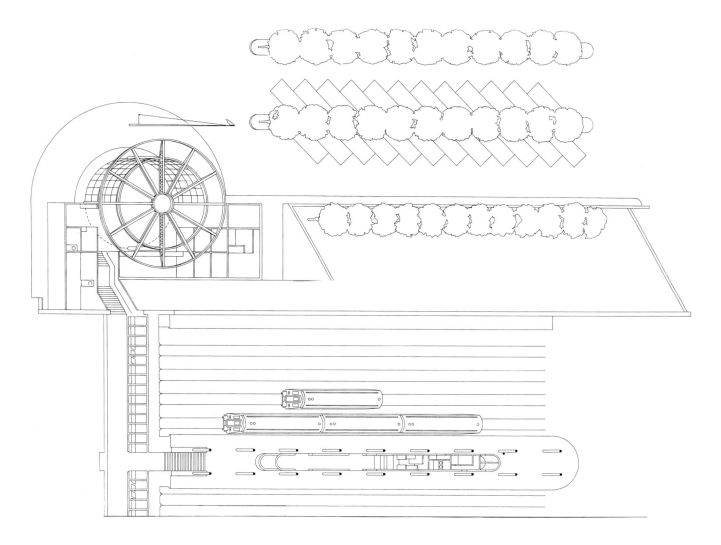

2.32 The glazed rotunda booking hall at Redhill Station in Surrey, England, designed by Troughton McAslan, provides a worthy identification for this suburban station.

The island station

Of the three suburban station types this is the most familiar. Island stations are generally isolated structures set within car parks and service spaces needed to support stations where part of the journey is taken by car, bicycle or bus. As it is set apart from the fabric of the town by these open peripheral spaces, this type of station is frequently designed as a free-standing landmark. Such stations have the advantage of being instantly recognizable as buildings serving railway needs, and hence the need for secondary signing is reduced. In reality, the three station types adopted here are often combined to various degrees, leading to a range of subtypes and hybrids.

A good example is Slependen Station, another Norwegian station, designed by Arne Henriksen on the commuter route into Oslo. The station is small, with a pedestrian bridge serving the two platforms and doubling up as a public route between the two sides of the town. A large drum contain-

ing a circular ramp provides access to the bridge and a high-level path to the east of the station.[12] The drum or rotunda acts as marker for this unmanned station, signalling its position in the relatively featureless suburbs. The drum is lit at night (an important consideration this far north), adding to its status as a local landmark.

Slependen Station uses simple but bold geometries to create a structure that stands out from the crowd. Circles, angled bridges and the long arms of parallel platform canopies are effectively combined to produce a composition of sculptural appeal. The station is not cluttered by shops, ticket offices or staff accommodation but stands as an elegant railway halt. Simple shapes and dramatic lighting ensure that the public are left in no doubt that this is a building of civic importance. Though modest in scale it carries the symbolism and meaning of railway architecture in its approach to design. The materials too are simple and derive their justification from the local landscape. Timber is widely used in vertical slats suggestive of the pine forests

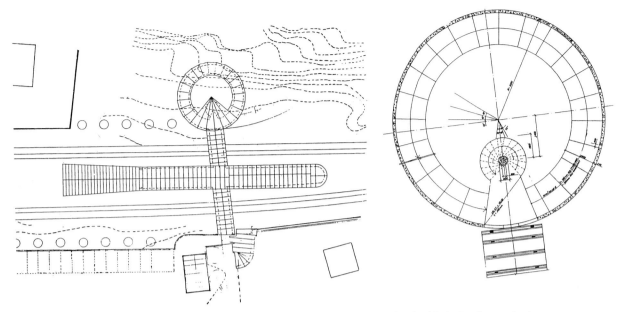

2.33 The drum and bridge of Slependen Station in Norway readily landmark the station in this featureless suburb. Architect: Arne Henriksen.

nearby, and smooth concrete is combined with steel to allude to the high-tech ambience of the trains.

The integration of station, community and trip demand

The concentration of housing, offices and mixed-use development around suburban stations increases the appeal of the station for both commuters and other travellers. Density of development within a 5 minute walk of stations greatly increases the number of trips made by rail as compared with other transport systems. In San Francisco, a study has found that people living near (within 500 m) of the Bay Area Rapid Transit (BART) stations were three times more likely to use the rail system for general journeys and over six times more likely to use it for commuting than were Bay area residents generally.[13] Two factors are, however, important in achieving the popularity of suburban railways. First, the availability of free parking at the destination of the journey acts as a deterrent to the use of rail. If an employer or shopping developer provides a parking space without charge then travellers are more likely to use their cars rather than the train. Hence urban planning policy and the development of railways need to go hand in hand. Second, the popularity of rail is helped if most kinds of trip origins and destinations are clustered around stations.[14] It is the linking of origin and destination that is important; it is of little value to group dense housing around a station and then provide dispersed shopping and job opportunities where they can only be reached by car.

The San Francisco study highlights the need for metropolitan areas to have multi-centred urban form, where each node is interlinked by efficient transit services (heavy, light rail and bus). This pattern, evident in Moscow, Paris, Toronto, Rotterdam and Stockholm, ensures a steady demand for rail-based journeys across a broad spectrum of journey types – commuting, shopping, leisure. The implications of the study are threefold:

- Mixed-use, dense development within a 5 or 10 minute walk of stations is only effective in increasing rail usage if the wider metropolitan pattern is structured in multi-centred nodes.
- Railway development and parking policy are related factors. The availability of free parking at destination points (as at suburban business and retail parks) discourages rail use.
- Stations need to be 'transit friendly'. Access should not entail complex changes in direction or level; should be perceived as safe even late at night; and should encourage access by walking and cycling.

Focusing mixed-use development near stations and designing communities to be centred on 'their' station has benefits in terms of the levels of car versus railway use. People's choices of travel type are, however, influenced by the nature of the destination in terms of its location to a station and the availability of parking. Perceptions of safety and ease of access are also important considerations. There are ramifications here for how urban and suburban areas are planned, how stations are designed, and how station and adjacent development are structured.

Rural stations

Railways in rural areas can do much to sustain small towns in the countryside by reinforcing the local economy and providing a magnet, albeit on a small scale, for future growth. Country stations are often the main social and business focal

2.34 The rural station, whether existing or new, has the potential to become a local business centre and focus for tourism development. This station at Sheringham in Norfolk, England, serves mainly as a heritage centre.

point of rural areas, locations where tourist services are promoted, and where local people can gain access to fax machines and telecommunication facilities. The linking of rural stations to telecottages means that the station can become a regional resource centre, providing a range of services to businesses and community groups. Where the station develops this new role, it can become a point for attracting new businesses to the area.

Rural stations are therefore both a means of access to other places and a centre for local enterprise and cooperation. As many rural train services are operated as a partnership between railway companies and local authorities, the station is pushed further towards a resource base of wider community and economic advantage. This potential is best exploited if the station contains business development facilities, information about training and grants etc., and is connected to the telecommunications superhighway. The accommodation of the rural station needs to contain these additional areas in order to provide the necessary business and social support. Such rooms are best placed alongside the booking hall so that the local tourist information stand and that related to local business opportunities are integrated.

The station is an important element in the creation and sustaining of local business enterprises. It has a crucial role to play as well in reinforcing a rural area's sense of community. While the station provides access to jobs in towns further afield, it can also help to attract jobs back from the city to the countryside. With rural populations growing in much of the UK, the railway infrastructure and particularly the stations have a key role to play.

Government itself recognizes these advantages. In the UK Department of the Environment's *Planning Policy Guidance on Transport* (PPG 13, 1993), emphasis is placed upon promoting corridors of growth along public transport corridors and around railway stations. The latter are encouraged to become nodes of economic activity supported by park and ride schemes, and cycle facilities at stations. Rather than close rural stations and abandon uneconomic lines, current thinking is towards bands of development along railway lines and magnets of growth at stations. Just as nineteenth-century railways opened up the countryside to fresh economic potential, so in the age of sustainable development rural railway stations are seen as vital economic and community magnets.

The implications of this change in emphasis have effects upon the design of new stations, the rehabilitation of existing ones and the development of land surrounding stations. As mentioned, if stations are to be hubs of business and travel life, then they need additional space and electronic information services to allow this to occur. High-technology communications contained within a business centre at the station can do much to activate local

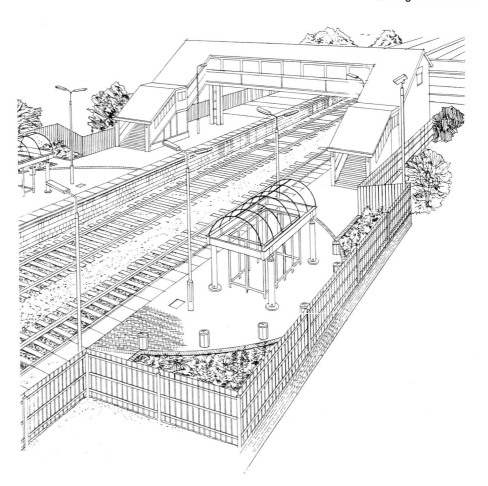

2.35 The key ingredients of a rural station (particularly those unmanned) are security, enclosure, lighting, platform shelter and pedestrian bridge.

people into becoming entrepreneurs. Running a business from a home in the countryside (to many people the rural idyll) could be assisted by the facilities available at a local station. Land around the station could be developed for local industry, particularly by exploiting the interface between service and light manufacturing jobs. The station could also provide a meeting room for local businesses to share. Where a local authority subsidizes the line (as in parts of the Netherlands or Denmark) the station could house an office where information on local services of various kinds is distributed.

Just as the nature of urban stations is changing, so too is the small country station. The migration to the countryside of the middle class has usually entailed the dependence upon car-based commuting. A new generation of rural stations could make this less necessary by encouraging more sustainable means of transport, and by providing the business facilities of the city within the station itself.[15]

Underground stations

Underground railways have traditionally provided the most aesthetically consistent systems of any railway type. This consistency often spanned the design of rolling stock, the engineering and design of stations, and graphics. The undergrounds of Paris, Moscow and much of London illustrate the point. The extension of the District and Central Lines in London in the 1930s under the architectural guidance of Charles Holden is a good case in point. Here, at stations such as Arnos Grove, Chiswick Park, Sunbury Town, Hounslow West and Ealing Common, simple geometric forms and modern functional materials betray the influence of architects in mainland Europe, particularly those in the Netherlands and Germany, whose work was inspected by London Underground designers in 1930.[16] Holden's designs employ smooth, mainly horizontal lines balanced by powerful primary forms – mostly cubes and cylinders. Each station was not a separate entity but part of a wider whole employing a recognizable language of shapes, colours and materials. It was consistency bred of ideology: Charles Holden reported in 1929 that he sought station designs that were

'as pure and as true as a Bach fugue; an architecture as telling of joy in plan, structure and material; joy, too, in all the human and mechanical activities which make up architecture today.'[17]

The 'human and mechanical', expressed delightfully in clocks, ticket machines, seats, lighting and abstracted sculptural panels, extended a rigorous philosophy from concept to detail.

The Holden and Pick tradition

Charles Holden and his mentor Frank Pick represented a shift from the perception of underground railways as primarily a matter of engineering with design embellishment to one of architecture buttressed by sound engineering. In other countries where engineer and architect were less professionally separated, the integration of both skills was more familiar in railway systems (for example the Berlin U-Bahn of the 1920s). Holden was concerned to ensure that the enduring elements of station design, namely the 'plan of service and the planes and massing arising out of that plan',[18] had priority over surface decoration. It was a departure from the pattern of much of London Underground, which on the Metropolitan Line for instance carried a latent fondness for surface embellishment. The functionalism of the extensions to the London Underground between the First and Second World Wars contrasts even today with the visually cluttered stations nearer the centre of the capital.

Holden and his team also carried through a revolution in the use of materials. He replaced wooden mouldings by brass trim; decorative colourful tilework by plain cream tiles, fair-faced brickwork and smooth limestone; timber strips on escalators by rubber; wooden handrails by metal ones; steel framing by smooth reinforced concrete. The effect was to add light, simplicity and openness to the interiors of stations. Added as a language to various line extensions, the effect was also to give London Underground a distinctive corporate style. For many travellers, these stations were their first experience of 'modern' design. This gives Holden's work particular value in terms of cultural rather than merely architectural history, and is one reason why so many of his stations have been listed as architectural monuments.

The example of the Moscow Metro

Now over 60 years old, the Moscow Metro is arguably the greatest flowering of public investment in underground railway systems. It is remarkable for the scale and lavishness of the station interiors, the degree of artistic collaboration in the installation of frescos, stained glass panels and sculpted decoration, and the implied contract between public transport and civic well being. Today the Moscow Metro carries 9 million passengers a day at an average speed of 26 mi/h (42 km/h), as against 2 million a day at just over 20 mi/h (32 km/h) on the London Underground.

The stations were designed as examples of socialist design under Andreo Zhdanov, Stalin's chief cultural commissar, in the official style of 'revolutionary romanticism'. Most were built in what is today called Stalin's Empire style, though other stations adopted the Constructivist and Art Deco languaged. Sculptors such as Pavel Korin were encouraged to create monumental works to inspire the travellers (such as the Jump of the Parachutists in Mayakovskaya Station), and elsewhere granite, marble and dazzling chandeliers testify to the extent of state patronage. Not only were the stations conceived with spacious subterranean interiors and furnished with scenes of industrial progress and heroic proletarianism, they were constructed on a cinematic scale and have become monuments to their age. As a result, 44 of the stations (nearly a half) are now designated as architectural landmarks and as a consequence are pleasantly free of advertising, even in the 30 miles of staircases that are such a pleasurable feature of the system.

The Moscow Metro has remained popular with the Moscow public. It has continued to be extended periodically since its birth in 1933, and today a new line and stations costing £127 million is under construction east of the capital. Mosmetrostroi (Moscow Metro Construction), the partnership of state and private contractors carrying out the work, is maintaining the tradition in the stations of creating opportunities for contemporary artists. This, and the grandiose scale of the stations (compared with those in the West), helps to uphold the popular appeal of mass public transport in the city. Interestingly too, the decision to build the metro helped to underpin the Moscow Plan of 1935, the first in a series of five yearly plans which linked city growth with the provision of public transport and other amenities such as parks.

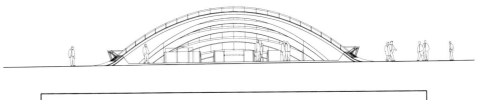

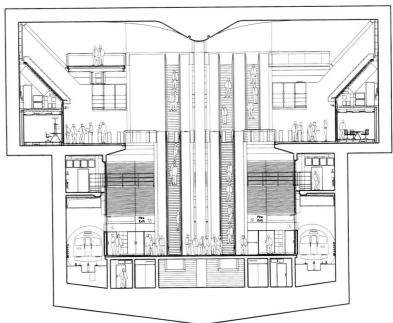

2.36 The escalator is a key element in the design of underground stations. Here at Canary Wharf Station, designed by Sir Norman Foster and Partners, it forms a central axis beneath a dramatic glazed canopy.

Underground railway stations today

Holden's approach to design has enduring qualities as a philosophy. He was as concerned with spreading a corporate image along a length of line as with ensuring that each station reflected honestly the arrangement in plan. To Holden, ideals of functionalism, honesty in the use of materials and clear geometric forms infuse both the overall design and the details of stations. He sought to control all aspects of design, which, even when appointed engineers or artists were employed, had to subscribe to a consistent whole.

To achieve consistency four conditions need to apply.

- The client (the railway company) needs to value design and be conscious of the benefit of corporate image.
- A single coordinating architect is required, armed with the ability to produce design guides and influence briefs.
- All design skills (from graphics to structural layout) need to subscribe to the same basic aesthetic ideals.
- Over time, the changes required of stations need to be carried out in sympathy with the original aesthetic aims.

Holden's stations subscribe to these ideals, as do those designed by Sir Norman Foster and Partners for the Bilbao Underground, Sir Richard Rogers' Metro extensions in Berlin, and Renzo Piano's in Genoa. They represent examples where the first three conditions converge, and hopefully with good patronage future changes will respect the values of their designers.

Large and complex railway systems cannot so readily be undertaken by a single design practice, and here there is a tendency for greater pluralism to occur. On London's Jubilee Line extension the 11 stations have each been designed by a different architect under the direction of Roland Paoletti as architect in chief. Here the intention is to form a design language based upon an exploitation of structure, light and public processional space. The language is not prescribed in construction details but exists as an open system capable of different interpretation by the separate architects. Even where the kind of aesthetic ideals promulgated by Holden cannot be universally applied, there remains an ordering strand uniting the stations.

It could be argued that the station should reflect the characteristics of the neighbourhood it serves, so that the nature of the architecture below ground mirrors that above. Holden and Pick's best underground stations personify the measured suburban landscapes that they served. There is not a great deal of difference between Ealing, Acton and Enfield, and it is perhaps inevitable that the new subway stations serving them should adopt a similar architectural approach. Today, however, underground railways are taken into urban landscapes of quite different character. The Jubilee Line extension, for instance, travels from the centre

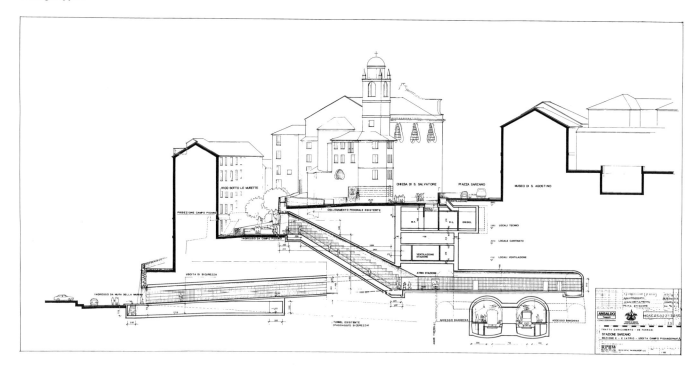

2.37 Connecting underground stations to the urban areas they serve requires skill in the handling of level changes and pedestrian movement. Architects: Renzo Piano Building Workshop.

of London to the fragmented wastelands of London Docklands. East London is marked, not by suburban order, but inner city disjointedness. It could be argued that a railway system should reflect this in the detailed development of designs for different stations. The advantage of using a different architect for each station is that local conditions can more forcibly shape the design than if the same architect was responsible for all the stations. By adopting a more open philosophy of design for the stations, a particular language can be translated with diversity and richness, rather than dogged uniformity.

The Jubilee Line extension

The Jubilee Line extension (JLE) is one of the most significant geographical enlargements of the London Underground system since its beginnings in 1862. Its importance lies not in the length but the move eastwards into areas marked by industrial decline and large areas of water. In fact, the 9 miles of track (14 km) crosses a widening Thames four times on its journey from Green Park in London's West End to Stratford in East London (with direct rail links in the future to the Channel Tunnel and CrossRail).

Claimed to be the largest single inner-city contract in the UK for 25 years, the investment of nearly £2 billion has provided the opportunity to explore new approaches to underground station design. Whereas earlier stations were fully enclosed, artificially lit structures based upon subterranean tubes of space, the new stations bring daylight down into public concourse areas and exploit double- and

triple-height spaces in an attempt to give drama to the volumes. New tunnel-boring machines, which have reduced in relative terms the cost of excavation, and the need to address the psychological welfare and safety of passengers have combined to give greater weight in the design of stations to interior space and how it is lit. This is particularly true of the stations designed to carry the heaviest passenger loads, such as Canary Wharf by Sir Norman Foster's office and London Bridge Station by architects Weston Williamson. Both stations are by no means inexpensive (£32.5 million and £76 million respectively), and involve elaborate interchange facilities either beneath water level (as at Canary Wharf) or below a Victorian railway station (as at London Bridge). In each station large spacious booking halls and circulation areas, criss-crossed by escalators with, at Canary Wharf, a shell-like roof deflecting daylight into the underground spaces bring architectural qualities to station design. As structural arrangements play an important part, the basic construction of the new stations is not disguised behind engulfing walls or advertising hoardings, but left to provide directional legibility for the users of the stations.

Each of the 11 new stations is designed by an architect working within a broad landscape of design ideas established by Roland Paoletti, JLE's architect-in-chief. Three elements in particular make up the language: the expression of constructional and structural elements; the manipulation of light, particularly daylight, to give spiritual uplift to public spaces; and the exploitation of types and sizes of interior volumes to give clarity and legibility to the

2.38 Underground railways present a complex challenge to both engineers and architects. Threading new lines beneath existing buildings requires considerable skill. Architects: Michael Hopkins and Partners.

stations.[19] Alsop and Störmer's design for the station at North Greenwich is less impaired by existing railway infrastructure than most, and consequently makes bolder expression of the guiding principles. It consists of a trench 20 m deep, 20 m wide and 400 m long, into which the station is suspended from the concrete roof. Above the station, provision exists to build a six-storey building to take advantage of the potential commercial benefits of the new station. Suspending the concourse and ticket hall allows light and view to be glimpsed around and through elements that are normally sealed visually. This not only creates a better grasp in the mind of the traveller of the layout of the station; it also leads to bold structural arrangements, which give scale and a sense of direction to interior volumes.

Each station is differently designed by separate architects.

To avoid excessive regularity, the 11 stations are the subject of distinct building contracts. Paoletti is keen that the various firms of architects and engineers do not talk greatly to each other but develop their designs in isolation.[20] For this reason no working group representing all the architects exists to coordinate designs. Only contracting working groups exist, and these are to ensure that the different contracts are completed on time.

The JLE has adopted a clear approach to design based broadly on Holden's guiding principles. There is not, however, an attempt to impose a corporate style, as occurred in the work for London Underground in the 1930s. Instead, variety and pluralism exist as detailed translations of a more open design language. Whereas Foster, Alsop, Weston Williamson and Ritchie develop their own interpretation of a rigorous philosophy, creating space, light and structure in their own distinctive ways, the details of finishes and graphic design impose a standardizing order. Platform surfaces, the design of many finishes at booking halls and around escalators, signage and seats will bring a familiar range of recognizable parts to unify the 11 new stations. However, the philosophy of exposing the civil engineering structures at each station means that applied finishes will take second place to expressed steelwork, concrete frames, brickwork and bronze.[21]

The stations will be the first in the UK to provide retractable glass barriers between trains and platform. They are being provided as an experiment (CrossRail will also use them) and follow a trend world-wide towards physical segregation of platform from track with busy subsurface railways. Designed to prevent passengers falling in front of trains and as part of the air-conditioning strategy, they will add a further unifying element to the stations. The use of toughened glass screens extends the range of applications of various types of glass. As a material glass is favoured by JLE architects, as it provides high graffiti resistance and ease of cleaning, and helps to filter daylight down into station concourses. When lit at night, the glazed elements of stations provide a welcoming glow, and help to landmark the stations within the urban scene.

The JLE is such a departure from practice elsewhere that it is worth listing the main characteristics of station

2.39 Identifying the station entrance is particularly important with metro systems. Here at the La Défense Station in Paris a small square is formed to help signal the presence of the station.

design. Generally speaking, the design of stations and their finishes subscribe to the following rules.

- Keep it dry (for speed of construction).
- Maximize prefabrication (for quality control).
- Keep it simple (for 'classic' elegance).
- Design for replaceability.
- Use light, particularly daylight, to guide passengers.
- Use structure to uplift the spirit and define routes.
- Exploit varieties of space.
- Define zones with materials (platform, ticket office, routes).
- Provide variety and richness at each station, rather than dogged uniformity.
- Employ a language of design from concept to materials.
- Integrate space, light and structure as unifying elements.
- Use materials that are easily cleaned and durable.
- Use light-coloured finishes for lighting energy conservation and good appearance.

These rules allow stations as diverse as MacCormac, Jamieson, Prichard's design for Southwick, Troughton McAslan's for Canning Town and Michael Hopkin and Partners' for Westminster to be read as a coordinated system of architecture below ground, rather than as isolated monuments. It is consistency within a fairly open language, not the dull repeating of a single style from station to station.

A renaissance in underground railways

As an urban form of railway, the underground system offers the following advantages over surface railways.

- They can be built with less obstruction to communities and business above ground.
- They are generally competitive in cost terms to elevated railways.
- With modern forms of tunnelling (that is, the New Austrian Method – see Chapter 4) a variety of profiles and sizes of tunnel can be constructed economically.
- They can be taken right into the heart of central business districts, with direct access beneath ground between station and building.
- They are less damaging to the aesthetic landscape of cities than are overhead railways.

These advantages need to be set against three disadvantages.

- Designing for fire escape limits the opportunity for fluid spatial architecture.
- Environmental problems, particularly toxic brake dust and fumes from trains, mean that a high level of physical or air separation is needed between trains, platforms and concourses.
- Underground railways are more prone than conventional railways to terrorist attack.

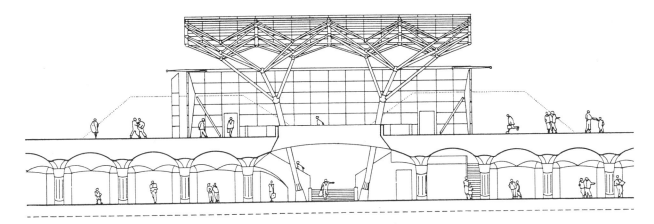

2.40 Structure and light are the two elements used to guide passengers from ground level to underground platforms on the Lyon Metro. Architects: Jourda and Perraudin.

Two aspects of underground station design have emerged of late to increase the architectural potential. First, designers have developed ways of bringing daylight down into the dark caverns of underground stations. This has obvious benefits for the welfare and amenity of travellers. By using deep underground cuts rather than enclosed tunnels, by exploiting angled walls in section, and by using tall 'light' walls that project out to the sky, it is now possible to bring natural light to underground concourses and platforms. This adds to the travellers' sense of direction and of time. The other recent breakthrough in underground station design has been the introduction of new tunnelling techniques. Changes in practice and technology have allowed larger-diameter tunnels to be constructed more economically and also those of sections other than circular bores. Elliptical and egg-shaped tunnel profiles are now possible, which allow the designer to set a variety of curved shapes in juxtaposition. On the Jubilee Line extension, for example, tunnels have been built as circular bores within egg-shaped section stations. The train sits within the pointed end of the 'egg' with the station platform occupying the more spacious round end. The difference in height between the two volumes gives a sense of drama to the station and allows the movable platform screen to slide upwards into the roof space.

Underground railways are generally the preferred option when transit authorities decide to construct new urban railways. Unless ground conditions are such that an overhead system is more economical (as happened with the elevated Bangkok railway), underground railways are an efficient and relatively cost-effective means of moving large numbers of people (up to 90 000 passengers an hour) through a congested city. Normally lines are taken beneath streets, but of necessity they have to pass under buildings from time to time. Where they travel beneath important developments above ground, the opportunity is normally taken to form a new subway station with a direct connection underground. The Metro station Louvre: Rivoli in Paris, for example,

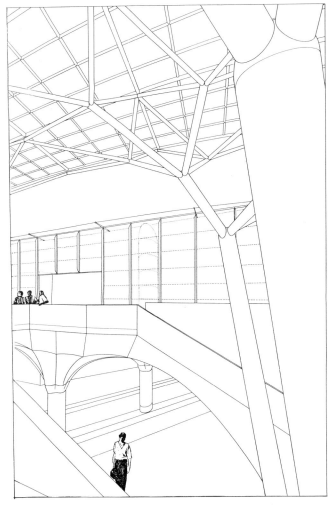

constructed in 1994, now serves almost exclusively the new system of underground shopping malls at the Louvre Museum. Similarly, the new Liverpool Street Station designed to serve CrossRail forms a direct connection with the commercial buildings centred on Moorgate.

There are commercial and cultural advantages in linking underground lines into important developments above ground. Not only does this better serve public transport needs, it also allows underground railway developers to

2.41   (left) Entering underground stations is usually a descent into darkness. Pulling daylight into underground concourses should be an objective of station design.

2.42   (above) One of the functions of walls and roof canopies of underground stations is to pull light down into subterranean concourses. Curved ceilings are particularly useful in this regard. Rotterdam Blaak Metro Station. Architect: Harry Reijnders of Holland Railconsult.

seek a financial contribution from those who own real estate above their lines. Meshing public transportation and private development interests is a crucial aspect of planning urban railways at the outset and, when station design is under way, in ensuring that direct links are made to each.

Light rail

In the past few years light rail has become the preferred option for suburban railway investment in many European cities. This is because it is relatively cheap (about 15–20% of more orthodox rail investment), utilizes wasteland and obsolete railway track, and has lower environmental impacts. The main disadvantages of light rail are its limited capacity in terms of carrying passengers (Docklands Light Railway illustrates this point) and the congestion caused by utilizing existing streets for new track. In Sheffield, England, the construction of Supertram has caused widespread obstruction to the highway system and inconvenience. In roads such as West Street, the laying of the track has also jeopardized the viability of many small businesses along its route.

Light rail is widely considered cost effective, flexible in operation, and environmentally friendly. As it often utilizes existing road space, the visual impact of light rail is fairly small. It is the most likely form of public transport to break the dominance of the motor car in journeying to work. With well-designed tram stops and quiet electronically powered rolling stock, light rail has enormous potential in easing urban congestion and reducing air pollution. In 1992 some

45 light rail schemes were under investigation in British towns.[22]

There are obvious advantages in civic design terms of light rail, whether independent or street-based systems. By using the space between buildings it provides access to the existing architectural infrastructure (and their communities) more effectively than either conventional (heavy) rail systems or metro (underground) systems. Trams, buildings and people form a continuous web of connecting tissue when lines are taken along streets, not beneath them. Proximity breeds the civic dimensions of livability and neighbourliness. The main disadvantage of light rail is that poor design of poles, signage, stops and canopies can disfigure once handsome lengths of cityscape.

The success of light rail depends to a large measure upon the level of design expertise and how early architectural and industrial design skills are brought into the procurement process. Too often architects have been used once the engineering of stations and track has been decided. Then the designers' role is one of cosmetics: instead of fashioning the whole undertaking, architects are used as 'environmental enhancers'. Early design input is essential if the objectives of transport engineering and urban design are to be reconciled. Without a strong 'design' presence, light rail will not be an aesthetically unified undertaking but a collection of disjointed and poorly coordinated actions. This point cannot be overstated with street-based transport systems, where the spaces between buildings are the main channels of public perception. Streets are the medium of the urban

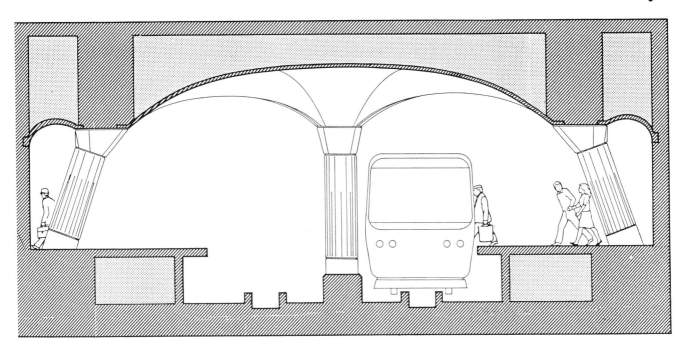

2.43 New tunnelling techniques and approaches to structure have expanded the opportunities for designers on underground railways. Architects: Jourda and Perraudin.

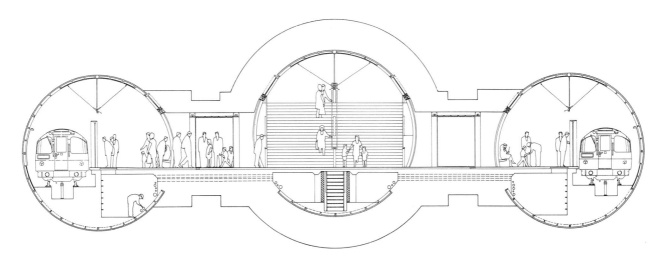

2.44 Safety on underground railways increasingly requires the separation of platform from track. Here at London Bridge Station on the Jubilee Line Extension a sliding glazed screen protects passengers until the train arrives. Architects: Weston Williamson.

experience, and to spoil them through poor engineering and design (as has tended to happen at Manchester) will probably undermine the enterprise.

With many recent light rail systems, architects have been brought in at the outset for these very reasons. The extension to the Docklands Light Railway from Canary Wharf to Beckton was designed by Ahrends Burton and Kolarek (ABK). The role of the architects was to provide a consistent kit of parts and aesthetic language for the dozen or so new stations. They also advised on the design of rolling stock, viaducts and other aspects of trackside engineering. In its appointment of ABK the London Docklands Development Corporation (LDDC) sought a strong and coordinated image for the new railway system. As it ran through areas undergoing great physical upheaval, the need was for clarity and legibility.

Deciding between heavy rail and light rail

As a rule of thumb, 'heavy rail' refers to the normal urban and inter-urban railway systems operated by a national or regional company. To allow for international networks the rolling stock is designed and built to agreed standards (normally UIC) covering not only track but train dimensions

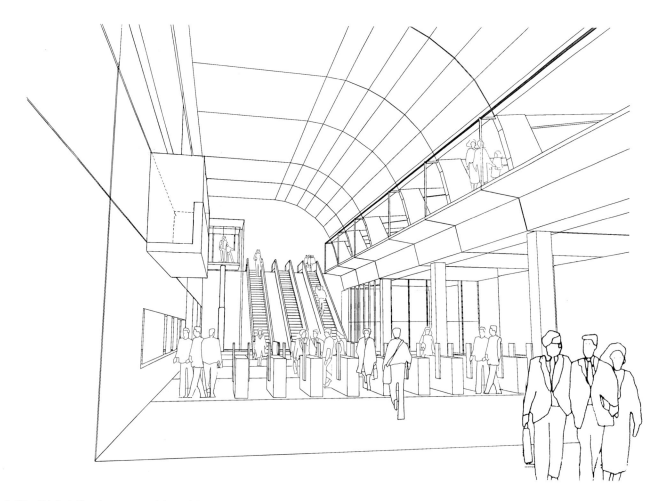

2.45 Well-defined routes and the minimum of barriers are essential to both safety and amenity. Dean Street Station, CrossRail, London. Architects: Troughton McAslan.

and coupling. Heavy rail also encompasses 'heavy rapid transit', which often shares technical standards with conventional railways. Heavy rapid transit (of which both London Underground and Network SouthEast are examples) usually consists of diesel or electrified urban railways, with frequent stops and heavy-duty rolling stock.

By way of contrast, 'light rail' is a guided transit system, which combines the vehicle technology of trams and buses with the characteristics of steel-rail engineering. Light rail, and particularly its modern manifestation (light rapid transit – LRT), employs steel track laid in existing streets, and quiet, relatively high-tech, rolling stock. There is no easy dividing line between light rail as represented by the Docklands Light Railway, the Manchester Metrolink or Sheffield Supertram. Generally, tram systems are street based, and light rail is a combination of track laid in streets and separate tracking systems.

If heavy rail and light rail represent the two main divisions whose characteristics depend mainly upon the degree of segregation and scale of engineering, there remain other refinements. As countries develop international rail networks (as is happening in the EU), a further classification of heavy

rail is appearing. The automated, high-speed railway with integrated traction and signalling (as represented by the French TGV system) represents a fast-growing subsection of heavy rail. At the opposite end of the scale, automated light systems, computer controlled (such as BART in San Francisco), reflect a distinct category of LRT systems.

Light rail has the advantage of flexibility, and is normally cheaper to install and maintain than heavy rail systems. It is well adapted to city and suburban needs but is less cost-effective than heavy rail in dealing with the heaviest traffic flows. Compared with heavy rail, light rail can operate cost-effectively at offpeak times, and effectively spans the demand load from the level of buses to medium-use heavy rail. If light rail cannot compete with heavy rail at periods of peak traffic load, it is less disruptive environmentally, and for many image-conscious cities projects a better picture of urban life. For this reason light rail has been the preferred option for urban regeneration projects from London Docklands to Manchester, and from Rotterdam to Grenoble.

Generally speaking, likely passenger flows determine which system of urban railway to adopt. There is a wide range of operational efficiencies and overlap between sys-

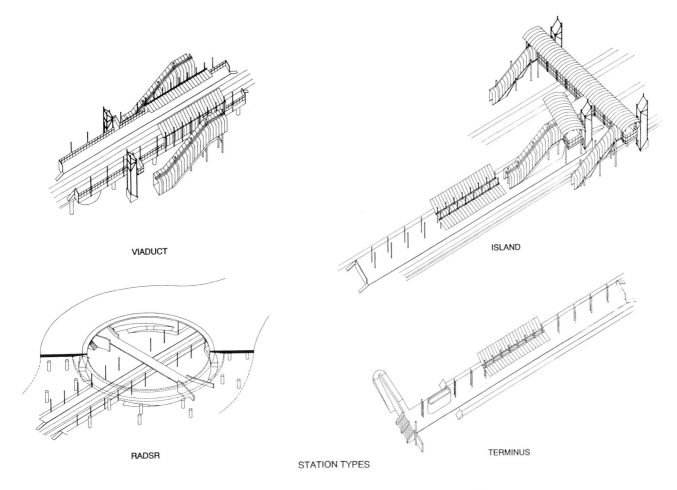

VIADUCT

ISLAND

RADSR

TERMINUS

STATION TYPES

2.46 Different station types on Phase 2 of the Docklands Light Railway. Architects: Ahrends Burton and Koralek.

2.47 At its most modest, light rail in the form of trams can be an effective substitute for polluting urban buses.

tems. It is generally accepted that light rail can operate effectively at flows between 2000 and 20 000 passengers per hour, whereas for heavy rail the equivalent flows are 10 000 to 50 000.[23] French experience suggests that surface light rail is difficult to operate above 9000 passengers an hour, whereafter segregated systems (normally heavy rail) become imperative. These traffic flows suggest that light rail is economic only in terms of populations over 200 000: a point confirmed by experience in Germany, where public funding for LRT is available only to cities in excess of 300 000 people.[24] Such calculations derive from likely population densities in corridors (normally a walking distance of 1 km) and their length. Concentric cities with randomly dispersed, radiating corridors (such as London) are clearly less effective than towns where population densities and public transit systems are considered as one. Where a grid of public transport routes is linked to compact corridors of population, the threshold of viability comes down to levels as low as 100 000.

Having selected the appropriate railway system, transport planners need then to decide upon the spacing of stations. This depends partly upon method of access (by bus, park

and ride, cycle or walking), the perception of the passenger, and political factors. Where most people drive to stations they can be fairly widely spaced, as the car driver expects a rapid journey for forsaking the motor car. A pedestrian, however, accepts greater stops as his or her perception of speed is much slower. Generally speaking, a journey from town edge to city centre should entail not

53

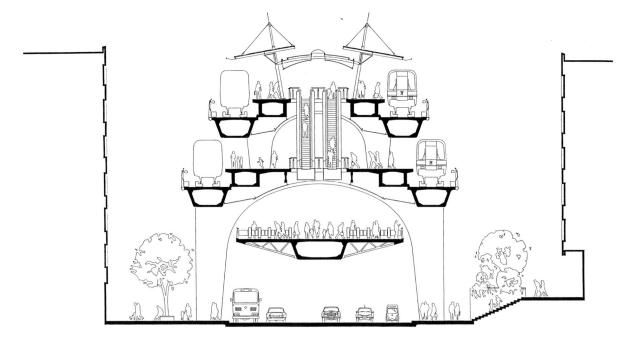

2.48 Elevated light railways provide powerful engineering statements and worthy urban landmarks, as here in Bangkok. Architects: Building Design Partnership.

2.49 Well-designed railways can enhance the development potential of redundant urban land. Architects: Ahrends Burton and Koralek.

2.50 Typical elevated station on the Docklands Light Railway. Architects: Ahrends Burton and Koralek.

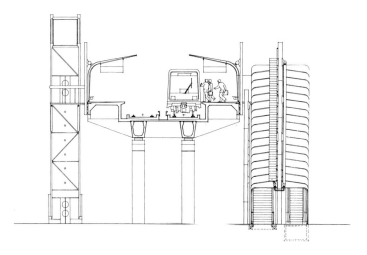

more than ten stops. Beyond this level the journey becomes frustrating. However, station spacing is also a matter of the number of people who wish to alight or join the train. With less than ten boarders or alighters the station is not adequately used, and with over 100 it is over-used. Hence the spacing of stations, the frequency of trains, and the 'speed' perception of passengers are all related factors.

Heavy rail and light rail are the two main categorizations employed for railways, but these are only part of what, in theory at least, should be an integrated transport system. At its upper end there may be links to airports or ferries: at the lower end links to buses, cars, cycles and walking. Integration requires building design, transport and land-use policies to be considered as one, and transport systems to be supportive of each other rather than locked in competitive battles. The cult of privatization that dogged the 1980s and 1990s effectively prevented the UK from developing an integrated transport policy. Elsewhere, particularly in Japan, France and the Netherlands, governments show greater interest in providing a framework whereby different private transport operators each play their part in providing a balanced and efficient public transport system.

The integration of other modes of transport with railways requires stations to be planned to accommodate effective access. Hence bus/rail links are important, as are park and ride and car park/rail links. In the provision of these

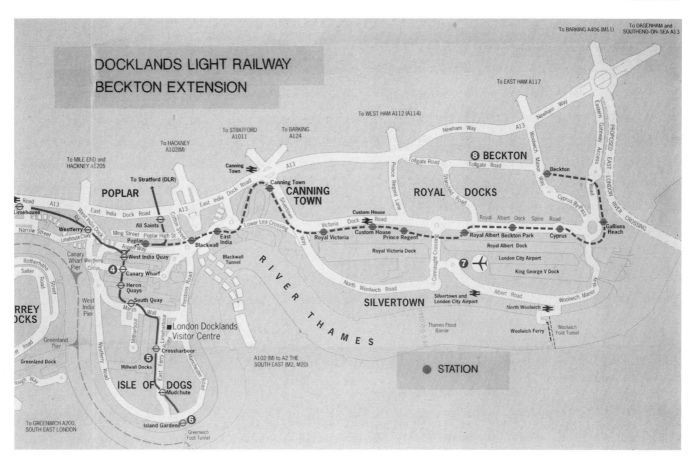

2.51 Plan of the Docklands Light Railway. The regeneration of inner city areas depends upon effective public transport provision.

interfaces the pedestrian and cyclist often suffer; yet the passenger arriving on foot is often by far the most important numerically. Formal provision is frequently made for ready access by taxi, but often at the expense of pedestrian safety (as at Waverley Station, Edinburgh and King's Cross Station, London).

The type of railway chosen, and whether other transport systems are set in competition or effectively integrated, are key considerations in the planning of transportation. The designer's task is greatly helped if the policy framework is well established at the outcome. Making subsequent provision for bus stops, taxi parking or cycle storage can undermine the elegance and operational simplicity of a railway station. As enthusiasts battle over the relative advantage of heavy and light systems, one should not forget that integration across the modes of transportation is what passengers seek. Although sustainable transportation will lead to greater use of both heavy and light rail systems, the railways on their own will not provide all of society's movement needs.

An integrated system is not only good for reducing energy use (by providing an attractive and well-coordinated framework of public transport, which lures passengers away from their cars); it is also beneficial in terms of environmental quality. To have bus, cars and railways in competition is not only inefficient but makes town centres unattractive by adding to congestion. With competition, no system works to maximum efficiency; there is duplication of service, over-provision, under-use, and frequent gridlock. An example is Newcastle Metro, which, when light rail and buses were integrated, attracted 60 million passengers a year. After deregulation, when buses and trains ran in competition, only 50 million were carried by the Metro. The increase in buses led to city centre congestion and subsequent decline of the older urban centre in favour of out-of-town car-based shopping and office developments. Current plans (in 1995) to revive the town centre entail restricting bus use where the Metro provides an adequate service. With hindsight, integrated public transport served business and commercial needs (as well as environmental ones) more effectively than under deregulation.

References

1. I am indebted in the general argument here to Peter Davey, 'Places of transition', *Architectural Review*, February 1995, pp. 4–5.
2. Thomas Markus, *Buildings and Power: Freedom and Control in the Origin of Modern Building Types*, Routledge, London, 1993, pp. 8–13.
3. 'Getting to the Airport', *Architects' Journal*, 30 March 1995, p. 51
4. *Ibid.*; the list is paraphrased and expanded in part.

2.52 Light rail can be
effectively threaded through
existing towns, utilizing parks,
street space and derelict land.
Croydon Tram Link. Architects:
Weston Williamson.

2.53 The Sheffield Supertram
introduces high-tech rolling
stock and stations into a city
engaged in post-industrial
reconstruction.

2.54 The elegant wavy roofline of the tram-stops at Rotterdam Blaak help to identify where to board the trams. The design and construction provide the minimum of hiding place for potential attackers. Architect: Harry Reijnders of Holland Railconsult.

5. 'Charles de Gaulle Airport: The Exchange Module – the TGV Station', press release, 12 September 1994, p. 1.
6. *Ibid.*, p. 2.
7. *Ibid.*
8. Kevin Lynch, *The Image of the City*, MIT Press, Cambridge, MA, 1960, pp. 62–66.
9. Nik Randall, 'Motive forces', *International Architecture and Construction*, No 1. 1993, p. 4.
10. Peter Davey, 'Station to station' *Architectural Review*, February 1995, pp. 48–49.
11. Dennis Sharp (Ed.), *Santiago Calatrava*, E & F N Spon, London, 1992, p. 65.
12. Charles Rattray and Graeme Hutton, 'Spanish steps', *Architectural Review*, February 1995, pp. 50–53.
13. Robert Cervero, 'Transit-focused development', *Universe Journal*, Vol. 4, No. 2, May 1994, p. 3.
14. *Ibid.*, p. 5.
15. In this section I acknowledge my debt to the arguments in *New Futures for Rural Rail* by Paul Salveson, Transet, London, 1993.

16. David Lawrence, *Underground Architecture*, Capital Transport, London, 1994, p. 77. See also *RIBA Journal*, 24 January 1931, p. 108.
17. *Ibid.*, p. 78.
18. *Ibid.*
19. The three points were made in an interview with the author at JLE's offices in London on 19 April 1995.
20. This was apparently Paoletti's intention as communicated to the author in the above interview.
21. *Building*, 7 April 1995, p. 75.
22. Alan Brookes and Michael Stacey, 'Making tracks', *Architects' Journal*, 8 April 1992, p. 30.
23. Phil Haywood, 'Heavy or light rail' in Nigel G. Harris and Ernest W. Godward (Eds) *Planning Passenger Railways*, Transport Publishing Company, Glossop, 1992, p. 38.
24. *Ibid.*, p. 39.

Station layout and design

CHAPTER 3

The design and planning of railway stations

The station acts as an interchange between systems. Here the traveller experiences the transition between the train and the rest of the world – the city, other transport systems such as buses and taxis, and the complexity of street life. Like the airport, the modern railway station is an urban gateway marking both entrance and departure.

To the railway engineer and designer the station consists of six main elements:

- railway track and signalling;
- the platforms;
- circulation areas;
- ticket sales and retail space;
- post and parcel areas;
- station forecourt.

Each has to be clearly defined for safety and ease of circulation reasons, with the connections evident through signing and good design. Hence for the travelling customer the path from station forecourt to ticket office past a newspaper stand and onto platform and thence train needs to be a smooth, legible and well-engineered sequence. For the railway employee the relationship between train, platform and parcels depot is equally important. Where the station management offices are located, the integration with closed-circuit television (CCTV) systems and computerized controls represents another ordering framework that railway station design increasingly has to acknowledge.

Generally speaking, the railway track and signalling systems have fixed engineering parameters which the station designer is rarely able to modify. Upgrading of lines (as for instance in connection with the Channel Tunnel) may involve changing the pattern of platforms or extending them, and this has design ramifications. But generally the architect accepts track as fixed elements, which naturally dictates the arrangement of platforms. The number of platforms and their length is determined by the operation pattern at the station. There is clearly a world of difference between a main-line station and a suburban one serving the same line, and between a terminal and a through station. The number of

3.2 Avoiding obstructions in platform areas by careful design helps with the smooth traffic of people. Here at Duivendrecht Station in the Netherlands the barrier is torpedo-shaped to avoid sudden obstacles. Unfortunately, the litter bins have not been given the same thought.

3.1 Duivendrecht Station, the Netherlands. Architect: Peter Kilsdonk of Holland Railconsult.

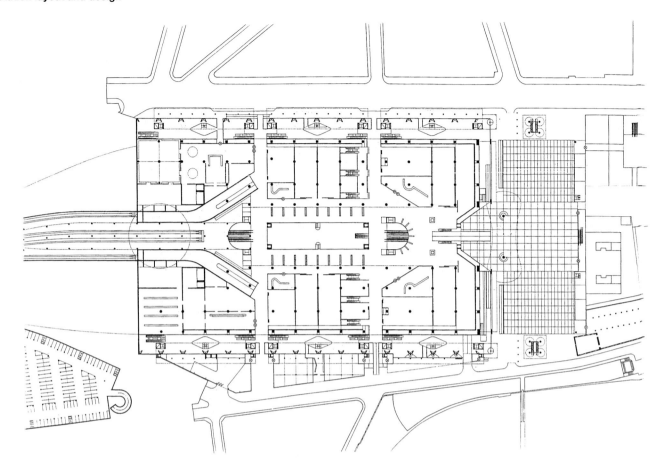

3.3 Stations are highly complex building types that, as here at Abando Station, Bilbao, are small cities in their own right. Note how the station is organized on the basis of streets and squares, which connect with the larger urban area. Architects: Michael Wilford and Partners.

trains to be handled determines to a large degree the number of platforms. As turnaround times reduce (from 50 minutes in the 1950s to 35 minutes today at terminals and 2–4 minutes at intermediate stations[1]) the capacity of stations to handle larger numbers of passengers increases. A greater throughput of trains means more travellers to exploit in shops and cafes in the station, and greater passenger flows in circulation areas.

Table 3.1 Platform widths

Minimum width from platform edge to nearest obstruction	2500 mm
Minimum width overall of island platforms	4000 mm
Recommended width for busy station	8000 mm
Clear platform width to obstruction with train speeds in excess of 100 mi/h (160 km/h)	3000 mm

Source: BR Platform Construction Guide, 1992

Table 3.2 Platform dimensions and design

Length	Maximum train length plus 12 000 mm
End ramps	Not steeper than 1 in 8
Crossfalls	Normally 1 in 40 Min 1 in 100 Max 1 in 12
Height (above top of rails)	915 mm
Recess (below platform coping)	300 mm
Maximum platform radius	360 m
Maximum track gradient (at platform)	1 in 260
Finish	Platform copings to be slip resistant and marked by continuous grooving and lighter colour

Source: BR Platform Construction Guide, 1992

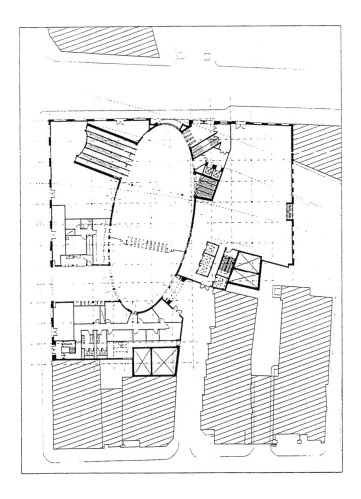

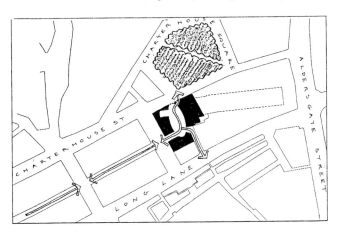

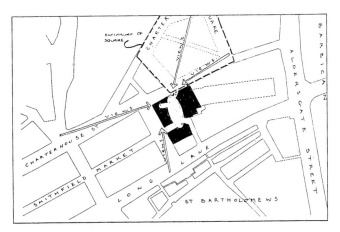

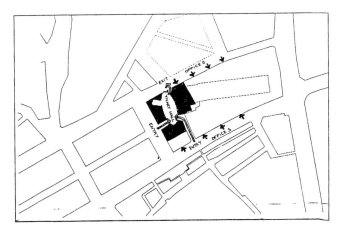

Platform length is determined by train length. In the UK, platforms cannot be shorter than the length of the train serving them. With InterCity trains the maximum platform length is normally 300 m. The width of platforms is a product of anticipated passenger density, usually calculated at one passenger per square metre.[2] Platform width has also to accommodate non-travelling station users (such as those meeting passengers), disabled travellers, and parcel vehicles. Normally a platform of at least 4 m width is required. The width, length and configuration of a platform are products of the level of usage and the type of train the platform serves.

The design of circulation areas is dependent upon a number of factors – density of use, ticket dispensing and control systems, the complexity of levels, whether passengers are regularly carrying luggage, the fluctuations at peak times, and access needs for disabled people. Different strategies exist to deal with the layout of such areas. Rather than design for maximum density, some stations (particularly in underground and metro systems) restrict the number of passengers using a station at peak times by introducing barrier controls. Other strategies involve the elimination of queues by having speedy ticket-dispensing systems, and the avoidance of obstructions (such as flower stalls) within the circulation areas. Commercial pressure to exploit the volume of passenger traffic occasionally runs counter

3.4 Linking the booking hall to the outside world and that of the trains requires considerable building and site-planning skills. Architects: Terry Farrell and Partners.

to the efficient movement of people, and can raise questions of passenger safety, particularly at peak times. Normally circulation areas are zoned into:

- ticket and information areas;
- waiting areas (for meeting passengers);
- dwell areas for intending passengers;

3.5 The station concourse needs to have clearly perceived functional zones and signs, which leave no room for ambiguity. Lille-Europe Station. Architect: Rem Koolhaas with Jean-Marie Duthilleul.

- cafes, bars, shops and bookstall;
- toilets;
- telephone and office facilities (fax, etc.);
- tourist information boards.

Such a list suggests a degree of linking and sequence between the parts. For instance, a passenger usually buys a newspaper after the ticket has been bought, and a person meeting a traveller will need to see the arrival board. Similar connections exist between the cafe area and toilets, and between telephone points and tourist information.

At suburban stations most people reduce the waiting time to a minimum. At intercity stations travellers tend to give themselves greater leeway, and here 'dwell time' is actively exploited. Hence the extent of circulation areas and their complexity are products not only of passenger volume but also of station type. Also, where the station connects with other transport systems (such as intercity linking with underground or metro) the circulation areas are connected both horizontally and vertically. The provision of both clarity and safety are prime considerations in station design, for which the exploitation of architectural means (light, space and structure) is often essential. Stairs, escalators, lifts and ramps are the means by which vertical level changes are achieved. It is clearly important that the design and zoning of circulation areas and the appreciation of means of changing from one level to another are integrated. This is best

3.6 Computer-generated drawings are often necessary to display the complexity of routes in underground stations. Here at the proposed Jubilee Line Extension Westminster Station, banks of escalators are crossed by lift and ventilating shafts. Architects: Michael Hopkins and Partners.

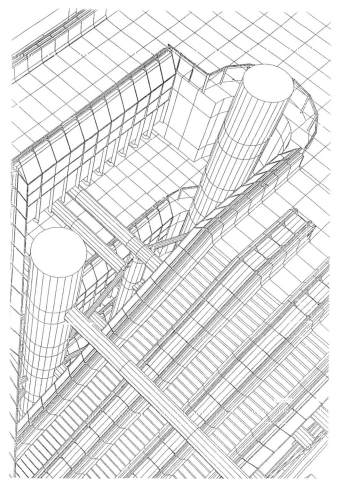

achieved by establishing hierarchies of movement at the outset and relating these to the most important activities (such as ticket booths and train information boards), using principal stairs and escalators as direct extensions to the major routes.

Changing direction is as inevitable at stations as changing level. Again, architectural cues can be employed to deflect movement. Construction, materials and lighting are key elements to exploit, not only to highlight the point where a circulation route changes angle, but to give recognition of where the deflected corridor or access stair is going. A good design is one in which the passenger knows where

3.7   The station entrance is well sheltered at Rotterdam Blaak Station, and the forecourt is arranged with pedestrian priority. Architect: Harry Reijnders of Holland Railconsult.

to go without the need to read direction signs. The role of structure (column, wall and roof) takes on more than a constructional function; it has a secondary role in giving meaning to the circulation pattern adopted.

Ticket sales and retail areas occupy the main circulation concourse of most stations. For railway companies, revenue from shops and restaurants is an important secondary source of income. In 1993/94 British Rail made some £153.7 million in rents from enterprises trading in stations.[3] Creating a range of retail outlets (pharmacy, bookshops, florists, etc.) has benefit for the traveller, but increasingly the shops in stations are being used by the local community as ordinary shops. The effect is to change the character of the railway station, and to encourage its perception by people who live nearby as a neighbourhood shopping centre. As with airports, the distinction between land uses has become blurred at many major railway stations. With a growth in conference facilities at mainline termini, the difference between station, office and retail centre is sometimes hard to make.

Generally speaking, ticket purchase occurs before other sales are made at stations. A passenger queuing to buy a sandwich to eat on a journey tends to have bought the ticket first. This pattern allows the ticket sales point to have primacy in terms of station layout. The first point of contact in the station's concourse is the ticket office; other retail or leisure activities are between ticket point and platform barrier. Shops and restaurants also tend to be more visible than telephone points and toilets. There are both practical and commercial reasons for this. Telephones need aural privacy and are often well away from major circulation areas and points where train announcements are relayed. Toilets too are often discreetly hidden, and increasingly at stations admission is by payment. As stations are usually under cover, cafes and restaurants often exploit the space at their perimeter by taking seating into the public concourse. This gives life and sociability to many stations but can pose danger to passengers hurrying to their trains. Clear zoning of the space nearby is an important consideration, not only at food outlets but also at other shops where queues regularly form.

Stations are central to the distribution of post and parcel services. Scheduled train services provide much of the distribution of the UK's mail. Parcel traffic at stations is often by van and trolley. Conflicts with passenger movement occur, and the station designer needs to zone circulation and office areas to reduce operational friction. As much of the post handled is of value, a secure area is needed at the station. Direct loading onto vans and sometimes larger lorries requires the provision of ramps.

The station forecourt provides direct vehicular access to the station for private vehicles, for other forms of public transport, for deliveries of various kinds, and most importantly for passengers arriving on foot. The station entrance often provides shelter for people waiting to use buses or taxis, or merely lingering before being met. Forecourt, station canopy, entrance and concourse are therefore related elements in the progression from town to train. An increasing trend is towards park and ride schemes, whereby car parks are provided alongside stations. Where this occurs, a distinction needs to be made between long-stay parking and short-stay parking for set-down and pick-up purposes. Since as many as a quarter of typical rail travellers have started their journey in a car, the design of the station and its forecourt are important elements in easing the transition from one mode of travel to another.

The majority of rail travellers arrive at stations on foot. While other forms of public and private transport are of growing importance in terms of delivering the passenger to

3.8 Providing inadequate car access at station entrances may lead to illegal or antisocial parking. Duivendrecht Station. Architect: Peter Kilsdonk of Holland Railconsult.

forecourt space will normally lead to more satisfying arrangements from an urban design viewpoint.

Station design: practical considerations

Stations are collections of structures performing different but sequentially related functions. They are rarely single buildings enclosed by a unifying roof; instead, they consist of various types of engineering and architectural structures grouped around the dictates of railway lines. As stations are usually approached from one side, they have a logical procession of spaces and buildings from town to train. This linear sequence is counterbalanced by the parallel geometries of the trains and platforms. Hence the station is a combination of symmetrical and asymmetrical patterns, each with its own unique structure. The task of the station architect is to establish a clear relationship between the parts, to signal the hierarchies of movement by architectural means, and to present a favourable technological and environmental image of the railway company.

Different types of station have their own preferred pattern of accommodation. The distribution and arrangement of the parts mirrors both the internal functioning of the station and the external patterning of the streets in the town. Irrespective of these patterns, most stations consist of a combination of the following elements, each with its own technical requirements.[4]

External circulation

Smooth connections in and out of the station are an important aspect of customer satisfaction. Travellers should be presented with clear routes to pedestrian ways, access roads, car parks, taxi ranks, bus stops etc. Ideally, these routes should be under cover, well lit, and safe to use. External signs and directional maps are also important, with the size, design and positioning of signs in direct relationship to their priority.

Architectural means should be employed to signal the significant access points (such as suspended canopies over main station entrances). Station layout should also ensure that sightlines in major circulation areas are not

the station, the foot traveller remains numerically the most important. Avoiding conflicts at the station forecourt is largely a matter of design and of ensuring that space for movement is fairly allocated for the different modes. At some stations, such as London's Charing Cross, the foot passenger is herded into over-narrow roadside pens in order to create space for taxi and minibus access. Here at least half of the forecourt is given over to wheeled traffic, yet by the author's estimate at least 90% of the station users arrive on foot. Greater equity in the allocation of obstructed. The width of routes needs to reflect their relative importance within the functioning of the station. Pedestrian paths should not be less than 1800 mm wide and should be kept free of hazards such as litter bins.

Segregation of movement is important. Those arriving and departing should not have to share a narrow entrance, and pedestrian, car and cycle movements should be zoned into distinctive areas. Where cross-flows occur, pedestrians should have a clearly recognized right of way – perhaps with the use of a raised paving area. The design of details such as handrails, stair or ramp nosings should be such that, by using contrasting colours, textures or materials, they are clearly discernible to those with disabilities.

The architectural quality of larger stations is determined by the attention given to circulation areas, both within the station and in its environs. Paving design and planting are both important factors. Block-paved pedestrian routes and parking areas are preferable to asphalt, and trees mixed with groundcover planting are better than mass shrub planting. With external surfaces and planting, attention needs to be given to initial and long-term appearance, particularly bearing in mind maintenance costs and the replaceability of materials.

3.9 Handling great and often irregular flows of people demands large uncluttered spaces and clearly identified routes. Dean Street Station, CrossRail. Architects: Troughton McAslan.

Lighting is an important consideration for both amenity and safety. A mixture of lighting is needed from lighting bollards illuminating pedestrian routes, to feature lighting around the station entrance, and street lighting for station approach roads. Where CCTV is in operation, lighting

Table 3.3 Platform access: stairs

Going	300 mm
Rise	150 mm
Width	1200 mm (min)
	1800 mm (max without intermediate handrails)
Headroom	1850 mm (measured normal to the pitch)
Number of steps	Max 16
	Min 3
Disabled access	Maximum number of steps between landings: 8
Handrail	Continuous on both sides at 850 mm above nosings and 50 mm in diameter

Source: BR Platform Construction Guide, 1992

Table 3.4 Platform access: ramps

Ramps needed	For all level changes up to 500 mm
Ramps needed	For level changes above 500 mm in conjunction with stairs
Gradients	1 in 12 max
	1 in 20 preferable
Length	10 m max
Landing (between ramps)	1800 mm
Width	1200 mm (min)
	1450 mm (preferred)
Finish	Slip resistant

Source: BR Platform Construction Guide, 1992

3.10 At Lyon-Satolas Station, the voluminous interior of the ticket concourse is both welcoming and reassuring to travellers. There are no columns or obstacles to interrupt movement or provide hiding space for potential attackers. Architect: Santiago Calatrava.

levels must be significantly higher, and poles capable of mounting both lighting and cameras should be installed. Directional signs, timetable boards and station maps also need supplementary lighting.

Internal circulation

Once inside the station, travellers need to be able to find their way from ticket hall to train without obstruction, frustration or ambiguity. Progression through the four main zones of stations – access and entrance, tickets and information, waiting areas, platform and trains – needs to be clearly defined.

The most significant features, such as the ticket office, need to be given the strongest architectural form. The language of design should signal functional hierarchies. The width of routes should reflect not just the scale of movement but their symbolic role. Station entrances, for example, may be wider

than passenger flows alone would indicate, ticket areas higher than function alone dictates, and platform canopies more elegantly engineered than is technically necessary.

Circulation through the station should achieve ease of movement, comfort and speed. As not all travellers are ambulant, and some have children in tow, movement needs to cater for all levels of mobility. Comfort is dependent upon shelter and warmth. Covered routes are necessary, and the use of glass may allow the designer to exploit passive solar gain to provide warmth at no direct cost (see the

Table 3.5 Main functional zones of typical station

Departure:	Parking, access and entrance	Arrival:
Rapid egress	Tickets and information	Smooth progression
from train to	Waiting and commercial	with clearly defined
entrance	Platform and trains	points of transition

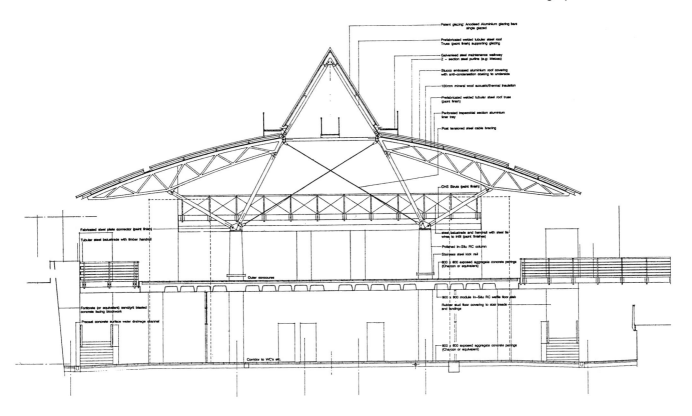

3.11 The open structure of Manchester Airport Station and the central rooflight provide the means to deal with smoke extraction – an important consideration after the King's Cross fire. Architects: Austin-Smith: Lord.

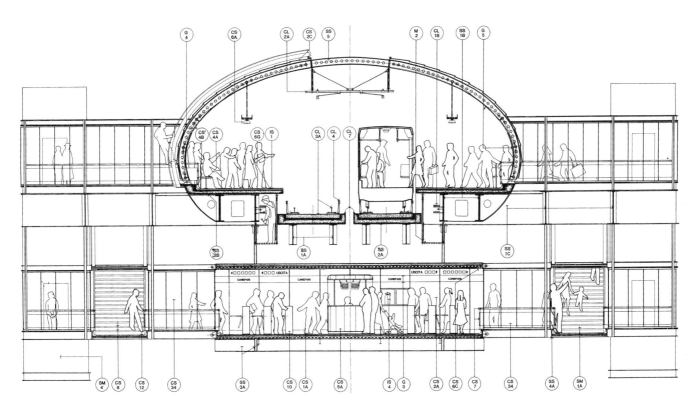

3.12 Stations are busy and often congested places. This section of Brin Station, Genoa, by the Renzo Piano Building Workshop shows the range of age groups and the various speeds of ambulant travel that designers need to accommodate.

3.13 At Lyon-Satolas Station, the escalators ascend towards the light from a large column-free concourse. Space, light and expressive structure provide the means by which travellers are guided through the station. Architect: Santiago Calatrava.

Table 3.6 Platform finishes

Clay tiles	Poor slip resistance when wet
	Good appearance
	Repairs relatively easily undertaken
	Not suitable for vehicular traffic
Concrete paving blocks	Good visual impact
	Excellent wear qualities
	Good slip resistance
	Repairs easily undertaken
Terrazzo tiles	Only suitable where kept dry
	'Up market' appearance
	Excellent wear qualities
	Repairs expensive
Hot-rolled asphalt	Average to poor appearance
	Good resistance to wear
	Requires expert laying
	Repairs tend to 'show'
Dense bitumen macadam	Available in a variety of colours
	Good resistance to heavy wear
	Repairs tend to 'show'

Source: BR Platform Construction Guide, 1992

Dutch station case studies in Chapter 7). Where glass is used for walls and doors, the design of mullions and glazing bars needs to help identify the position of the glass. Direct sunlight can cause glare, overheating in summer time, and can obscure information displays. Deflectors and solar screens may be needed.

The spatial experience of circulation areas should reinforce the functional priorities. Voluminous concourse spaces where shops, ticket points and information displays are located can usefully be used in conjunction with narrower corridors or routes to private offices. The gestures implicit in the design of the station need to mirror the intended functioning of the parts, especially the distinguishing of major and minor spaces, and public and private routes.

Floor finishes need also to help define routes and the transition between the main functional zones of the station. Brick paving, non-slip stone finishes, terrazzo and textured ceramic surfaces could all be used to guide travellers at both perceptual and practical levels. Finishes that are robust and easy to clean are essential, especially when trolley traffic has to be accommodated. At entrances, matting may be necessary to restrict the spread of dirt or to prevent interior surfaces becoming wet and slippery. Finishes of both floors and walls should be selected to aid the identification of circulation areas. Geometric patterning of carpets and other floor finishes helps to maintain good appearance even when the surfaces are stained or worn. Such patterns can also provide directional guidance.

It is important to ensure in the planning of stations that pedestrian routes are not impeded by seats, litter bins, poster displays and vending machines. The travellers' real and perceived sense of progression from station entrance to train is the main priority. Internal circulation should also not be obstructed by discarded trolleys or the activities of parcel services. Care given to the storage of trolleys and, through good planning, the avoidance of their being deposited near stairs or ramps will prevent passenger bottlenecks and accidents later.

Ticket offices

Customers should readily be able to find their way to the ticket sales area. It is here that financial transactions are made and hence where travellers and staff come into direct contact. The quality of environment, the ability to talk comfortably on a one-to-one basis, and the layout of the ticket hall should all create a favourable and reassuring image.

Individual ticket positions where ticket sales, reservations and the supply of published information are dispensed should be designed so that they can be served by a single queue. This saves on space and gives a sense of privacy at the point of sale. A single queue also allows waiting travellers to be given supplementary information in the form of advertising or train timetable displays. Space for automatic ticket machines should also be provided.

Normally the station manager's office overlooks the sales floor for efficient monitoring and supervision of the staff–customer interface. The staff offices behind the ticket screen should not be in evidence at the point of sale but screened from the customers' view. As large amounts of cash are stored, questions of security and safety of staff need to be considered, particularly at larger stations.

Ticket halls should be spacious areas where the quality of materials, finishes and lighting is of the highest specification. Along with the interior of trains, it is here that customer perceptions of quality are forged. Well-coordinated interior design, from seats to the layout of ticket sales points, helps to establish the image of the railway company. Consequently, ticket halls tend to employ more expensive materials than elsewhere in the station, particularly right at the point where cash is dispensed.

Commercial areas

Shops and restaurants within station areas serve customer needs and add greatly to the railway company's revenue. It is important that a good balance of commercial facilities is provided without jeopardizing the efficient running of the station. There are space, hierarchical and station management issues involved in this balance.

Signing of retailing units is often a problem. The standardized logos of many familiar retail names can disrupt the harmonized signing of stations, and where traveller information should be paramount it is often the case that shop signs prove the most visible. Another problem concerns the use of space outside retail units. Many shops and station cafes adopt this space as their own, sometimes jeopardizing movement along concourses.

Other facilities serving customer needs, such as telephones, post boxes and vending machines, may be located near circulation routes. They are best placed as alcoves just outside main passageways rather than as islands that travellers have to negotiate.

Shops and cafes often have their own shopfront design and external furniture. The coordination of these elements into the station environment requires design cooperation between railway and retail companies. Similarly, seats and tables placed outside cafes can jar with well-maintained station interiors. Litter, too, deposited around fast-food outlets poses a hazard to travellers, who may slip on discarded hamburger wrappings, and raises an issue of responsibility for the removal of refuse. A useful deterrent is to insist that all retailers use well-marked plastic cups and bags, thereby helping to identify the offending material.

Waiting rooms

Waiting areas need to provide shelter, comfort, amenity and travel information. Such areas may be alongside buffets or may be self-contained spaces. Waiting rooms are normally heated, carpeted and (unlike platforms) provided with upholstered seating. As passengers here are waiting for trains, waiting areas are normally equipped with train departure and arrival monitors, public address system, clock, litter bin and interior planting. As many travellers pass the waiting time reading, the level of lighting is high. Also, as these are travellers about to board trains, the impression of quality is important. Waiting rooms are normally finished in cotton-backed vinyl, hardwood trim, carpet, linoleum and stainless steel. Painted finishes are also commonly employed, especially where problems of vandalism necessitate regular upgrading.

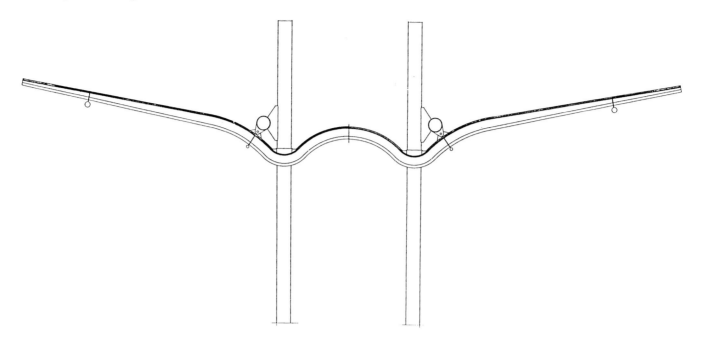

3.14 Structural design is a key element of station architecture. Simple, elegant and easily maintained canopies can do much to enhance the station environment. Architects: Ahrends Burton and Koralek.

Station enclosures and platform shelters

Passengers need to be protected from the elements while waiting for trains, and staff need a reasonably sheltered working environment. Station enclosures need to exclude rain, provide shelter from wind, and allow for daylight penetration. The traditional qualities of large glazed atria-like spaces in nineteenth-century stations provide an admirable example today. Glass is preferable to polycarbonate sheets, which are easily scratched and tend to discolour. Modern glasses can provide a measure of solar protection and insulation.

Glazed roofs combine good appearance with flexibility in both plan and section. They are generally fairly lightweight and self-maintaining. They are rarely entirely waterproof, but glazed station canopies provide the shelter and good appearance needed. Solid roofs deal more effectively with driving rain, but the lack of light beneath means that energy is consumed to light signs and routes. Stringent fire requirements limit the use of glazed roofs or require the introduction of special protective glasses and jointing systems. Fire and smoke hazards vary with situation, but extraction systems and means of escape require to be considered at the outset.

Station canopies need to project as far as the platform edge and signal sightlines permit. With curved platform layouts, roofs cannot usually project to the same extent as with straight platforms. Station canopies do not usually extend for the full length of platforms. About 50% of platform

3.15 The provision of access for roof maintenance, without disrupting the life of stations and impeding pedestrian flows along platforms, needs to be considered at the design stage. Architects: Austin-Smith: Lord.

lengths are normally covered, the remainder being open with separate station shelters provided every carriage length or so.

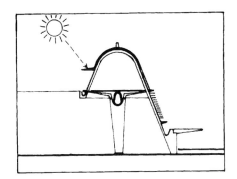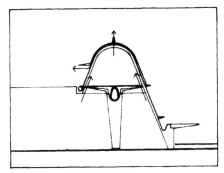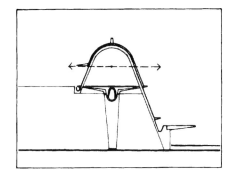

3.16 Bridges over railway tracks need to provide solar protection (left), ventilation (centre) and views (right). Architects: Weston Williamson.

Preventing water penetration is an important feature of station safety. Floor finishes can become dangerous when wet. Where water may be driven in around the edges of canopies (as at platform edges), care should be taken to specify finishes that are non-slip even when saturated. As driving rain is a problem on exposed stations, canopies need sometimes to have a skirt to prevent water reaching the platform horizontally.

The structure of canopies, shelters and enclosures is what gives many stations their characteristic appearance. The grid of columns, beams, glazing bars and panels of glass and cladding establishes the backcloth for other station activities. The columns and beams have both an aesthetic and a practical role. They give stations their sense of direction on foot; their rhythmic spacing helps establish the speed of trains for seated travellers; and the refinement of their details helps to establish (as at Waterloo International) a relationship between station and train design.

Lightweight station canopies do not perform well as acoustic enclosures. Their very thinness means that sound is not absorbed but echoes from surface to surface. This means that public address systems need to have closely spaced speakers to prevent announcements being drowned by the noise of passing trains.

Toilets

Although most trains have their own toilets, their provision in stations is an important measure of customer satisfaction. Toilets need to function well (even when subject to frequent vandalism), look good, and be kept clean. Good appearance can help to deter vandals, who appear to be attracted to the cheap and shoddy within stations. For this reason toilets are normally expensively detailed, with hardwoods, ceramic tiles and good quality door furniture specified. Better quality materials tend to be more vandal-proof than cheaper ones, and make the task of maintaining good appearance and cleanliness easier. Where possible, natural light and ventilation should be exploited, as artificial light and mechanical ventilation greatly increase cost and risks from vandalism.

The planning of toilets should separate WCs from the sanitary zone (where wash-handbasins are located) with spacious internal areas. Queuing space away from circulation areas should be provided at the busier stations. Soap-dispensing, hand-drying equipment and mirrors should all be provided (preferably not over basins), as should facilities for disabled travellers. The provision of toilets for disabled people, with special handrails, extra width and integral washing facilities, should be provided as a matter of course (especially as they are rarely installed on trains). Likewise, parent and baby rooms should be provided at most busy suburban and mainline stations. Where payment for the toilets is made, the provision of turnstiles and separate entrance and exit points will need to be provided.

Passenger bridges

Bridges are generally preferable to pedestrian tunnels as a means of crossing over the tracks to distant platforms. They are usually cheaper to build and offer greater amenity than artificially lit tunnels. Bridges are normally enclosed to deter stone throwing (which is one of the most common forms of vandalism on railways) and suicides. The view out of passing trains is an entertainment for many, and gives travellers an idea of the arrival of their train. Bathed in sunlight, railway footbridges are important station landmarks, making them easier to find than tunnels. The natural light and external views give passengers using bridges a greater sense of direction than those crossing the tracks by other means. Normally footbridges are located near the centre of platforms not far from the entrance to ticket offices, and are usually provided with ramps and lifts.

Access for disabled people

There are many forms of physical and sensory disability that stations need to cater for. Many travellers have limited mobility, vision or hearing, which affects their ability to use station facilities and board trains. Stations must be designed so that disabled people can travel by train with ease, comfort, dignity and safety.

Disabled provision is a legal and moral responsibility. In their customer care policies most railway companies place emphasis upon providing access for all. The statutory duties under the Chronically Sick and Disabled Persons Act 1970, the Disabled Persons Act 1981 and the Disability Discrimination Act 1995 require provision to be made at stations for a variety of impairment. In addition to disability, architects need to design stations so that people can cope conveniently with young children or heavy baggage (the latter is a particular problem at mainline termini and airport stations).

Disabled travellers represent an important market for railway companies, and providing for their needs projects a favourable image for other customers. Also, the special standards needed for disabled passengers raise the general level of provision for all.

By good design it is possible to limit or even eliminate the difficulties faced by disabled travellers. Typical measures to ease access for disabled people at stations are:

- providing lifts to supplement stairs or ramps;
- avoiding short flights of steps by installing ramps;
- increasing the width of routes and doorways;
- increasing the level of lighting, especially at entrances and staircases;
- using textured paving to define safe limits;
- installing clear warning and directional signs (some may be in Braille);
- providing additional handrails for staircases;
- providing special disabled access ticket desks;
- providing disabled toilets and telephone;
- providing screens and barriers that are solid at ground level for detection by people using canes.

Information signs

Rail journeys often involve passengers' changing trains to reach their destination. Timetable information, the expected arrival of trains etc. need to be presented in a coherent and organized fashion. There are three main ways in which this information reaches the traveller:

- by poster display for main timetables;
- by electronic screen for imminent train movements;
- by voice announcement.

Information screens, illuminated monitor displays and announcements keep passengers waiting at platforms informed of the arrival and departure of trains. Many travellers will seek this information in the tickets and information zone. It is here, after they have bought a ticket, that they usually begin to plan their journey. Poster displays and leaflets are normally the first point where travel information is sought.

Main indicator boards provide information in the waiting and commercial zones. Being electronic they can be quickly updated to inform passengers of, say, late-running trains. The main indicator boards are normally supplemented by smaller electronic monitors at platform entrances and near food courts. Separate arrivals and departures monitors may also be provided at larger stations.

Travellers making connections will normally search out the full timetable monitor, which, placed near to waiting areas, provides more extensive information about a variety of destinations. The system, though details may vary at each station, should provide a visually coherent and structured approach. The three main means of giving customer information at the station are dependent upon the provision of well-sited clocks. Also, as customers who have missed their intended connection often need to telephone, the placing of payphones near to information areas is vital.

As a single display screen may not be adequate for the volume of passengers, it is common practice to place repeater monitors along platforms and in different locations in waiting or commercial areas. This is particularly true for 'connections' display material.

Station types, facilities and standards

Of all building types, stations are amongst the most technically demanding. As at airports, the architect has to balance strict programmatic and engineering requirements with the need to address the needs of the travelling passenger – both aesthetic and practical. Increasingly also the designer

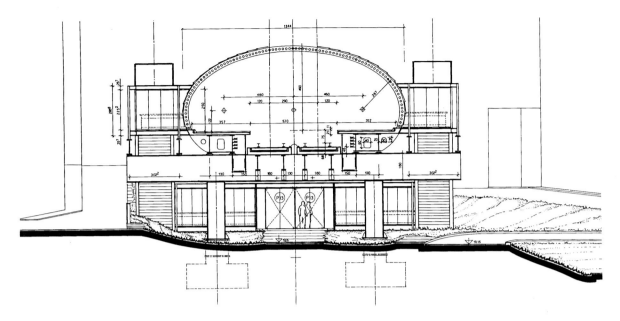

3.17 The sectional design of stations as well as their plan should help to identify key station areas, such as entrances, ticket areas and platforms. Architects: Renzo Piano Building Workshop.

of stations has a range of health, safety and environmental standards to face. To make the architect's job easier when confronted by such complex requirements, most client bodies produce briefing guides, which provide invaluable technical information and organizational parameters.

Stations are normally classified into eight types based upon functional requirements and passenger throughput. These are:

- mainline terminal;
- mainline interchange station;
- mainline station;
- busy suburban station;
- typical suburban station;
- suburban interchange station;
- quiet suburban or rural station;
- unmanned station.

The technical demands of each, whether heavy or light rail, vary, as do the needs of passengers. Briefing guides, such as Network SouthEast's *Core Area Station Guidelines*,[5] embrace both practical and logistical questions on the one hand and issues of passenger amenity on the other. For relatively simple stations the footprint plan is generally given to the architect. Tried and tested layouts of booking hall, station entrance, platform configuration and staff offices normally accompany the designers' brief. This avoids unnecessary reinvention of the wheel, and once a layout has become preferred operationally it is clearly a nonsense to depart from its broad spatial and hierarchical principles. However, as station design is an evolving craft, with ever stricter safety and environmental factors to incorporate, no two stations are ever alike in spite of facing similar constraints.

The role of briefing guides raises aesthetic and ethical questions. As each railway company (such as InterCity or ScotRail) has its own briefing manual there emerges quite naturally a house style for the station on a particular line. This extends superficially to graphics and colouring, and more deeply to station layout and architectural style. Conflicts of interest can occur in two ways. First, consistency across a large number of stations can prove tiresome for travelling customers, whose only clue to a station is in its name. For some this may be reassuring, but the lack of variety and richness could be considered a failure of enlightened patronage. Second, architects appointed to design a particular station find their room for aesthetic innovation curtailed by over-rigid prescription. In earlier times (as with parts of the London Underground) the station designer was part of an in-house team, and this reinforced the sense of corporate identity. More recently (as with London's CrossRail project) private architects have been appointed, each noted for their freshness of design approach. In these circumstances, there can be a conflict between aesthetic freedom and the strict parameters of briefing guides. However, where rules have been interpreted freely (as with the Jubilee Line Extension in London), there can emerge a collection of stations with little direct consistency except for the signs. Outside the UK there seems less concern for corporate regularity: Renzo Piano's Brin Station in Genoa (see Chapter 8), for instance, has little in common organizationally or aesthetically with the other stations on the line.

The position of a particular station within a category is a question both of location and of the throughput of passengers. A small station that attracts large ticket sales has the effect of pushing it up to a higher categorization, as revenue for tickets can be exploited to achieve sales elsewhere, such as in shops. Conversely, a large station (such as Clapham Junction in London) that is mainly a passenger interchange and does not regenerate large ticket sales will move down the list. With privatization, ticket sales are increasingly used as an indicator of further development potential.

The main facilities to be considered at the different station types are as follows.

Mainline terminal:
- waiting concourse;
- travel indicator board;
- retail and refreshment shops;
- travel centre;
- ticket hall;
- parcels depot;
- toilets, including facilities for disabled people;
- security point;
- first-aid point;
- telephones and business area;
- Suburban rail, bus, taxi and metro interchange;
- tourist information centre;
- staff accommodation.

Mainline interchange station:
- waiting concourse;
- travel indicator board;
- retail and refreshment unit(s);
- travel centre and ticket hall (combined);
- parcels point;
- toilets;
- telephones;
- suburban rail, bus and taxi interchange;
- customer car parking;
- staff offices.

Mainline station:
- waiting area;
- travel indicator board;
- retail and refreshment unit;
- travel centre and ticket hall (combined);
- parcels point;

- toilets;
- telephones;
- bus and taxi connection;
- car parking;
- staff offices.

Busy suburban station:
- waiting area;
- travel indicator board;
- retail and refreshment unit;
- ticket hall;
- parcels point;
- toilet;
- telephones;
- bus and taxi connection;
- car parking;
- staff offices.

Typical suburban station:
- waiting area (sheltered);
- ticket office and ticket machines;
- telephone;
- taxi area;
- car parking;
- bicycle storage;
- staff office.

Suburban interchange station:
- waiting area (sheltered);
- travel indicator board;
- retail and refreshment unit;
- ticket office and ticket machines;
- telephone;
- staff offices.

Quiet suburban station:
- waiting area (sheltered);
- ticket machines;
- car parking;
- bicycle storage;
- telephone.

Unmanned station:
- waiting area (canopy);
- ticket machine;
- public address system;
- car parking;
- security lighting and CCTV;
- telephone.

The above list may vary according to circumstances, but it remains a rough guide for establishing the range of facilities according to the hierarchy of station type. Also, as new station types occur, such as airport stations, they will require a separate categorization with facilities specific to their generic needs.

Where two or more systems overlap, as for example when a mainline terminal station gives direct access to metro or suburban services (as happens at London's Waterloo Station), the complexity increases. This leads to the exploitation of various levels for different operational needs (with all the implicit difficulties of moving travellers safely along stairs and escalators) and to people crossing between systems to use facilities rather than to travel. The more retail, leisure and catering units are provided, the more non-travellers are attracted to stations. This may benefit the owners of railway estate, who can earn up to 20% of their total revenue from retail-type sales, but it can impede the smooth movement through stations of legitimate railway travellers.

Once a station's position has been established on the checklist, the range of facilities naturally follows. The architect therefore has a firmly established schedule of accommodation and other guidance to follow. Although the technical parameters are usually well defined, what is often lacking is a philosophy to follow. Whereas a designer will be told how many toilets to provide, there is less likely to be a statement of what a railway station is, and what overall form it should take. The station concept is often largely left up to the architect. Austin-Smith: Lord, who designed the new railway station at Manchester Airport, were instructed to use architecture as a means to guide travellers through the various platform and concourse levels, thereby avoiding signs that necessarily had to be in several languages. Such guidance at a more philosophical level is rare, however.

From an operational point of view, though different stations may fit into separate categories, they are part of a network managed as an integral unit. Staff often interchange between stations much as passengers do. Also, staff may not be present all of the time but merely man the station at peak travel times (that is, the morning and evening rush hour). Hence suburban and light rail stations need to be operationally effective when manned and unmanned. This affects the policy and design approach for dealing with vandalism, theft, personal attack and car crime on the one hand, and ticket sales and travel information on the other. Unmanned stations, though they are less intensively used than others, suffer more vandalism and travellers more personal attack. The designer needs to specify materials, lighting and security systems with this in mind. Bearing in mind that over 60% of Network SouthEast's stations fall into the category of unmanned or partially manned stations, the problem of maintenance and its increasing cost has implications for both design and estate management.

Aspects of station design

Though the design of stations is undertaken on an individual basis, there are principles and constraints that apply across types and locations. Of these the most important are as follows.

Site choice
Stations should be located where they are well connected to other aspects of the urban or regional infrastructure. This means a good central location in a town, a position where bus and road access is direct in the suburbs, and where interchange is easy with other forms of public transport in a large city. It also makes sense to choose a site with good visual links, as actual prominence helps with the travellers' perception of where the station is, and how it can be reached. Such considerations lead to public gathering space at the perimeter of stations (as in London's Euston Station) and, in Haussmann's Paris, to stations being sited where they form terminations to major boulevards or landmarks on the riverside.

Station layout and design

3.18 The new station at Rotterdam Blaak was formed at a crossing of existing underground metro and tram lines, making the station a convenient interchange between rail systems. Architect: Harry Reijnders of Holland Railconsult.

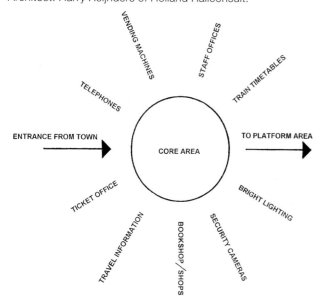

3.19 Typical facilities within core area.

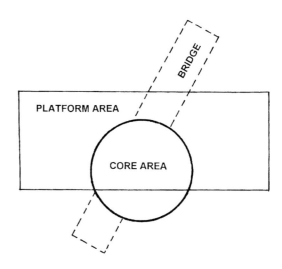

3.20 Diagrammatic layout of station showing the three main zones: core area, peripheral (platform) area and bridge.

Location of station is therefore a matter of practical connection and visual perception. The choice of site also opens up opportunities for subsequent urban design or architectural expression. The expansion of London's Charing Cross Station by Terry Farrell and Partners in 1989 allowed the building known as Embankment Place to landmark the position of the station on the Thames waterfront.

Site choice, public access points and station layout are connected factors. These are not matters that should be left to transport planners, as their engineering dictates may, if immoderate by urban design concerns, militate against a satisfactory site choice and layout of station.

Choosing a site is also a matter of size and shape. Simple rectangular sites are easier and cheaper to develop than irregular ones. Order, procession and legibility – key factors

in moving people through complex structures – are difficult qualities to achieve where sites lack geometric regularity. Size is also important; the station exists as an enclosed, territorially bounded structure, and as an external gathering space. There needs to be adequate space outside the station entrance for bus stops, taxi ramps, car parks, and public meeting areas. Much greeting of friends occurs at stations, and this social function needs to be accommodated with a sense of style, not cramped onto noisy concourses.

Core and peripheral areas

Stations large and small consist of core areas, where ticket halls and the like are located, and peripheral areas with platforms, bridges and subways. The core area is most people's understanding of the centre of the station. Here ticket sales are made, newspapers bought, travel times checked and staff offices located. The core area is linked to the station forecourt via an entrance area that handles the transition between the external and internal worlds.

Conceptually, the core area can usefully be considered as a circle within a rectangle. The outer ends of the rectangle represent the far distance of the platforms.

The elements that make up the core vary according to station type. Mainline stations have elaborate facilities and location; small suburban stations may have a core area of little more than a fixed timetable board and a ticket machine. Defining the core area is a matter of architectural treatment. Glazed central halls, which were a feature of nineteenth-century railway stations, have recently been reinterpreted (see for instance Calatrava's Lyon-Satolas Station) as architects have sought to define internally and externally by way of skyline punctuation the location of the core area. In small stations it may be sufficient simply to define its presence by a change in paving material or a circle of lights.

76

3.21 Typical facilities within platform area.

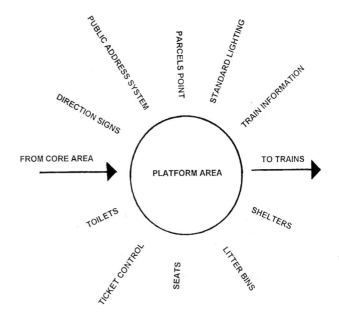

3.22 The main zones of a typical station are well defined here: entrance to left, ticket areas and shops around a central space, and platforms to the right. Architects: Austin-Smith: Lord.

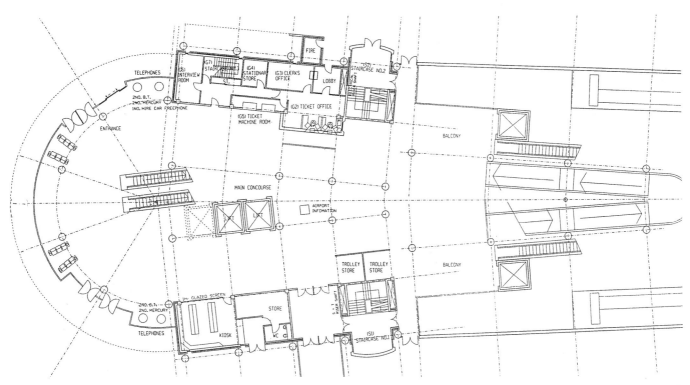

Core areas are spaces where complex activities take place. They have special significance in terms of the running of the station. Simple shapes in plan, such as circles, squares, hexagons or triangles, accommodate more easily the diverse functions that have to be housed. Offices, ticket points, toilets, shops and cafes can be provided as perimeter functions that share a common public space. Such an arrangement reinforced in the architectural language gives expression to the management of the station, which is to the travellers' benefit. Knowing immediately where to buy a ticket or a cup of coffee saves time and frustration.

Peripheral areas are mainly the platforms, footbridges and service spaces. As with airports there is a clear distinction between public and private, between trainside and trackside areas restricted to railway staff. As they are some distance from the core area, these parts of stations pose particular security threats. Hence proper consideration of lighting, the design of shelters, and the position of closed-circuit television (CCTV) is imperative. The outer edge of the peripheral areas also defines the division between railway estate and landownership by others. How this is defined depends upon circumstances and location. Ideally, the

3.23 Identifying the edge of platforms with changes in texture and pattern is an important safety factor. Architects: Ahrends Burton and Koralek.

walls of buildings should form physical barriers, rather than fences, which require regular maintenance and often deteriorate quickly. The design of walls and the position and type of landscaping have implications for security and personal safety (see later).

Public entrance, gathering space, core provision and peripheral areas are related into a logical sequence. The transition from city street to railway seat is a complex system of controls, movement in different directions and at various levels, and opportunities to spend money. The role of design is to make railway customers conscious of the routes and points of access, and so attracted by the spaces that they are willing to dwell long enough to buy a sandwich, newspaper or a tie. For the station manager, the smooth movement of people who arrive and depart in great floods is the main concern, coupled with ensuring that they have a valid ticket and the necessary information to reach their destination.

Security and public safety
One of the principal purposes of station design is to generate in the travelling customer a sense of security. This is achieved in four main ways: by careful attention to layout and detail, by design that encourages people to adopt a territorial attitude and exercise surveillance, by good lighting, and by the use of CCTV. Station layout is of crucial

importance. Platforms and waiting areas should be fully open to the view of onlooking travellers and train crews, overlooked where possible by local residents, and designed without blank corners or walls behind which muggers or burglars could hide. Defining boundaries of the station and of platform areas is also important if one is to expect passengers to 'police' the area themselves and avoid accidents. Similarly, providing surveillance opportunities by, for instance, ensuring that waiting rooms look directly onto platforms and that the ticket office has a window overlooking both, can be beneficial to safety. Lighting positioned with pedestrian needs in mind creates a sense of security: good overall lighting is better than pockets of brightness and relative darkness.

The design of walls, fences and planting is also important. Criminals do not like thorny shrubs to push through (as the scratches and cuts can help identify them), but they do take advantage of high walls where provided. On the whole, slatted fences are better from a security viewpoint than solid walls, as criminal activity can be detected through the slats, and with correct design fences are more difficult to scale than walls. Fences are also less prone to graffiti than walls. Although planting at the back of platforms can be an amenity, it is generally discouraged, as it provides just the cover that muggers or other personal attackers desire. Where dense planting is provided it is better outside walls and fences (that is, on the public side) not on the train side. Planting creepers against walls and fences can enhance their appearance and deter graffiti.

CCTV is of great benefit in reducing crime. The position of CCTV cameras and the design of stations need to be considered together. To avoid a proliferation of poles, CCTV equipment is best located on lighting standards or fixed to the sides of buildings. As most thefts and attacks occur after dark there are clearly related decisions spanning station layout, lighting design and the position of security cameras.

The objective in designing for security is to reduce station crime and to give travellers a greater sense of their own security. Both objectives are important, but the response to each is slightly different. With fear of attack, greater emphasis may be put upon ensuring natural surveillance opportunities, high levels of lighting and frequently positioned

3.24 Platform lighting and traveller information voice systems are normally pole mounted. Integrating them into the architecture of the station is not always easy. Duivendrecht Station. Architect: Peter Kilsdonk of Holland Railconsult.

CCTV cameras. With actual crime, rather than fear of crime, the strategy may involve extra window and door locks, security grilles and alarm systems. Dealing with theft from railway property leads to quite a different response to increasing the passengers' sense of their own security.

Station management is also an important factor. Passengers are most at threat when they are away from the core area, particularly at the far end of platforms. Keeping travellers near to ticket offices and newspaper stalls should be the designer's and station manager's objective. Having attractive and highly lit central areas, whose boundaries are clearly marked and readily perceived, is as important as having them well used and overlooked. The design of such areas has to impart a sense of safe zone upon the traveller.

Being able to observe other people is crucial. Lighting needs to ensure that faces are lit. Vandals and burglars will be deterred from entering stations where they think they may subsequently be identified. People also need to be able, at some distance, to recognize the age and gender of fellow travellers, and take appropriate action if they feel ill at ease.

It is important to avoid corners where attack can occur. Walls need to be designed to avoid recesses where a person can remain hidden, and columns of sufficient slenderness to do the same. Thick, chunky piers may give a station a feeling of engineering bravado, but if they hide a mugger the design priorities are clearly wrong. Waiting shelters on unmanned stations pose a particular risk to travellers. Criminal activity can be reduced by ensuring that shelters have all-round visibility. Any obstruction, such as a timetable, is best positioned elsewhere. With relatively vandal-free armoured glass panels on roof and wall, modern transparent shelters have proved safer than traditional more ornate designs. Ideally, two or more shelters should be employed, each providing natural surveillance of the other.

Mention has already been made of the importance of station lighting to safety and security. Lighting conveys a sense of ease and allows people to use platforms and staircases without fear. In general, people perceive a brightly lit area as less hazardous than a gloomy one, and this can be turned to the station designer's advantage by increasing the intensity of light in the safe core area. Night-time use of CCTV

is also dependent upon adequate artificial lighting levels and well-placed fitments.

Travel information

Travel information by way of electronic displays and traditional timetable boards is normally provided in the core area fairly close to ticket points. They are placed at or above head height to allow groups of people to use them at once, and this also reduces vandalism. Platform indicators are also needed, particularly on larger stations, and this is usually provided by liquid-crystal equipment or flap indicators.

Travelling customers need to be kept informed of the running of trains, the platforms to use, and whether any delays are to be expected. Customer-care policy places great emphasis upon rapid dissemination of train information to travellers. As this is usually electronic, the cabling and upgrading of the facility need to be taken into account at the design stage. The position of electronic train information boards is also constrained by two factors: the need to ensure that all travellers are kept informed, and that the equipment does not pose a danger to through trains.

The three forms of providing travel information – printed timetables, public address and electronic display – are serving slightly different needs. Travellers planning journeys need access to timetables, while the regular commuter is interested in knowing whether his or her train is late and on

3.25 Projecting signs and clocks have greater visual impact than those integrated within the station structure, but elegant supports are needed to avoid visual clutter. Lille-Europe Station. Architect: Rem Koolhaas.

3.26 Information signs are best integrated into the architecture of the station, and positioned where they have maximum impact. Potsdamer Platz Station, Berlin. Architects: Hilmer and Sattler with Hermann and Ottl.

which platform to expect to board it. Hence the position of travel information needs to be considered in relationship to likely use. Temporary boards may also be needed, to inform travellers of engineering work, or other exceptional delays. In positioning temporary and permanent timetable boards (and advertising displays) care must be taken to avoid obstructing visibility (essential for effective surveillance) or impeding pedestrian flows.

Customer facilities

A range of secondary facilities is required to make the traveller's journey more comfortable. This includes such things as bench seating, litter bins, vending machines, telephones and toilets. Some of these are best located in or adjacent to the core area, others along the platform. Some of the facilities need to be placed under cover (such as vending machines) while others can be in the open.

Factors to consider are the grouping into loose units of certain of the facilities (such as seating, vending machines and litter bins) and the logical siting of others (such as telephones near the station entrance). Robustness of design

is also important: bench seating, for example, has to survive being in the open, the effect of pollution at trackside, and vandalism. The position of vending machines, toilets and telephones should be such that they can be monitored by railway staff, either directly or via CCTV. The relationships established by the designer have implications for subsequent running of stations. Hence integration between facilities management and design is important at the outset.

The question of toilet provision is an important one because of the cost, maintenance and potential vandalism problems. As most trains have toilets on board the case for station toilets is less easy to defend. Normally, toilets are only provided in larger stations where volume of traffic or length of waiting times (between trains) justifies their presence. Where toilets are provided they need to cater for disabled users and for nursing mothers.

To avoid having a cluttered appearance, signs should be grouped together into well-coordinated units. The style and location of signs are a design issue, not a matter to be left till the end. Multiple plank signing with reference to

Table 3.7 Platform lighting

Uniformity ratio (between minimum and average luminance)	1 to 2.5
Recommended level	Minor station 100 lux Major station 150 lux Underground station 150 lux

Source: BR Platform Construction Guide, 1992

other facilities besides trains (such as toilets, telephones and tourist information) is preferable to a collection of ad hoc poorly positioned signs.

The same is true of station branding signs. This is the most important information sought by most travellers: such signs are confirmation of their arrival. The signing for the station name and local directional signage should be clearly separated in position, scale, colour and graphic style. Often the station name is integrated into the canopy structure of platform waiting shelters and fixed onto walls at the back of platforms. Where such support does not exist it is common to use free-standing 'goalpost'-type station name signs erected within platform areas. The core area also provides points where station signs can be located, such as the blank walls of booking offices. Lighting of station name signs and directional signs also needs to be considered at an early stage in design evolution.

Lighting
The importance of lighting has been discussed several times already, but it remains a crucial factor in station design. Lighting impinges upon customer safety and satisfaction, upon effective station management, on energy consideration, and on the smooth operation of the trains themselves (particularly for driver-only trains).

The policy is normally to have two levels of lighting intensity – brightly lit core areas and less brightly lit platform areas. How the lighting is to be designed, and the relationship between natural and artificial sources, are matters for the architect. However, in reducing levels of lighting at platforms, it is imperative not to reduce the num-ber of lighting poles and fittings, but to use lower wattage levels of lamps. One does not want pools of brightness and relative darkness, but a good spread of lighting along the whole length of the platform. As most platform shelters do not contain integral lighting, the positions of lighting poles, shelters and bench seating are related considerations. Energy-efficient luminaires should be used as a matter of course.

Lighting is an important element in providing legibility for the traveller. The relative brightness of the core area will naturally attract passengers embarking from trains in that direction. Effective lighting design may reduce the need for secondary signage, or at least make the role of directional signage merely one of confirming what appears obvious in the architectural and lighting treatment. Lighting needs also to take account of train drivers' needs, to ensure that station illumination and signal lights are not in competition.

Environmental standards
Stations are not always heated, though heating is provided by indirect sources, for example lighting, the people themselves, and local heat sources such as shops, cafes or offices. However, heating is often needed to avoid condensation on glazed canopies and to provide welcoming currents of warmed air at station entrances, in sitting areas, and alongside ticket offices. Rather than heat the whole station, it is more common to provide localized sources of heat (by radiator or convector) in specific areas.

Heating is also an important consideration in the pressurization of air for ventilation or smoke control. Mechanical ventilation linked to heating installation in the winter and cooling in the summer may be needed. Casual gains from equipment may be such that all-year-round comfort is best achieved by packaged air-conditioning units in specific areas (such as the ticket office). The maximum permitted recirculation of treated air and the use of heat pumps is a sensible way of reducing energy costs.

Smoke venting is sometimes required, depending upon the size and type of station. Large concourse areas often require to be separately smoke vented: this has serious consequences for the visual appearance of the space, and is an obvious constraint upon design. Fire separation of 1–2 hours between concourse and ticket office and between enclosed platforms and restaurant areas is sometimes required. Fire screens, doors on self-closers and sprinklers may all be necessary in larger stations. As a general rule designers should zone and separate fire-risk areas as much as possible, rather than tackle the problem as an engineering and constructional issue later.

Fire prevention is a matter of design and management. The use of a concourse area for housing a temporary exhibition with fire-risk screens changes the assumptions upon which the design for fire safety may have evolved. Likewise, litter can pose a problem to fire or smoke spread if it is allowed to collect. Effective management of stations is an important consideration in reducing fire risks.

Specific environmental standards exist for railway staff accommodation. Typical of these are Network SouthEast's environmental criteria for ticket offices (Table 3.8). In meeting these standards there are implications for the overall environmental strategy of the station, and for the proximity of adjacent activities.

Fire protection
Various statutory regulations determine the level of fire risk and how protection is best achieved. Stations pose fire problems from three distinct perspectives:

- fire safety for passengers;
- fire safety of the structure;
- fire safety of the cladding.

Designing for fire protection is a matter of considering the dictates of each perspective and evolving strategies accordingly. Passengers caught in a fire need to escape, and here smoke is the principal hazard. Safety and stability of the station structure in a fire is also important, as is that of the cladding. Materials behave in different ways in the event of a fire and their relative toxicity varies. After disasters such as the fire at King's Cross Station in 1987, regulations have been tightened. Stations present particular hazards in the event of fire: escape routes are curtailed by railway track; there are usually a multitude of levels; and access for fire crews is not always easily provided. Added to this, stations

Table 3.8 Environmental standards for ticket offices

Heating	20°C by local appliances or central heating system
Ventilation	Minimum of two air changes per hour or 28 m^3 per hour, whichever is the greater. Cooling should be provided where the temperature is likely to exceed 25°C
Lighting	Standard service illuminance at task level General 500 lux Workstation 750 lux
Acoustic	Noise level at workstation should not exceed 60 dBA Noise level from ventilating equipment to be less than 50 dBA at nearest workstation Ticket office floors to be carpeted; ceilings to be sound absorbent

experience great flows of passenger traffic, thereby exposing large numbers of people in the event of a fire.

Understanding where fires are most likely and where risks to safety and structural stability are greatest is of concern to the designer and engineer. Station design cannot evolve in a balanced fashion without fire risk being integrated at the beginning. The management of fire safety influences the articulation of the station into its constituent units, the choice of structure, cladding and finishes.

Voice announcement systems
Graphic displays – both traditional signboard and electronic – and voice systems provide the means by which travellers are kept informed of where and when to board trains. Public address voice systems need to be readily audible and clearly understood. As many stations use voice announcements in emergencies, the public address system has to be capable of effective communication under normal operation of the station and in the event of fire or terrorist attack.

Delivering clear intelligible speech messages depends upon the quality of the equipment and the acoustics of the space. System design and architectural design need to be related if travellers waiting at platforms are to receive clear messages. In 1991, BS 7443 *A specification for sound systems for emergency use* was introduced, which also provides a basis for establishing a minimum standard for train messages. The British Standard introduces the speech transmission index (STI) measured on a scale of 0 to 1, where 0 is very poor and 1 is excellent. Stations should achieve an STI of 0.7 or above.

Stations normally use messages recorded by trained orators, which are relayed at predetermined times to waiting passengers. Only rarely are ad hoc messages transmitted. The sound received by the public is dependent upon the quality of message as relayed, the spacing of speakers, and the characteristics of the space. The space influences how much direct and indirect sound is heard. The physical qualities and level of background noise of an enclosed booking hall and an open platform vary greatly. The address system needs to respond to these different conditions, with architectural design helping to improve the intelligibility of the relayed message. Unfortunately, for safety and maintenance reasons railway station surfaces are normally hard, thereby increasing the reflected sound. Good sound reception is dependent upon maximizing direct sound and minimizing reflected or reverberant sound. The use of perforated metal cladding to absorb reverberant sound aids the clarity of public address systems at stations.

Those who install public address systems at stations are cautious about guaranteeing compliance with BS 7443 where the architectural arrangements preclude measures to achieve reverberation targets.[6] For the Jubilee Line extension in London, the client body requires architects and engineers to meet minimum STI standards as part of briefing instructions. This is to allow subsequent public address system contractors to give quality assurances under the British Standard.

References

1. Ernest Godward, 'Design for passenger interchange', in N.G. Harris and E.W. Godward (Eds), *Planning Passenger Railways*, Transport Publishing Co Ltd, Glossop, 1992, p. 52.

2. *Ibid.*, p. 55

3. British Rail, *Annual Report and Accounts for 1993/94*, p. 36.

4. For this list and the technical requirements the author is indebted to the design manual *Gateway to the Train* written in 1992 by British Rail's InterCity Company to guide appointed architects.

5. *Core Area Station Guidelines*, Network SouthEast, London, July 1991, p. 10.

6. Neill Woodger, 'Voice alarm systems', *Architects Journal*, 8 June 1994, p. 23.

1 Providing parking spaces and access for buses at station entrances encourages the smooth transition between transport systems. Duivendrecht Station, the Netherlands. Architect: Peter Kilsdonk, Holland Railconsult.

2 Stations have traditionally provided city centres and suburbs alike with distinctive public buildings. This station at Redhill in Surrey, England, by architects Troughton McAslan won the Brunel Award for the best small European station in 1992.

3 Daringly wide-spanned roofs with bands of glazing are one of the characteristics of great railway stations. Amsterdam Central Station.

4 View of Roissy Station at Charles de Gaulle Airport: platform level. Architect: Paul Andrew.

5 Crossing the tracks via underground routes is less inviting than via bridges. Here, at Stadelhofen Station, Zurich, Santiago Calatrava has used elemental concrete structure to provide interest in the concourse beneath the tracks.

6 The platform canopy is a key feature of suburban stations, exploited here to provide a rhythm of light and structure. Stadelhofen Station, Zurich. Architect: Santiago Calatrava.

7 The station needs to be identified in busy streets. Here at Bilbao the metro station designed by Sir Norman Foster and Partners has a distinctive canopy to catch the eye.

8   Changing level and direction occurs at all stations. Light, structure and space should be employed to guide passengers. Lille-Europe Station. Architect: Rem Koolhaas with Jean-Marie Duthilleul.

9   (Below, left) Crossing the tracks on bridges provides welcome views, and is generally more elegant than tunnels. (Below, right) Stations can be dangerous places. Architectural design should seek to create a sense of security, particularly at night. Docklands Light Railway, London. Architects: Ahrends, Burton and Koralek.

10 At Lyon-Satolas Station, the low-level platforms (necessarily below ground as a means of reducing airborne noise) are bathed in rhythms of sunlight taken down through breaks in the roof canopy. Architect: Santiago Calatrava.

11 At airport stations, ramps are needed to cater for those passengers using trolleys. Notice how the rooflight guides travellers towards the exit. Manchester Airport Station. Architects: Austin-Smith: Lord.

12 (Above) One of the functions of walls and roof canopies of underground stations is to pull light down into subterranean concourses. Curved ceilings are particularly useful in this regard. Rotterdam Blaak Metro Station. Architect: Harry Reijnders of Holland Railconsult.

13 (Left and below) Sloterdijk Station, Amsterdam: structural elegance. Architect: Harry Reijnders of Holland Railconsult.

14 Two views of Lyon-Satolas Station at Lyon Airport. The platform canopy (left), concourse roof (right), provide travellers with a clearly differentiated set of station spaces and structural landmarks. Architect: Santiago Calatrava.

15 The asymmetrical curving platform canopy at Waterloo International Station provides a fine spectacle outside and inside the station. The design, by Nicholas Grimshaw and Partners, won the prestigious Mies van der Rohe Award for Architecture in 1994.

16 (Left) Docklands Light Railway, Phase 2. Architects: Ahrends, Burton and Koralek.

17 (Below, left) The renaissance of the railway has led to a new generation of stations and station types. This building, at Manchester Airport Station, provides a worthy landmark at a busy airport, based upon elegant roof canopies. Architects: Austin-Smith: Lord.

18 (Below, right) Modern stations are a fusion of architectural, engineering and industrial design; their creation requires considerable interprofessional cooperation. Lille-Europe Station. Architect: Rem Koolhaas with Jean-Marie Duthilleul.

Technical issues

Assessing the environmental impact of railways and stations

New railway lines and associated stations come within Annex 2 projects of the EU Directive on Environmental Assessment (85/337/EEC). They are classified as 'major infrastructure projects', for which developers must submit an environmental statement (ES) quantifying and ranking all environmental effects. The ES is then the basis on which the environmental assessment (EA) is undertaken.

Measuring the effects of railway lines and stations upon the environment consists of considering (a) the construction effects and (b) the operational effects.

Normally, to reduce the environmental impacts railway developers should avoid disturbance to areas of recognized environmental richness or scarcity such as sites of special scientific interest (SSSIs), national and local nature reserves, national or regional parks, ancient monuments, listed buildings and conservation areas. Impacts on these designated areas can be indirect, such as upon the water courses that run into a protected wetland, or upon the visual setting of an ancient monument. The Victorians ran their lines along the banks of estuaries or immediately against walls of ancient castles, but today's laws prohibit (or at least discourage) such practice.

Those planning the route of new rail systems, whether heavy rail (such as the Channel Tunnel link) or light rail (such as the Sheffield Supertram), need to minimize their adverse impact upon the environment. It may be possible to obtain consent to cut a new line through an ancient woodland, but the developer is likely to face delay in obtaining planning permission, and in the process may attract unfavourable publicity.

The EU Directive and national laws based upon its principles subject developers, at least by implication, to a close scrutiny of alternative routes at the outset. Feasibility studies normally help to identify routes of least environmental impact. Although the ES procedure is mainly restricted to environmental factors, they correlate to a degree with social and economic considerations. A new rail line may have environmental impacts, but the benefits to local business and tourist development could (in economic terms

4.1 The station canopy at Wemys Bay Station in Scotland, designed by James Miller in 1907, bathes the ticket hall in daylight.

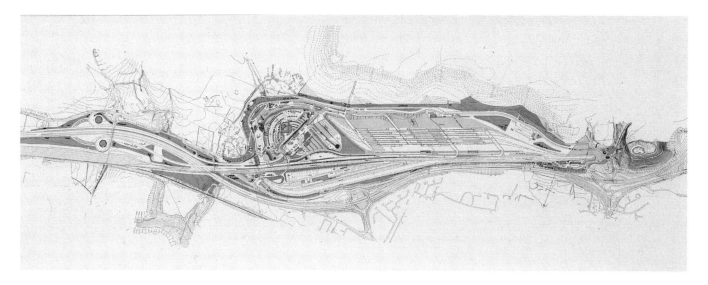

4.2 The scale of impact of modern railways is often large. Measures (as taken here at the Channel Tunnel terminal) to reduce visual, noise and heritage intrusion include careful choice of line route, earth modelling, extensive tree planting, and landscape design based upon sound ecological principles. Architects: Building Design Partnership.

at least) outweigh the disbenefits. Ignoring the social impacts when undertaking the ES can lead to a lack of balance when seeking development consent. The new rail interchange, for instance, at Lille (called EuroLille) had significant environmental impacts, but the economic regeneration brought about by the railway's expansion has been of great benefit to this region of northern France.

Normally, the ES will categorize and quantify the following environmental impacts:

At construction stage:
• land take;
• agricultural land loss;
• severance of communities;
• impact upon heritage resources;
• impact upon natural resources;
• visual intrusion.

At operation stage:
• noise;
• vibration;
• pollution;
• journey disruption (by other modes);
• impact upon ecosystems;
• impact upon effective land use (such as agriculture).

There are overlaps between the two stages: an impact upon a nature reserve can consist of direct loss of habitat (at construction stage) and a loss of species richness by the impact of the trains upon the animals and birds that remain. Similarly, a farm may be severed by a new line, leading to agricultural land loss, but the pollution and inconvenience to the farmer of a bisected farm lead to environmental impacts during operation.

Questions are often asked at public inquiries into new rail lines (usually as part of the environmental assessment procedure) about the wider benefits of rail as against road construction. No new railway is impact free, and often promoters of lines set local environmental impacts against wider ecological and economic benefits. Generally speaking railways have:

• potentially less noise and visual pollution than roads or airports;
• a safety record better than roads and arguably also better than airlines;
• less air pollution along their routes than roads;
• less global warming gas generation per passenger mile than transport by road or air;
• less land take for infrastructure than roads;
• broad benefits to local communities in moving freight, compared with roads.

That railways are less damaging in environmental terms in moving people and goods than road or air is seldom disputed. Unfortunately, in restricting the ES and EA procedures under EU and UK law to the local impacts, the wider questions of sustainable development are too rarely addressed.

Normally stations are considered as integral elements for which planning consent is sought for new rail lines. There may be situations, however, where the station's impacts are greater than that of the connecting lines. With the Channel Tunnel, the new interchange at Folkestone designed by the Building Design Partnership had arguably greater impact – particularly visual – upon the Kentish landscape than the lines, tunnels and embankments of the new railway line. Similarly, the much expanded Waterloo Station designed by Nicholas Grimshaw and Partners brought about a scale of

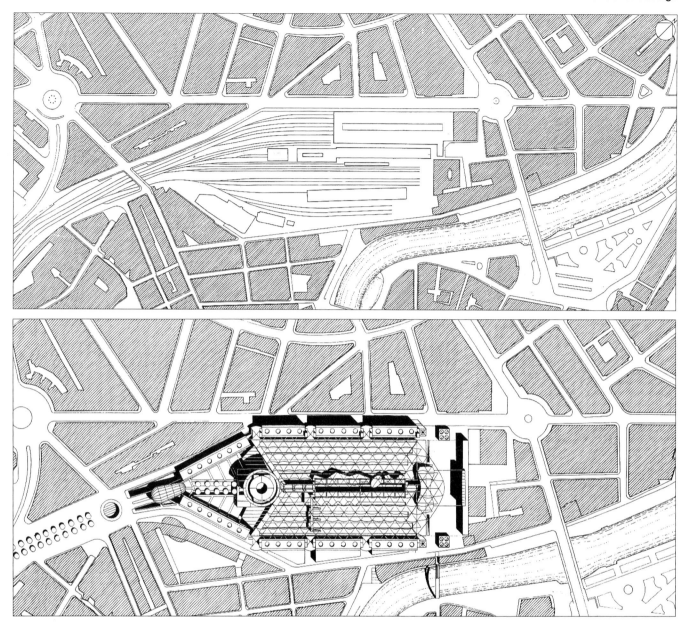

4.3 Larger stations are as much exercises in urban design and site planning as they are architecture. Above, existing station plan; below as proposed at Abando, Bilbao. Architects: Michael Wilford and Partners.

changes to the urban structure and environment of this part of London greater than that of the upgraded railway lines. Where impacts are of this magnitude, those who design stations need to be able to present their proposals in a fashion that allows the likely effects to be readily assessed by others. Increasingly, the use of computer visualization is used to help in quantifying and relaying the impacts to interested third parties. At Waterloo International, Grimshaw's office modelled the station using advanced computer graphics, which allowed the effects of the structure to be assessed within its urban context both during the day and at night. The programme was also used to 'fly through' the public concourse areas to give a ready impression of how the new international station would be

experienced by travellers. Such methods help designers to make the best visual and urban design judgements, but equally importantly they allow those who have the public interest to uphold to assess accurately the visual aspects of environmental impact.

Stations and urban design

As Eero Saarinen's Helsinki Railway Station (1904) clearly demonstrates, stations address the city at two levels: at the macro-scale and at the micro-scale. The first impacts as a series of bold, heavily engineered geometrics, which are superimposed onto the urban fabric with much drama and contrast in scale. Whether station or railway track, the

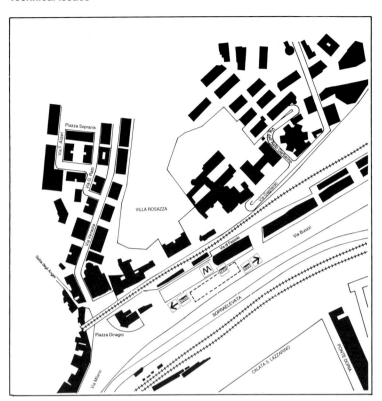

4.4 Suburban stations provide the opportunity to link quarters of towns segregated by railway lines and major roads. Architects: Renzo Piano Building Workshop.

4.5 Forming space at the station entrance, identifying the station with a simple canopy and providing a transparent yet visible structure, all help to encourage use of public transport. Architects: Allies and Morrison.

4.6 Redeveloping obsolete railway land provides opportunities, as here at London's King's Cross, to form new interchanges, parks and commercial development. Architects: Sir Norman Foster and Partners.

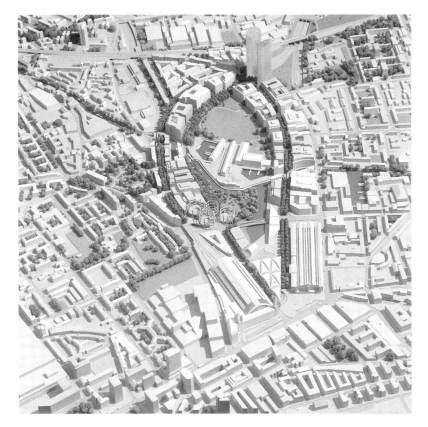

4.7 The immediate hinterland of stations needs to provide access, security and amenity. Combining all three requires skill in landscape, urban and building design. Architects: Austin-Smith: Lord.

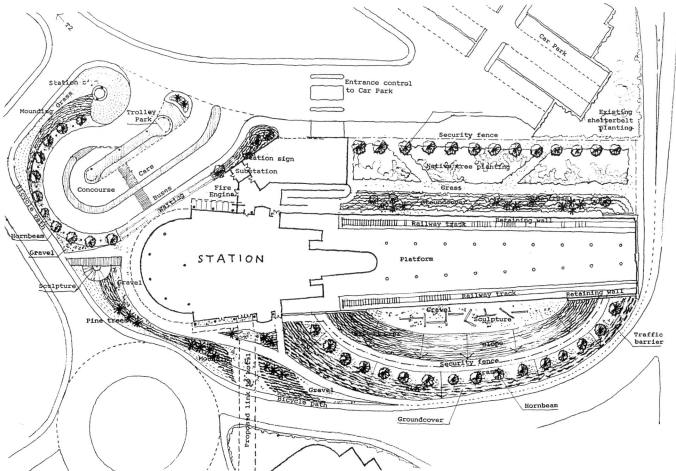

city scene and its patterns of movement are greatly altered by the arrival of railways. At the micro-level, small but significant impacts occur, altering the character of neighbourhoods, shopping patterns and social life.

If the railway station is an urban gateway, with all the ramifications of architectural scale, expression and public space that this implies, the elevated railway viaducts and river bridges needed to serve them involve enormous urban intrusion. Where the first opens the railway to the city, the second forms barriers, both real and perceptual. At the level of urban, as against building, design railways are rather a mixed blessing. They bring economic benefit but at the cost of environmental intrusion and community disturbance. The task today is to reconcile the scale of engineering and visual impact of modern railway infrastructure (stations and track) with the civilizing human qualities that cities have traditionally represented.

This can be achieved in a number of ways. One cannot hide away large railway stations, but it is possible to celebrate them publicly and turn them into worthy landmarks. To do this it is necessary to:

- Treat the station as a quasi-public building, linking internal volume to external space with a sense of procession, dignity and scale. The management of external public space, often outside the confines of the station, is an important consideration. Public squares adjacent to station entrances allow the transition in scale and movement patterns to be reconciled.
- Accept that large stations consist of two principal elements: the train shed with a large transparent canopy over platforms, and the station itself. The nineteenth-century station took the separation of these two distinct railway zones to its logical conclusion, with the engineer responsible for the first and the architect for the second. Today engineering and architecture are better integrated, but there remains a case for allowing the station to address the interests of the city and the platform canopy that of the trains. Such a separation, at least at a conceptual level, will lead more naturally to a legible sequence of spaces for the traveller from urban street to railway seat.

- Avoid seeing the station as a mono-culture of activity. Large modern railway stations are a mixed-use, multipurpose megastructure where much retail, banking and office floorspace has an almost predatory relationship to the social node that is the station. This trend should not be resisted but turned to advantage by the urban designer. Embracing a wide definition of what is a railway station allows the designer to provide greater richness of experience and form. The implications of this are important, particularly at the briefing stage of projects.
- Exploit surplus railway land (such as redundant goods yards) to help heal the rift between railway stations and their urban context. When railways were constructed over a hundred years ago few sought, beyond the station and hotel, to stitch the complex railway and warehousing activities of stations into the physical and social web of cities. Today the release of large tracts of railway estate (as at London's King's Cross) provides almost unprecedented opportunity at an urban scale to connect dislocated communities and introduce much needed green space into the city.

Without the intention, stations have become the hearts of many neighbourhoods. With car-based travel denuding towns of their traditional central social and retail activities, the station has emerged as one of the enduring magnets of community life. This is true not only of large terminals but also of smaller town and underground stations. Much can be done to reinforce the role of the station as a public building in an age increasingly dominated by private ambitions. Forming sheltered routes into stations (as at Hammersmith Station) could lead to the regeneration of local shops and businesses along its path; the creation of a square at the station entrance (as at Leiden Station in Holland, or Lille-Flanders Station in France) could encourage the relocation of offices and community services. Pushing fingers of potential outwards into decaying or overcongested streets (as at Gloucester Station) could allow the station to assume a civilizing role upon the city it serves.

Many architects are currently engaged in translating these principles into the design of new stations and the

4.8 At Lille-Flanders Station a new square with fountains and only limited car access ensures that the station connects pleasantly with the town centre. Effective urban design around stations often requires the redefinition of public space.

restructuring of existing ones. In the UK, the architects Terry Farrell, Nicholas Grimshaw and Sir Norman Foster have taken a leading role. At various locations, mainly in London, these architects have widened the debate about the future of railway architecture in a number of projects and built schemes. One of the most notable is Embankment Place, completed in 1990, which exploited the air rights over Charing Cross Station.

Charing Cross Station is typical of the urban design problems posed by stations. Positioned on an important bend in the River Thames opposite the Royal Festival Hall, the station faced away from the river, with its rather bleak backside overlooking it. Station entrance, hotel and square looked northwards towards Trafalgar Square, with narrow service streets to the side. In spite of the layout, much pedestrian movement was southwards to the Thames and to the east and west. Farrell had the task of giving the river a landmark that addressed London's need for a civic presence along this corridor, and of organizing a complex web of pedestrian movements to riverside theatres, water buses and offices.

The river frontage was addressed by building a large and architecturally dramatic office building above the railways in the form of an enormous arch. Facing south, it looks directly across the Thames to the arts complex on the South Bank, thereby meeting wider civic duties and helping to 'repair a gap in the sweeping riverscape of the north bank'.[1] Farrell's masterplan structured new pedestrian routes between existing and intended buildings and parks, using view and changing scale to orientate users. To ensure that the new routes are safe, they are well overlooked by a variety of activities and served by shops and restaurants that remain open for long hours. The main strength of the redevelopment of Charing Cross is the way in which issues facing both the city and the pedestrian are reconciled in a scheme that is dramatic yet rich in detailed consideration of urban design.

Some of the same qualities are evident too at Hammersmith Broadway Station on London's Underground. Here the plan was to reinforce the station as a point of connection at the heart of the neighbourhood. The station is buried within a large traffic island surrounded by busy roads, with little movement through its centre at ground level. The new station is based upon an intricate pedestrian domain (rather like the village centre that existed here before the station was constructed) with 'gardens, shops and cafes that connect routes across the site with the transport facilities'.[2] Life below and above ground is reconciled with the aid of new squares, malls, lanes and concourses. The same approach is found at the remodelled South Kensington Station, where the new design structures the interchange into a connecting web of routes, open squares and public spaces. The latter serve not just users of the Underground railway station, but those intent upon visiting shops and the host of public museums in the area. As at Hammersmith, the scheme involves bisecting the city block with glazed sheets and making access to the site easier at its edges.

The station as new urban object

With their scale and ability to animate towns with human movement and life, stations are essentially urban buildings, even where they occur in suburban locations. Stations are expressions of spatial organization, with bold, often sculptural architectural forms held together in the presence of light.

More than most building types, stations are a question of space, and movement systems materialized into diverse architectural elements at different levels.

The building technology of stations is one of the means whereby function and programme can be communicated in the language of materials. The technological meaning of stations is expressed through structure, construction and materials. The play of surfaces, lines and textures imparts significance to the various structural elements. Stations are experienced and savoured in movement and at rest. The appreciation and application of engineering and technology relate the speed and scale of trains to the human experience.

Form, space and articulated structure are the three main tactile elements of modern stations. They are perceived, enjoyed and understood through the medium of light – both natural and artificial. The approach to the whole and to the detail should be united by the same vigour, as should the architectural to the engineering elements. Harmony of conception, aided by clarity of layout, constructional honesty and rigorous detailing conspire together to create stations worthy of the new railway age.

Scale, invention, specificity and permanence are qualities of modern stations. As they mediate between public and private realms, stations engage more directly than most building types in questions of promenade and ease of passage. Stations are a question of relative movement: between the scales of train speed and human speed. They are points of interchange in journeys – of breaks in mode and technologies. The transition from the train to the platform and thence to the car, bus or cycle is a movement through technologies and designs. The idea of the station as cultural and social interchange gives poignancy to how changes in materials, technical innovation and references to historical precedents are handled.

Stations integrate, on the one hand, human scale with train scale and, on the other, human scale with civic scale. The station gives order to the city by providing anchor points and by resolving type and place characteristics. Stations are distinctive building types because they mediate between functional orthodoxy and the special qualities of places and sites. The sense of order and appropriateness derives from the relationship, often a complex one, between urban fabric and the discontinuity of different types of movements, between modern demands and historic precedents, and between public interests and private ones.

The public experience of stations, often expressed by civic grandeur, leads naturally to questions of cultural rather than functional life. Stations are consumer objects, where large numbers of passengers and non-travelling public converge to buy goods, watch and to undertake journeys. In larger stations the personal experience is subsumed within the wider cultural melée of shops, restaurants and tourist services. Stations, like museums and shopping malls, are inevitably part of modern life beyond the experience of travel. Just as many people who visit museums are not interested in the objects, so at stations many are there to experience the ambience, to soak up to tension without intending to travel themselves. These are people who see stations as leisure destinations where the urban dialogue takes place with particular sharpness.

Stations carry connotations of meaning, which imply positions of relative power. The different classes of traveller, the distinctions between the tourist and the worker, between salaried and unsalaried, are expressed (or suppressed) in approaches to design. Nineteenth-century stations, with their first-class lounges and smoking rooms, were deliberately class conscious. Today, stations carry meanings that are more about openness, flexibility and freedom of access. The platform barrier and waiting room class distinction has withdrawn from the station to the train itself, leaving the station as more conspicuously a building of the city. Being engaged in a dialogue between the public and private realm, and between building programme and urban context, the design of the modern station is essentially a question of order, integration and relationship:

- order – in the sense of distilling clarity from complex demands and programmes;
- integration – in the sense of balancing human experiences with technology, light and space;
- relationship – in the sense of striking a compromise between the needs of the individual and that of the city which the station serves.

Spandau Station, Berlin: the station as urban link

Spandau Station in Berlin (an unrealized project by Santiago Calatrava of 1991) is based upon the idea of the station as integrated urban element. The design consists of the station and two parallel office blocks, which are conceived as a unified whole. The station roof canopy in effect is suspended from two rectangular office buildings, each of which defines at its outer edge a landscaped city park.[3] Platforms are reached via escalators; these take passengers down to the trains, which run below ground at this point. To help stitch the station into the fabric of Berlin two devices are used. First, the station is arranged as part of a wider commercial redevelopment, with station entrance and office entrances directly related to each other. Second, the canopy of the station is about the same height as the trees in a nearby park. This allowed Calatrava to design his columns as quasi-trees, adding to the sense that station and park are related entities. Unlike other stations by the architect, Spandau is not a free-standing monument but part of a linked complex of public spaces and buildings.

Thameslink 2000: the station as bridge

The design prepared by Terry Farrell and Partners for British Rail in 1991–92 was part of a feasibility study exploring the architectural possibilities and urban design implications of a new railway crossing of the Thames in central London. The origins of the idea lay in British Rail's intention of linking the north of England to Europe with trains that ran through London without stopping at any of the capital's termini.

Farrell proposed a station straddling the Thames, sitting above the existing Blackfriars railway bridge. The concept involved remodelling Blackfriars Station and moving its main ticket and concourse onto the new station bridge, where they formed entrance portals. Part of the architect's task was to test the impact of the proposal upon historic views of London (particularly those towards St Paul's Cathedral) and to give evidence at the consideration of a Parliamentary Bill. As such, the outline design fulfilled BR's responsibilities under formal environmental impact assessment procedures.

4.9 The Thameslink rail crossing (at present unrealized) offered the addition of a dramatic and finely engineered bridge over the capital's neglected river. Architects: Terry Farrell and Partners.

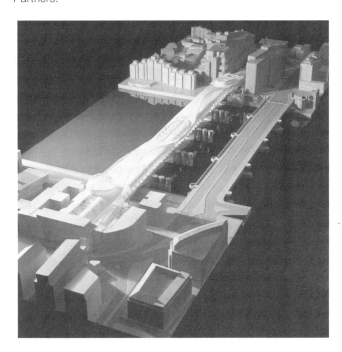

The design confirms trends already highlighted with regard to the changing nature of stations. The proposed Blackfriars Station is an integral station and railway bridge with a pair of pedestrian walkways hung onto either side of the structure. The station is divided between two booking hall and concourse areas, each placed on either end of the bridge, where they form links with adjoining urban development. The platform areas are housed on the bridge itself, with daylight entering via boldly sculpted curved rooflights. Throughout the proposal, light (which enters dramatically during the day and is emitted with equal gusto at night) and structure provide the basis for architectural expression. The promoters of the Bill recognized that such an important river crossing had to address the issue of landmarking the capital as well as providing a convenient new station.

Passenger reassurance and station design

Railway stations need to provide psychological reassurance for passengers often disorientated by the complexity of modern travel. The role of architectural design is to help

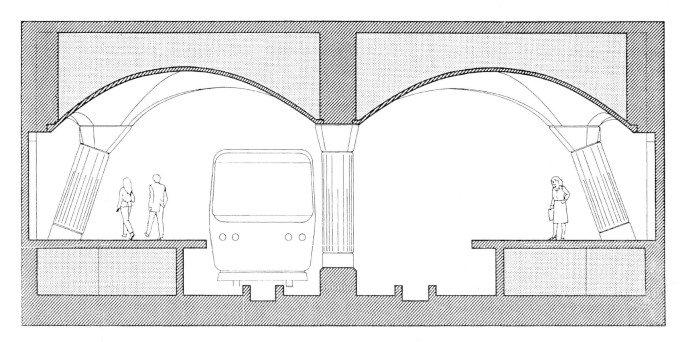

4.10 People travelling alone are particularly vulnerable at unmanned or underground stations. Architects: Jourda and Perraudin.

define patterns of movement in buildings that can be hostile and forbidding. Good station design ideally provides perceptual markers, which travellers can use to orientate themselves, and which through the use of structure, space and light also uplift the spirit.

Large modern railway stations are transport interchanges. Here passengers experience a change in mode of travel and a transition in speed of travel. As stations mediate between different scales of movement and methods of transportation, the experiential perception of travellers is crucial. The greater the complexity of the interchange (as for example at airport stations, where planes, heavy rail, light rail, taxis and buses may interface) the more difficult the task for the designer. Here, clarifying movement needs of travellers, who are each seeking a different mode of transport, demands great skill of the architect. Modern transport interchanges involve complex human transactions where perception is as important as reality. Being able to 'read' a key route, to identify the right escalator, to know the direction of trainside, to be guided to the right platform, is not about signage but about architectural design.

As railway tracks are great dividers of towns, the station has the further task of marrying two pieces of urban geography. Stations are social bridges for local communities as well as points of departure for travellers. Uniting two sides of a town has implications as great as conceiving the station as an urban gateway. While mainline termini should be designed as entrance portals containing large public gathering space in preparation for lengthy rail journeys, the typical station is more a linking element across impenetrable tracks of railway estate. The station has the task, therefore, not only of handling a transition in scales of movement but also of facilitating cross-city links. Necessarily, such movement is often

at right angles to that of rail travellers, and can interrupt the smooth handling of passenger movements. At Edinburgh's Waverley Station, the main concourse is crossed at high level by a walkway, whose main function is to link the Old and New Towns of the city. For many people, this is the main pedestrian connection between two distinctive urban areas. The station provides a public route quite independently of its main function as a passenger terminal.

The public component to stations can be as important as that of providing direct access to the railway system. In many ways the larger the station the more crucial are civic considerations. As railways are privatized the station may begin to lose its civic function. Franchising companies running the station as real estate need the public in order to support shops and restaurants, but paying for stations to serve as public bridges linking areas of towns offers little commercial advantage. When stations were automatically viewed as part of public services such conflicts of interest did not occur. If the station becomes not public estate but private property, only transactions involving money will be tolerated. Movement and urban linkage for its own sake, an essential component of station function for over a century, may be curtailed. Where it remains, good design is essential to allow passengers to distinguish between elements of stations that are merely to do with the matter of connecting urban tissue, and those that are to do with guiding travellers through stations en route to the train.

Safety and security at stations

Stations are dangerous places for staff and passengers. The danger stems from the trains themselves, from the pollutants that flow from trains to stations, from the dangerous

4.11 Creating safe stations for children is of growing interest to designers. Architects: Building Design Partnership.

nature of station structures, and from the risks to personal safety from antisocial human behaviour. Staff and travellers both have legitimate concerns over their own health, safety and security. The designers' task is to reduce these concerns to a minimum.

Safety is a matter of direct risk and perceived risk. Fear of crime at stations is often far greater than real crime, and removing the fear element through better platform lighting and safety-conscious design can readily allay anxieties.

Effective safety design needs to address station layout, management and training of staff, care over maintenance, lighting and surveillance. Many accidents are the fault of poor strategic design (such as placing trolley stands near staircases), poor detailed design (such as badly positioned lighting), poor management (such as allowing litter to collect), and poor maintenance (such as not repairing broken windows). Though new regulations (such as the EU's Construction, Design and Management Directive) place a statutory duty to design with safety in mind, many accidents at stations are the result not of construction but of their use by station staff or the public.

There is a cost, both real and architectural, in designing for safety. The engineering prowess of stations can be at the expense of the safety of site operators and those subsequently involved in maintenance. High-level glazed roofs with little in the way of access pose particular difficulties, especially when scaffolding is prohibited by railway tracks

underneath. The converse, however, of designing out all risks can lead to dull station architecture. Safety planning is a matter of balancing risks against real costs in financial terms and more tangible disbenefits in aesthetic terms. Risk evaluation is part of the process of design, where the cost of safety is set against other operational priorities.

Most railway companies have safety plans, which establish the means of achieving certain levels of safety and security. Most safety plans identify the areas of greatest risk, and suggest methods of risk abatement. The areas of greatest vulnerability in terms of fatalities – passenger falls from trains and the death of trackside workers – are outside the field of influence of station designers. However, other common sources of accidents – such as falling onto tracks from platforms, accidents at stations due to vandalism, personal attack, and slipping on wet station surfaces – can all be reduced by better design.

Generally speaking, the lower the level of station usage the greater the risk from crime and vandalism, and the greater the feeling of insecurity amongst passengers. High levels of platform occupation generally reduce both real and feared crime. Similarly, platform bridges, which pose a particular threat (from stone throwing, falling parts and graffiti), are less vandalized and consequently safer for passengers if there is a consistently high level of use.

The main problem with stations concerns the irregular pattern of use (due to the arrival and departure of trains), which results in lengths of platform, waiting areas, toilets, bridges and underpasses being alternatively filled with people for brief periods and empty for long ones. It is during the quiet periods that attack upon property and passengers is likely to occur. Both the design and the management of stations can play their part in reducing risks.

Another safety problem that station architects face is in the selection of materials. Ground surfaces need to be robust, non-slip, replaceable, and textured so that those with partial sight can feel the edge of platforms or determine routes to lifts. Textured or round-stippled finishes are normally used to define a band at the platform edge. For some the deliberate texturing is a useful guide; for others the surface can trip. The relative texturing of paving surfaces means that some areas are smoother than others: it is these smooth finishes that, when wet, can cause accidents, especially when people are rushing to or from trains.

Materials also need to be selected so that even when vandalized they do not pose a risk. Broken panels of glass can provide sharp edges, which could arm an attacker or blow down onto waiting passengers in a wind. The replacing of materials in a fashion that does not cause potential danger to operatives is part of the criteria for material selection at the outset.

Architects are increasingly required to take responsibility for project safety under wider safety plans. What Railtrack calls 'the cascade of safety responsibilities based upon customer/supplier principles' extends to designers and contractors.[4] The idea is to control risks imported onto the railway at source by better safety design and management. Those providing services including design to Railtrack are required to display the 'necessary competence, commitment and resources to safely plan and discharge their work'.[5]

Access for disabled people

Designing stations to be freely accessible to disabled people is a concern at all stages in the evolution of a new station (feasibility and site choice, strategic design, detailed design). It is no good leaving the needs of people with impaired mobility until disabled toilets are being designed: their requirements should influence the whole station concept.

Disabled people in the UK account for about 10% of the population (nearly 6 million people). They are not necessarily disabled in the sense of being wheelchair users, but they suffer from impairment of hearing or vision. Only 4% of disabled people are in fact wheelchair users, and of the total disabled population only 30% suffer from mobility limitations[6]. Hence the station architect has various levels of disability to accommodate, not all of which fall within definitions covered by statutory regulations (such as Part M of the Building Regulations 1989, or BS 5810). Designing stations so that they provide universal access is one thing; creating a travel environment that is 'welcoming and inclusive'[7] to all is another. Achieving the latter requires the architect to consider whether the design discriminates at a psychological level between able and disabled people.

The main points to consider in the design of stations for disabled people are as follows.[8]

Site choice
The site should avoid steep changes in level. As railway lines are often in cuttings or embankments, the location of the station should ideally be where the track is at grade.

Site layout
The layout of the station, and how changes in level are negotiated, should facilitate, rather than obstruct, disabled access. The perception of layout and station entrances should be friendly to all.

Car parking
Disabled access by car is needed at the station entrance. At least two parking bays should be provided for disabled drivers at the entrance and one per 100 elsewhere.

Station entrance
The entrance to the station should be clearly signed and well lit (disabled travellers are especially vulnerable to mugging). The entrance should also be level, with non-slip materials where they are likely to be wet. Automatic sliding doors are preferable to swing doors and should normally be at least 12 000 mm wide. Kickplates on doors are needed for wheelchair users, who tend to push into them with footrests. Glass doors should be readily identified.

Station navigation

The design of the station should help disabled people to find their way around. Navigation is a question of signage and the perception of station routes by architectural means. The use of lighting (both natural and artificial) should guide those with impairment to the key station areas (booking hall, platform). People with impaired vision tend to move towards the light, and this tendency should be reflected in the sequential passage through stations from entrance to platform. Similarly the use of floor finishes and patterning needs to distinguish major from minor routes, and safe from unsafe zones.

Station signs

The location of signs, their height and type are all related factors. The information needs of able travellers are much the same as those of disabled travellers, but the positioning and type of signs may vary. Wheelchair users, for instance, need signs nearer to their head level (say 1300 mm) than other travellers, especially where these are tactile signs. Illuminated signs should be lit to a level of 50 lux over the ambient light level. Raised lettering, Braille and tactile station maps all help to make travel more convenient for different levels of impairment.

Station surfaces

Surfaces need to facilitate ease of movement and define safety zones. The areas of potential danger are at the platform edge and around staircases. Textured finishes help disabled travellers to distinguish the safe from unsafe zones. However, the textured finishes that may aid some can become a hazard or inconvenience for others. Carpets pose a dilemma: for those with limited hearing carpets are beneficial in reducing general noise levels (which helps with the audibility of station announcements) but for wheelchair users carpets can obstruct movement and interfere with electronic steering systems.

Changes in level

Stairs, lifts, escalators and ramps are all needed if different levels of impairment are to be accommodated. The question of level changes is both a technical issue and a psychological one. Disabled travellers do not want to feel segregated but part of the life of the station. The provision of separate access for those with limited movement increases the sense of discrimination. Routes and level changes designed for disabled access should be available to all: in fact the higher level of provision with regard to details such as the width and provision of handrails makes travel easier for all. At station entrances, ramps for wheelchair users should be designed so that everybody is encouraged to use them, and the same is true of station lifts.

Toilets

Disabled toilets are needed in most stations, and the level of provision is specified in Part M of the Building Regulations. The minimum space for a disabled toilet with wheelchair access is 1500 mm by 2000 mm. Finishes and colours that are inviting are also preferable to the white and chrome vision of hygiene normally provided.

The design of stations from car park to train needs to evolve with disabled needs in mind. As railways provide the main means of transportation for an increasing number of people with impairments of one kind or another, the station environment is of central importance. Design is a question of providing a dignified and comfortable means of navigating the complex zones and changes in level of a typical station. It is also a matter of creating an accessible environment and one free of psychological barriers. In this the use of light, sound and materials plays an important part.

Levels of disabled provision

With an ageing population it is prudent to design in excess of the minimum statutory standards. Designers need to adopt a wide definition of disability, particularly at heavily used stations. Besides wheelchair users, consideration needs to be given to certain common conditions of colour blindness, the use at main terminals of Braille train timetable and lift call buttons, the provision of induction loop facilities for the hard of hearing, and ticket offices and desks that can be reached readily by wheelchair users. In addition, disabled toilets should be provided as a matter of course.

Although disabled access provision is expensive it does reinforce the social connotations associated with railways. Compared with travel by air or bus, railways have tended to be seen as a public service rather than as a private transport industry. Having an adequate level of disabled provision at stations provides evidence of this. Also, if standards are adequate to meet the needs of disabled users, they will be all the better for the able bodied.

Passenger space standards

As a general rule, designers need to allow for 3 m² per passenger in station concourses, 2 m² per passenger in core areas and 1 m² per passenger on platforms. Greater density of occupation at platforms is accepted, as passengers here do not wait for great lengths of time and are not usually moving in various directions. In concourse areas passengers may be buying tickets, newspapers, checking on timetables or using telephones. These rule-of-thumb figures will vary if passengers usually use trolleys (as at airport stations) or at termini where a large number of non-travelling people may be present.

A fine line exists between space that is congested through over-use and its efficient use. There is certainly an argument that with privatization of railway stations what is seen as one man's congestion may be viewed as another man's profit. There is likely to be pressure to increase income from concourse areas, and this means attracting more people past retail outlets: the slower they go the more likely they are to wander into shops and cafes. Efficiency and speed of movement can run counter to ambitions for maximizing retail profit from the public areas of stations.

As stations are subject to marked flows of people, the space guides vary in their impact throughout different times of the day. At mid-morning after the rush hour a station can appear quite deserted. Adjusting space levels to operational need is an important consideration in the design of different types of station. The problem is not merely one of balancing the efficient throughput of passengers with maximizing profits from secondary attractions; there are important issues of safety, fire escape and security surveillance. Capacities at some railway termini can approach 2000 passengers per hour in each direction, which amounts to about 5 million passengers per year. Passenger perceptions of space standards and dwell quality are important elements in customer satisfaction levels.

Integration of light, structure and detail

With complex stations, structure, light and detail are all necessary to guide passengers through various levels and in different directions. Details in particular, if near to eye level, provide legibility to interior spaces. The rhythms of structure too are important; a line of columns or a framework of beams overhead can guide passengers to preferred routes and give clear direction to organizational or spatial hierarchies. Light, especially natural light, has the benefit of focusing attention upon important spaces, such as booking halls, or of leading passengers towards platforms and entrances.

How structure, light and detail are used depends upon circumstances. With larger stations the role of architectural structure is often paramount. Expressive structural solutions can provide both exterior and interior landmarking, and with the introduction of light the eye is taken to the essential points. Hence structure and light are not separate concerns but two elements that need to be considered in unison. Daylight and sunlight, the latter necessarily diffused, are materials in their own right – as important as solid walls. How light strikes a surface and highlights a detail, how it throws structure into stark relief, are necessary concerns of railway architects. At its most essential the role of architecture in stations is to guide passengers to avoid the use of signs and direction boards. An ideal station is one where ordinary travellers grasp the logic of a station's design and readily comprehend its various functional and processional spaces.

With most railway architecture, light, space, structural philosophy and detail can be effectively manipulated. The problem is less readily solved with underground stations. Here natural light is not a tactile material to be exploited but an artificial material, which offers little scope for architectural invention. Without daylight, structure becomes lost in the gloom, and its logic is difficult to grasp against a backcloth of artificial lighting. A solution employed by many (such as Alsop and Stormer at their Paddington CrossRail station) is to deflect natural light down into the underground station by using glass walls or reflective shafts of translucent material. Such walls, set sometimes at angles, run from above the ground to platforms some distance beneath.

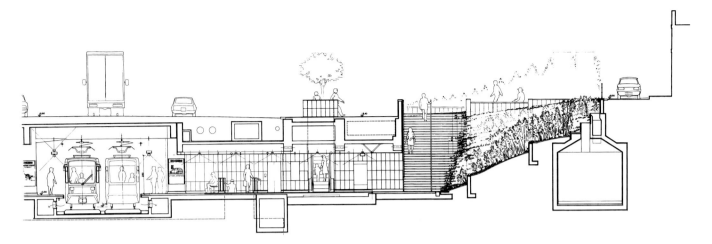

4.12 Planting on an angled bank helps to deflect daylight into the entrance of Dinegro Station, Genoa, by Renzo Piano Building Workshop. Notice the large ducting areas required for ventilation and smoke extraction in underground railways.

4.13 Uplighters fixed to the top of columns can do much to illuminate structural elements and hence give passengers a sense of space and direction in larger stations. Architects: Austin-Smith: Lord.

Deflected natural light is generally easier to manipulate than artificial light, and gives a more wholesome quality to subterranean transport.

If structure, light and detail are essential elements to exploit in order to give legibility to complex station interiors, their role takes on particular significance at the points where passenger flows are greatest. At stairs and escalators people are often disorientated by the changes in direction or level. Here the designer needs to ensure that the orchestration of architectural elements is helping, not frustrating, the passengers' appreciation of key routes and flows of movement. The functional planning of stations and the architectural and structural response require to be united by a common vision irrespective of the background of the professional players. Calatrava's Satolas Station in Lyon shows the benefit of designing a powerful, expressive structure in terms of the passengers' appreciation of space and route.

A problem can occur with stations containing large commercial areas. Whereas light, structure and detail may be used by the designer of a station to guide passengers through complex railway functions, where retail malls are incorporated into stations such elements may be exploited to deflect travellers into shops and cafes. At London's Liverpool Street Station the play of light and procession seems to guide travellers rather more towards local shopping malls than to the booking hall or platform. As the balance of power has shifted from public to private interests, the railway station has seen the architectural language of light and space exploited to serve commercial as well as travellers' needs.

Station design and building services

One of the biggest challenges in the design of railway stations is to achieve a close correspondence between the

shapes of space, enclosure and structure, and the various services of fire protection, air-handling, lighting and Tannoy systems. Unless thought about at the outset of design, these services can appear as ill-fitting adjuncts to an otherwise elegant concept. Integration of architectural and services demands is best achieved by adopting a building form that responds in a direct fashion to the physics of air movement, to the practicalities of lighting (both natural and

4.14   Good lighting in ticket halls – both natural and artificial –
helps with creating a welcoming atmosphere for customers.
Redhill Station, Surrey. Architects: Troughton McAslan.

artificial), and to the realities of fire fighting. It is also helpful
if the design of lighting, especially natural lighting, reinforces
the sense of legibility and orientation within the station.

Such integration can best be achieved by understanding the technical requirements of the different building
services that railway stations have to accommodate. As with
many public buildings there are complex questions of safety,
health and security to consider as well as the more normal
building services of heating, lighting and ventilation. There
are connections between the parts: dealing with the toxic
dust that is given off by train brake shoes (which impinges
directly upon health) has implications for air movement
flows and ventilation levels. Similarly, security and lighting
have a direct relationship. The effect of these connections
is to add to the difficulty of accommodating the aesthetics
of architectural form with the practicalities of services.
Moreover, as their needs vary over the lifespan of the station, what starts off as a successful integration between
structure and services may end up as a building of pro-
gressively greater mismatch.

As a general rule, designers should integrate the formal
requirements of architecture and building services within a
consistent and visually coherent station. This principle,
however, needs to recognize that the life of building services
is shorter than that of the station by a factor of as much as
3 to 1. This means that station lighting or ventilation systems
may be totally renewed several times, each upgrading
requiring new stanchions, fresh duct lines, or even com-
pletely new technical approaches. The cycle of changes,
and the different lifespans of individual parts of the building, suggest that accessibility and renewability are key considerations in the design process. Added to this, social
changes add fresh – sometimes unpredictable – demands.
The growth of terrorism in the 1980s led to the introduction of new lighting and camera systems at many stations,
and the current concerns over air quality at the trackside
are leading to changes in ventilation policy with enclosed
platforms.

Reversibility and accessibility of services suggest that
building them into the structure and fabric of stations (as
against placing them on the surfaces or hanging them from
separate poles) is a solution that is satisfactory for only a
short period. Some stations exploit exposed services for their
decorative qualities – particularly ducts that are brightly
painted. Elsewhere, lighting poles (which support also security cameras and public address systems) provide a kind of
forest of trees within the open malls of larger stations. Such
poles (sometimes called technical trees) can provide the
support for changing servicing technology without despoil-
ing the aesthetic of the station.

Station design is therefore based upon the concept of
permanent and less permanent parts. The move towards
more natural methods of lighting, heating and ventilating
buildings means that the basic design is less likely to be a
simple rectangular box. Working with nature as a source of
energy and visual delight is beginning to shape a new
generation of railway stations (as at Brin Station near Genoa
by Renzo Piano). Not only do these stations, evolved from
more ecological principles, entail fewer mechanical services (and hence fewer poles and ducts), but their
architectural form is more distinctive and as a consequence
the station serves better as a landmark. If they are stronger

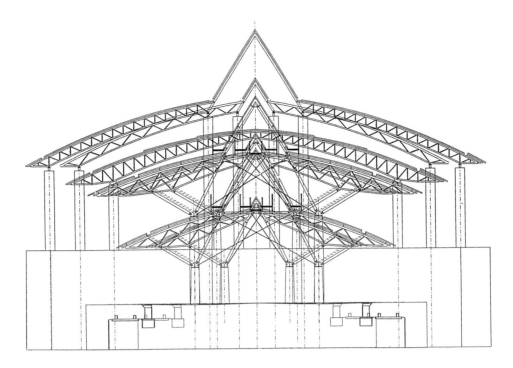

4.15 Platform and concourse roofs form an interesting juxtaposition in the multi-level Manchester Airport Station. Architects: Austin-Smith: Lord.

landmarks on the outside, they also provide improved legibility for passengers on the inside. Stations that use natural lighting to guide passengers through complex levels of building (as at the station at Manchester Airport) provide a more satisfactory fusion of architecture and services than an earlier generation of stations, of which London's Euston is a prime example.

Noise at stations

The introduction of a new generation of high-speed trains has meant that greater attention has had to be paid to questions of noise. New, faster trains and double-decker trains (now being introduced onto French and Dutch railways) have resulted in noise at stations being a greater problem than in the past. Faster, larger trains also mean that community noise disturbance needs to be addressed by the designer and engineer.

Noise can be controlled by three main means: by placing track and station below ground; by using sound-absorbing materials in the construction of tunnels, cuttings and station buildings; and by using noise deflectors. Contact noise between train wheels and track can be reduced by laying rails on a continuous ballast bed resting on rubber mats. New Dutch stations have also used grooved resonators beneath the platform edges to reduce the high-pitched noise caused by the contact between wheel and rail, and plywood boxes concealed in suspended ceilings of stations to dampen low-pitched noise.[9] Noise deflectors can be trackside free-standing screens, not unlike those

used at airports. At stations, designers can use angled walls to deflect noise away from sensitive areas. Walls, essential for structural purposes, can be either angled, curved or given greater substance in order to deflect or absorb noise. The most sensitive areas for noise are ticket offices, waiting rooms and platforms.

The problem of noise at stations is more acute where high-speed trains regularly pass through without stopping. Station layout and design need to consider noise and suction jointly so that air pressure and sound frequency are dealt with simultaneously. Noise is a matter of comfort, audibility of station announcements, and security. A noisy station is not a safe place, as cries for help cannot be heard. As trains become faster, the problem of noise becomes more complex to deal with, both at the level of station design and in terms of neighbourhood disturbance. Like energy conservation, noise control at stations is not a clip-on extra but an important element of strategic design.

Canopies: technical considerations

The fashion for glass station roofs raises the obvious question as to how they are to be cleaned, maintained and repaired. Health and safety regulations place restrictions upon methods of cleaning, and lay down standards at the design stage regarding access. Designers of glazed structures need to address at the conceptual stage how maintenance is to be carried out – both for replacement and regular cleaning. An example of the integration of design and

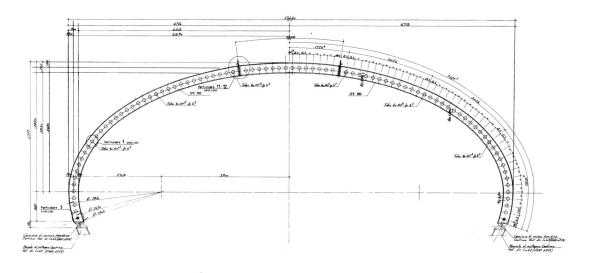

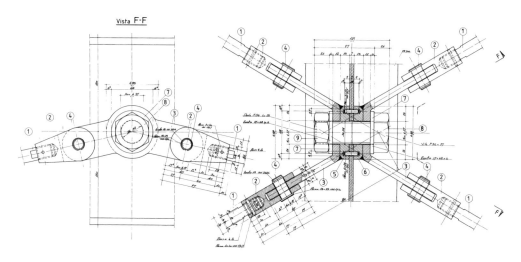

4.16 Graceful station architecture requires the use of elegant details. Waiting at platforms subjects station design to closer scrutiny than in many building types. These examples of canopy and assembly are from Brin Station, Genoa. Architects: Renzo Piano Building Workshop.

4.17 Station canopies have traditionally combined the design skills of the architect and engineer. This handsome station roof in Glasgow was demolished in 1976.

4.18 Brin Station employs a curved glazed platform canopy with an integrated cleaning system like a car-wash.

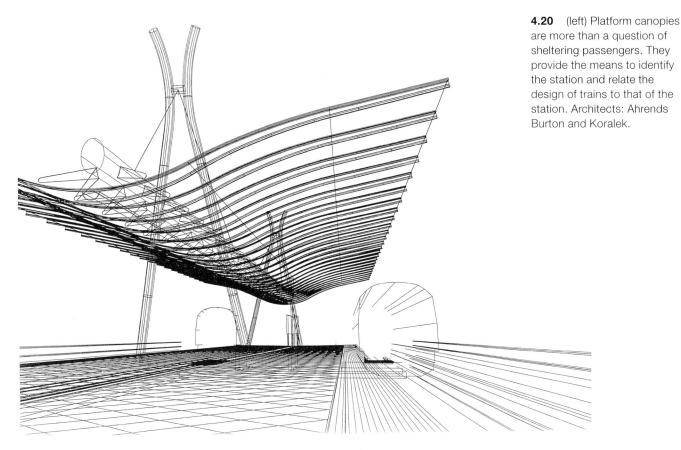

4.20 (left) Platform canopies are more than a question of sheltering passengers. They provide the means to identify the station and relate the design of trains to that of the station. Architects: Ahrends Burton and Koralek.

4.19 (right) Sophisticated glazing assemblies help to give modern stations an ambience approaching that of contemporary high-speed trains. East Croydon Station. Architects: Alan Brookes Associates.

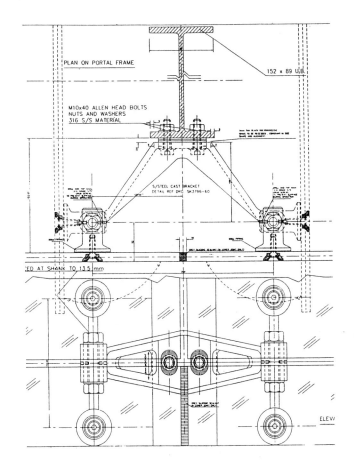

maintenance is Renzo Piano's Brin Station in Genoa, where the curved glazed roof and cleaning apparatus were considered as related problems at the start of design. The system adopted is similar to a car wash that travels the length of the train roof on a wheeled gantry.[10]

Cleaning the inside surfaces of the glass is equally important. The dust and fumes from trains quickly discolour glass, especially the areas directly above railway tracks. Brake dust is toxic, discolouring and adheres to glass. Regular cleaning is essential if the station is to retain its bright image.

Durability and maintenance are also related factors. Where painted steelwork is employed, designers need to provide the means for regular repainting. Steel structures above glazed roofs (such as at Waterloo International) pose a particular difficulty, and designers should consider whether aluminium can be substituted for steel. Again referring to Brin station, the specification for the painted steelwork consisted of four separate coatings, the final one being applied on site.[11] Within the life of a typical station the protective coatings on steel structures will need to be renewed perhaps a dozen times. How this is to be undertaken without disrupting the life and operation of the station is a design question, not merely a maintenance one.

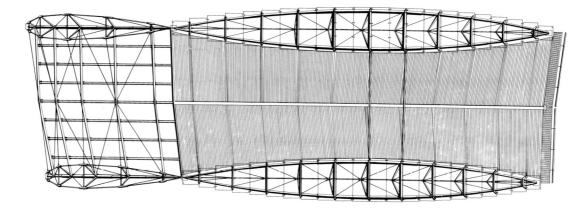

4.21 Roof canopies and glass assemblies need to be able to accommodate curves in the layout of stations and considerable structural movement. Architects: Nicholas Grimshaw and Partners.

Waterloo International Station, roof canopy

A combination of asymmetrical roof trusses and a shallow curve in plan meant that the glazed canopy over the station could not use standard manufacturer details. The twisting nature of the structure and the different angles of incline at different parts of the arch resulted in the decision to use a 'loose-fit' approach to glazing. Rather than adapt a standard glazing system by cutting sheets into different sizes with specially shaped fixing components, the architects decided to hold the glass in the frames along their length with overlapping sheets, rather as occurs in greenhouse construction. The cross-joints use concertina-shaped neoprene gaskets, which flex and expand to accommodate different widths, angles and degrees of movement.

The use of overlapping sheets of glass does not significantly reduce the transparency of the station canopy, nor views out to Westminster and the River Thames. It gives the station canopy a distinctive faceted look, particularly from the inside, and one that is reminiscent of a Victorian glasshouse. This effect is enhanced by the strut and ties that criss-cross the air space just outside the canopy line. The architect describes the roof as adopting the biomorphic qualities of an armadillo, where each section of glazing moves independently of the neighbouring pieces.[12]

The three-pin arch supporting the canopy is made up of two bowstring trusses, which are pinjointed asymmetrically. The tie rods run inside the canopy on the longer eastern-side trusses and outside the canopy on the shorter western-side trusses. The glazed canopy is mainly found on the west face of the arched station roof, as this is where the best views and least obstruction occurs. The eastern section of the station roof is clad with stainless steel decking between banana-shaped rooflights, which follow the shape of the trusses.

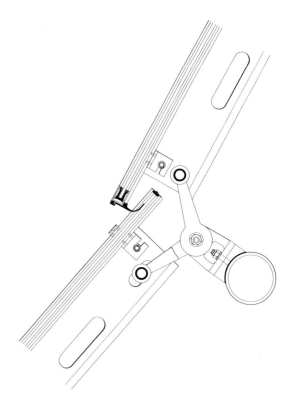

Glazing, jointing, framing and structure provide a well-integrated canopy over 400 m long above the station. The tapering span (from 50 m at the station entrance to 35 m above the outer lengths of platform), the changing geometries of the platform curve in plan, and the safety angles of trains, have resulted in a roof that provides the public face of the project. Yet the canopy cost only 10% of the total contract for the new station.

The decision by Nicholas Grimshaw and Partners to use 'loose-fit' glass assembly accommodates not only the asymmetry in plan and section of the station roof, but also the differential loads at different points in the canopy deriving from wind, train vibration and thermal expansion. The structure and glazed cladding had to be able to accommodate movements of up to 55 mm due to thermal expansion and 11 mm deflection due to the weight of trains. The overlapping tile-like assembly of each pane of glass is sealed by the use of a continuous neoprene gasket stiffened by an aluminium core, which is clipped to the outer edge of the lower sheet.[13] The use of neoprene gaskets and planar fixings exploits existing, not new technologies, yet the Waterloo Station canopy is as bold and expressive as the recent French stations by Calatrava or those in Italy by Piano. Ventilation and smoke extraction is provided by overlapping the eastern and western sections of roof at the apex. The two do not join but slide together with a deep airspace between each roof. Opening vents in the space allow comfortable environmental conditions to be maintained and emergency smoke extraction to occur, while in the winter months solar radiation warms the station concourse.

The station canopy is the main means by which the station announces the age of the Channel Tunnel. British Rail, through the Channel Tunnel architect Michael Edwards, encouraged the architect to create a building that was 'innovative, efficient and demonstrative'.[14] Waterloo International was intended as a flagship for the new railway age, and as the English counterpart to Lille station then maturing in France. The contrast at Waterloo between the old station and the new carries the message of quality and excitement that both client and architect sought, and which is communicated most forcibly in the design of the canopy.

Civil engineering matters

Crossing the tracks

Stations pose the particular difficulty of how to cross the railway tracks. Not many building types have to introduce changes of level to clear potentially dangerous corridors placed through their centre. There are two ways to cross the railway lines – either by tunnel or by bridge. Tunnelling is more expensive, but it has two advantages: tunnels can provide direct access to other transport systems, such as metro lines, and they are less prone to vandalism than bridges. The latter is mainly because of the materials employed – tunnels are a matter of civil engineering rather than architecture, with the robustness of finish this implies.

Bridges, on the other hand, are more about the architecture of stations than about their engineering. As they provide access to views and light, bridges are normally transparent structures. It is this quality that makes them particularly attractive to vandals, who seem drawn to the glass panels and, if the bridge is open, to dropping objects on passing trains. Where vandalism is high, tunnels are preferred to bridges in spite of their extra cost and lower amenity value for passengers.

With overhead power lines, bridges represent a greater climb than tunnels, thereby inconveniencing passengers, particularly those who are not fully ambulant. Ramp distances as a consequence need to be longer with bridges, and this can affect the layout of platforms. An increasing feature of station design (see the East Croydon case study in Chapter 2) is to provide the main station accommodation on the bridge itself. The advantages are obvious: ticket offices and waiting rooms can then provide the surveillance of the bridge necessary to deter vandalism, and the extra cost of a bridge can be justified by the other facilities it provides. Bridge stations have the advantage too of providing stronger landmarks than ordinary stations with underpasses to cross the tracks. This allows the station to be recognized within the wider townscape: a point particularly important in relatively faceless suburban locations. Bridge stations can also exploit the integration of structure, construction and glazing to enliven the experience of train travel, and by ramping down to platforms give a sense of arrival at the train platform.

Underground railways: a question of engineering or design

In underground systems, station design is directly related to the engineering of tunnels. For this reason many subway railways (such as those built in Hong Kong and Singapore in the 1970s) have tended to be determined almost exclusively by people with civil engineering rather than architectural skills. Here stations are adjuncts to the dictates of lines and tunnels, not worthy structures in their own right. In the case of the first underground railway in Hong Kong the design work was undertaken by engineers Freeman

105

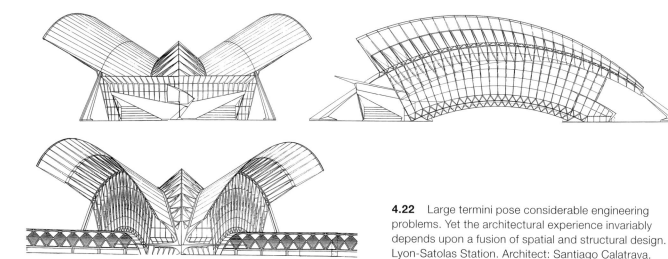

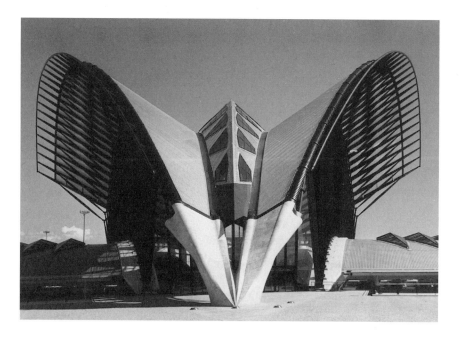

4.22 Large termini pose considerable engineering problems. Yet the architectural experience invariably depends upon a fusion of spatial and structural design. Lyon-Satolas Station. Architect: Santiago Calatrava.

4.23 At Lyon-Satolas Station, architecture and structural engineering become a seamless whole united by common expressive values. The station acts as a bridge above the low-level TGV lines.

Fox and Partners, with the industrial designer Misha Black providing largely superficial embellishment. No architect was involved until Roland Paoletti acting as chief architect helped to extend the system a decade later.[15]

As underground railways are an elaborate exercise in earthmoving, tunnelling and diversion of understreet services, they tend to be the province of civil engineers rather than of structural engineers or architects. This has implications for the approach to design and the ethical or philosophical position adopted. Civil engineering is a precise science with rules determined by the physics of structures and the condition of soils. On the other hand structural engineering and architecture is a question of construction and how it is read by the users of buildings. What has tended to occur in recent underground railway development is a better balance between civil, structural and architectural design skills, with the latter now informing the former rather than vice versa. The effect of these changes is to produce a generation of new stations where structural design, the forming of space and how it is lit are better integrated than in the past. Getting the fundamentals right means that less effort needs to be directed at the superficial aspects of station design, such as graphics, murals, colour coding and decorative finishes.

There is, however, a further problem with the relative role of professional advisers. As civil engineers are usually the first to be appointed (because the choice of line route often raises major issues in this area) they have the habit of staying on to design the stations and above-ground entrances. It is not a deliberate policy of railway developers but rather the result of perceptions of priority. Many believe that civil engineers resolve problems below ground with architects working from the ground up. As underground stations are necessarily positioned below ground they have tended to be seen as a tunnelling issue, not one of architecture. Hence in many countries underground stations

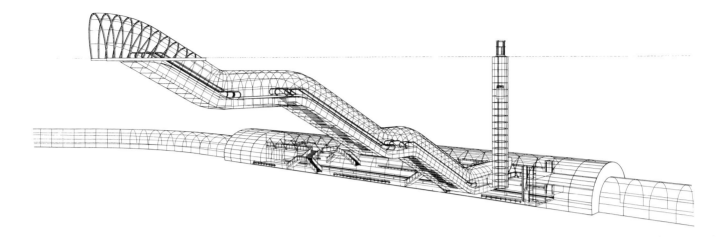

4.24 Underground railways were traditionally the preserve of civil engineers, but today architects are often the lead designers. Bilbao Metro. Architects: Sir Norman Foster and Partners.

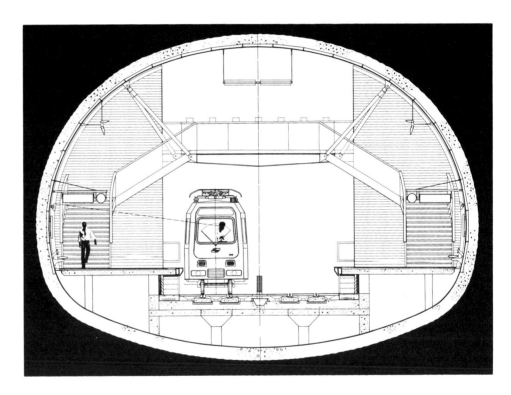

4.25 The New Austrian Tunnelling Method (NATM) has opened up fresh opportunities for underground architecture. Different tunnel profiles are now available, and the costs of large bores has been reduced. Bilbao Metro.

are designed by civil engineers, often with a subservient architect or designer in tow.

Recent underground lines have, however, broken with this pattern. In the UK the Jubilee Line Extension (JLE) and in the USA the new underground railway in Atlanta are particularly good examples of design-led, not engineering-led, station architecture. In both cases civil engineers are used as tunnellers only, with independent architects being appointed for the stations and above-ground development. This not only benefits station design but also encourages a better dialogue between above-ground development of station land and that of adjoining developers. Taken to its logical conclusion in Toronto and Vancouver, this led to a situation where developers took advantage of impending railway construction to undertake fresh construction, and were persuaded to make a financial contribution to the rail-

way works. Splitting underground and above-ground works sometimes discourages such dialogue.

The JLE follows the pattern of BART (Bay Area Rapid Transit), whereby different local architects were employed for each station. Rather than standardize the system, the policy in San Francisco was one of diversity bred of the idiosyncrasy of site and whims of different architects. The result is one of controlled variety, as a strong discipline of standard parts, details and movement systems also existed. The main problem with this approach is one of time: employing different designers for each station exposes the whole undertaking to the risk of time overruns. When there is the risk that politicians may renege on a commitment to construct a new underground line (as is often the case), any potential extension of time to get a project constructed can put the whole undertaking in jeopardy. This is why a

4.26 With underground railways, conspicuous signs are essential to identify the presence of stations. Note the three key elements: Metro sign, security camera and litter bins.

single firm of architects is often employed, frequently producing merely a sketch scheme and kit of parts, which becomes the basis for a design and build contract.

New Austrian Tunnelling Method

Although the New Austrian Tunnelling Method (NATM) was held responsible for the collapse of tunnelling at the London Underground extension at Heathrow in 1994, it remains widely employed in the UK and elsewhere. The NATM is simple in conception: rather than build the tunnel immediately after excavation, with NATM a temporary tunnel lining is formed using sprayed concrete, and then in-situ or precast concrete linings are built at a later stage. The advantage of this is that contractors have a larger area underground in

which to work, extra space to take services outside the perimeter of the tunnel, and the excavation and tunnel building operations are separated in time. With NATM the tunnel is stabilized with sprayed concrete as quickly as the excavated material is removed. This allows tunnelling to proceed more rapidly than with conventional methods, and tunnels can be built to larger sizes at little extra cost.

After the Heathrow collapse a modified form of NATM has been introduced in the UK to satisfy the Health and Safety Executive. The time delay between concrete spraying of the rough surface of the tunnel and the installation of the finished concrete lining has now been reduced. Contractors have a set time to link the two operations (generally reduced to weeks rather than months).

Different ground conditions affect the suitability of NATM. On the JLE a modified form of NATM was used to deal with waterbearing and collapsible beds (for example in the Greenwich area). Once the tunnel has been excavated and the temporary linings are installed, the next task is to erect the waterproof membrane and drainage fleece, which sits between the two tunnel linings. On JLE the 4.4 m diameter train tunnel consists of six segments, which fit together to form a 1.2 m long ring. Each section, which weighs over 2 tonnes, is lifted into position by a ring handler (a hydraulic arm that picks up each section, rotates it through 90° and places it against the tunnel wall) before it is bolted to adjacent sections.[16]

Using the NATM on the JLE, two tunnels are effectively built: an outer rough tunnel 5.3 m in diameter and a finished tunnel 4.4 m in diameter. The space between the two gives room to operate the equipment and a services channel while construction is in progress. Once a length of tunnel has been completed, cement grout is pumped into the space between the two diameters, forming a stable fill between the inner and outer tunnel linings, and fixing permanently the waterproof membrane and drainage system.

Much the same approach applies to the tunnels constructed to house the stations, which can be up to 12 m in diameter. Sprayed concrete secured with mesh reinforcement forms the outer tunnel, with in-situ concrete cast into formwork making the permanent inner lining. Waterproof membranes, strengthening ribs and a drainage fleece fill the gap between the two. With NATM, costs are reduced over

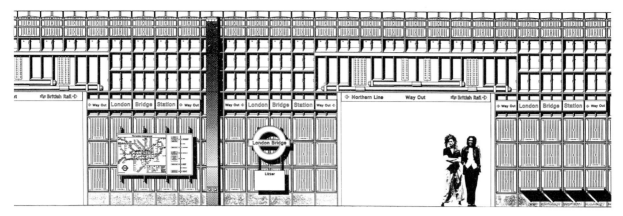

4.27 The incorporation of signage, advertising, directional panels and litter bins needs to be tackled at the design stage if the resulting station is not to suffer later. Here panels of vitreous enamel provide a grid that accommodates all the other elements. Architects: Weston Williamson.

4.28 Identifying stations requires attention to corporate signage. Brin Station, Genoa. Architects: Renzo Piano Building Workshop.

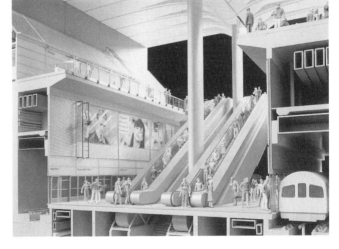

4.29 Poster advertising needs to be well integrated into the architecture of stations. Here at Canary Wharf the posters fit into a grid that corresponds with construction lines. Note too how a movable ladder provides ready access without obstructing concourses. Architects: Sir Norman Foster and Partners.

traditional tunnelling methods, particularly for the construction of large-diameter tunnels or tunnels of non-circular shape. The occupied public tunnel is normally 80% of the area of the outer tunnel, though the two tunnels do not need to be symmetrically placed in section. Egg-shaped or even doughnut-shaped public concourses are possible within round outer tunnels. The flexibility of shape and ease of forming secondary openings is an advantage of NATM that many station designers have exploited.

Advertising and public art

The coordination of advertising

The sale of advertising space is an important source of revenue for railway companies. Station advertising is also a means whereby the railway company can provide publicity about its own services. Commercial and railway advertising has a big visual impact upon the station environment. Poster displays provide colour, interest and sometimes amusement for the traveller.

Commercial advertising needs to be well coordinated. Poster displays need to be planned into the station environment, not added in a piecemeal fashion later. In terms of station communication, the priority is to give the travelling public information on station location and train services, not sell local hotel space or soap powder. Badly located advertising can lead to visual confusion, disruption in station movements, and the undermining of architectural integrity.

The location of advertising and its design are crucial considerations. Both station and commercial advertising need to be considered at the design stage, and related to

4.30 Ceramic murals are frequently employed at underground stations. Here at Bastille Station in Paris the scene depicted refers directly to the history of the area.

other questions such as the dissemination of essential travel information, the travellers' perception of the station zones, and the location of other commercial activities (such as shops and food outlets). Also, the impact of commercial advertising upon the three principal station design elements – structure, space and light – is an important aesthetic matter for the architect to consider. Advertising should not be ignored by the architect or left to others: it requires to be addressed at the initial design stage.

The four main station zones – access and entrance, information and tickets, commercial and waiting, platform and boarding – provide a framework for deciding on where and how to advertise.[17] As a general rule, advertising is most effective when it is sited perpendicular to pedestrian flows. The station designer should identify locations at each zone for advertising, and provide a means – well integrated with the architecture – whereby it can take place. Typical locations and opportunities for commercial advertising are as follows.

Access and entrance
Car parks and forecourt areas provide locations for advertising without impeding the main station signs. In some ways, commercial advertising can signal the presence of a station. The station entrance should normally be free of advertising. As car parking areas are often unattractive, advertising can add colour and interest, as long as it is well integrated with both building and landscape design.

Information and tickets
Commercial advertising is normally restricted in these areas, as railway – not commercial – information needs are paramount. Also, the lack of private advertising helps to signal this most important area of the station from the operator's point of view.

Commercial and waiting
Advertising is normally concentrated into this area. Two main types of commercial advertising exist: that to draw customers to the retail and food outlets in the station, and that advertising services or products further afield. In addition, there is normally advertising for the railway company. As the posters and signs used in this area are usually contained within spacious concourse areas or beneath lofty train canopies, there is height and volume to exploit in the location of advertising. Again, the architect should identify at the design stage where advertising should be located, and of what type (poster, panel, or illuminated signs). Incorporating advertising displays within a language of structural parts determined by the architect is preferable to ad hoc signage later.

Platform and boarding
This is another popular area for advertising, as it can be seen by those on trains and by passengers waiting at platforms. In certain types of railway, such as underground systems, this is the area of the station where most commercial advertising is located. Poster-type displays are the most popular. They can be incorporated into other platform structures, such as waiting shelters and canopies, or suspended from screen walls. At underground stations, large display advertising frequently lines the inside of platform tunnels, where it is often set between station signs or above seats. In the enclosed world of subterranean railways, commercial advertising can have large visual impact.

The design and coordination of advertising is a skilled operation. As a general rule, poster-type displays should be

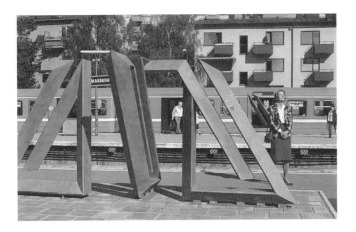

4.31 Stockholm Railways has commissioned major works of public art since the 1940s. Here at Skarwasbriuk Station steel sculpture is placed on the platform to amuse passengers as they wait for trains.

4.32 At Wakefield Station in Yorkshire, sculpture by Charles Quick enlivens a blank wall alongside the platform. The changing rhythms of the work capture well the movement of the trains.

4.33 Again at Wakefield Station, sculpture by students attached to Bretton College has added interest to a blank brick wall.

integrated with the station structure or furnishings of various kinds (seats, litter bins, lighting). Most advertising comes in standard sizes, whether it be illuminated signs or large posters. Station architects should incorporate these standard dimensions into areas specifically identified for commercial advertising. Also, as effective advertising requires well-lit signs, the architect needs to coordinate the design of lighting and display areas.

Public art

Public art adds to customers' enjoyment of travel and can, with thoughtful provision, ease the frustration of delayed journeys. Art adds nothing to the functional aspects of station architecture, but it can enhance the quality of the station environment and the image of the railway company, or titillate the curiosity of travellers.

Sites for public art exist widely within stations. At the entrance, art can enhance the aspect of car parks or brighten up blank gable walls. It can also be used to establish a theme that art in the station develops further. Inside the station, the main booking hall and central concourse provide further sites for public art. Art can also be used to brighten up dull platform areas, perhaps by expressing (as at Wakefield Station in Yorkshire) the sense of rhythm and movement of the trains.

Public art should not be confused with decoration. Art deals essentially with concepts and abstract ideas: it is not a question of painting a wall for its own sake. Decorative

embellishment that cannot be justified functionally or architecturally should be avoided.

As public art is a question of concepts, these should be accessible to the public. The visual benefits of murals, sculpture or light displays should ideally be of maximum impact and exploit fully the perceptions and interests of people using the station. It helps, therefore, if the subject

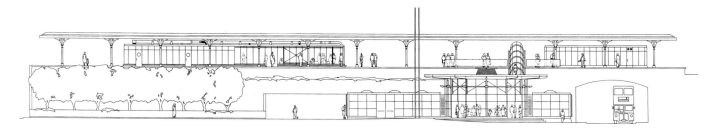

4.34 Good design briefing is essential to the making of high-quality railway architecture. Redhill Station. Architects: Troughton McAslan.

of a piece of public art makes reference to an aspect of the town or region it serves. It also satisfies public taste if the material employed is pleasurable in its own right (such as landscaping, lighting or carved stone). What should be avoided is work based upon such obscure abstraction that very few travellers understand it. Equally, art that uses shoddy materials such as cheap emulsion-painted surfaces is not likely to appeal for long.

Sites for public art should be identified at the design stage. Art should not be employed to remedy poor design. The selection of locations for artistic installations and the briefing of artists need to be undertaken as the station design is being evolved. Some of the most successful station art has occurred where architect and artist have shared values, employed similar materials and collaborated on concepts or themes at the outset.

Public art needs to have plenty of visual impact with a minimum requirement for maintenance or aftercare. This affects the choice of materials, the location and the timescale envisaged. On the London Underground and Moscow Metro, works of mural art and sculpture look as good today as when installed 50 years ago. But they were carved out of granite or marble, or constructed of cast bronze. Quality of materials is an important factor, not only in the question of long-term appearance but in the work's vulnerability to vandalism.

The client view: Railtrack Property

The landlord for the operational estate of British Rail is Railtrack plc. It has responsibility for the physical assets of 2500 stations, 1200 signal boxes and 40 000 railway bridges, and the welfare of its 22 000 tenants. Of the properties, about 1000 are listed, adding greatly to its need for specialized professional services.[18]

The main goal of Railtrack is to manage the estate of structures, to compile investment programmes for new stations, to refurbish existing ones, and to deal with day-to-day maintenance. It has the task of enhancing asset performance, and here the development of retail activities in stations has a key role. Railtrack and its divisional offices is the client for most architects engaged in the design of new

stations on the British Rail network. In its mission statement the company seeks amongst other things to:

- set industry standards that others aspire to;
- build an image within the railway industry and customer network;
- ensure that safety is paramount;
- develop effective partnership with suppliers, tenants and customers.[19]

Railtrack's property function extends beyond the railway station. It is engaged in retail and commercial expansion of its existing stations, the land round about them, and the air rights above them. Architects engaged by the company are as likely to be exploring the development potential of railway land at the periphery of stations as the spaces within them. As UK government plans are to involve the private sector in the running of certain stations, much attention is given to partnership developments and partnership funding. In this, Railtrack's own team of architects have an important role: they advise on technical, regulatory and aesthetic standards, thereby ensuring that station development adds to the company's asset resources. They are also involved in coordinating with the architects employed by the tenants of Railtrack buildings.

As Railtrack is concerned with image and standards, it communicates with its own regional offices and private firms through a variety of design guides. These establish performance standards, advise on safety and other complex issues, explain the regulatory framework for station design, and publish best practice guidelines. Independent architects, whether they be employed by retail tenants or by Railtrack itself, are therefore given firm guidance about the standards of design sought and the parameters within which they should work. For Railtrack this means that station design has an air of consistency from one end of the UK to another; for the architect or engineer it prevents wasted effort rediscovering what is already well known.

Privatization and design

The breaking up of the UK railway system under the 1993 Railway Act will result in 25 train-operating companies (which includes seven InterCity operators), three train-leasing companies (providing the rolling stock), and Railtrack (responsible for stations, track and operational land). Where British Rail once provided a comprehensive and aesthetically integrated system, the new arrangement will consist of diversity and, critics claim, fragmentation of the service. Putting aside political and economic considerations, the result of the government changes will be to free the different companies to pursue quite separate ambitions with regard to design. Gone are the days when standardized design guidelines operated from one region to another and led to a similar package of aesthetic ideals from rolling stock to waiting rooms. Under the new system each company will be tempted to outvie its geographical neighbour with a distinctive range of colours, shapes, materials and graphic symbols for trains and station alike.

As Railtrack will own nearly all the stations (although it will directly operate only 14 of them), this company has the largest task in maintaining some element of design consistency between the parts of the new railway system. Its head of architecture and design at the time of writing, Ian Hurst, says that there should be a corporate feel that allows diversity for designers working for different clients and in separate parts of the country, but within a familiar recognizable style.[20] This is to be achieved by effective design briefing and management of appointed architects, and by the issuing of design guidelines for key problems. In addition, Railtrack's *Design Standards Manual* will provide a broad framework of consistency at a technical level. The emphasis is upon variety within a system of preferred materials, products and standards.

Even when the architect is working for an operating company, the interests of Railtrack will be safeguarded through these guidelines. Effective design management, for which the brief and guidelines, are key instruments avoids the risk of compromising the clarity of the station as a functional and visual experience.

Design does not reside just within Railtrack, but it is here that the parameters are established. A company such as Burger King, with its distinctive logo and house style, will be encouraged to exist within a coordinated environment where the needs of passengers and the clarity of travellers'

perception are paramount. Without this controlling mechanism stations can become disorientating and potentially dangerous places. In controlling visual clutter and restricting the impact of competing styles, the station architect is upholding public values in what is increasingly a private world.

Railtrack recognizes in its various briefing documents that the perception of good design helps to promote effective marketing and image branding. Hurst has seen the balance shift at British Rail from a culture that traditionally valued engineering to one that equally values design. Although passenger surveys indicate that users appreciate well-designed trains rather more than well-designed stations,[21] the station environment is still one where perceptions of quality are established. The same surveys suggest that travellers value details as much as the whole, with clean toilets and accessible telephones as appreciated as the clarity of architectural space.

In order to achieve consistency of finish and efficacy in the use of materials, Railtrack's guidelines offer advice and establish performance standards. These have the effect of restricting choice, which – even allowing for different situations and the whim of designers – provides visual unity for what is increasingly seen as an important asset base for the company. The constraints upon the choice of materials from the dictates of vandalism, the need for replaceability, long-term robustness, safety, and accidental damage caused by luggage trolleys and skateboards, restrict finishes to a few familiar materials. Floor finishes, where strict slip coefficients have to be achieved, lead to specially treated terrazzo or semi-polished granite, just as stainless steel is one of the few materials that can withstand heavy damage and still look good. Technical and visual criteria limit the choice to an extent greater than at airports (where vandalism is less severe and costs usually higher). Stations with high levels of usage, such as London's Victoria with 1.6 million passengers a week crowded into narrow concourses, need to use surface materials that look good, wear well and can be readily replaced.

As most rail travel uses existing stations, the task of design is not one of abstract invention, but of upgrading the spaces and finishes that currently exist. While investment in the railway system still creates stations with flair, such as Waterloo International, Railtrack is rather more preoccupied with refurbishing stations. Whereas, in the design of the new, architects can exploit structure, space and light to create classic timeless stations, much of Hurst's time is spent reusing space and considering maintenance options within the confines of buildings often over a century old. Train-operating companies often see the older stations as presenting a poor outlook from the train window, and are anxious to upgrade their appearance. Too often, as on London Underground in the 1980s, a concern for enhanced image leads to cosmetic changes that address not the fundamentals of use or user legibility but surface embellishment. Coloured tiles, patterned paving and super-graphics are the ingredients usually exploited by those worried about image. Refurbishment, Hurst believes, needs to go further than decorative enhancement to address the real quality issues in travel – safety, visual unity and perceptive clarity.

The separation of operators of trains from those who own stations needs to be managed to ensure that there is no clash of interests. The free movement of people at stations and the opportunity of seeing the trains from concourses is leading to the progressive removal of ticket barriers from many stations. The interests of those who run the trains (and hence need to ensure that all travellers have tickets) and those who provide the stations are not the same. Station managers want passengers to be able to progress smoothly from ticket offices to platform without interruption to flow, either visual or physical. These divergent interests and priorities can lead to quite a different approach to station design, depending upon which party the architect represents. Just as the design of airports is constrained and often confused by passport control, so too the ticket barrier adds to the design complexity of stations. Hurst uses his coordinating function to marry the different objectives into a uniform, high-quality end-product.

Gateway to the Train design principles

In order to ensure that the importance of design is recognized at every level of station architecture, British Rail's InterCity company produced *Gateway to the Train* in 1993.

This consists of a number of design principles, and lays down expected standards regardless of which architect is employed for different InterCity stations. Though InterCity is now a private company, the principles have value irrespective of franchising arrangements.

The *Gateway to the Train* report written by Ian Hurst, then head of architecture and design at InterCity, recognizes that 'good design is good business'.[22] His concern was to ensure that 'identity, station environments, architecture and design... from tickets to trains, stations to stationery'[23] are of the highest standard. The report divides stations into four design zones:

- the arrival point;
- the access and ticket zone;
- the commercial and waiting zone;
- the platform and boarding zone.

Each has detailed requirements, which are more than a schedule of accommodation or technical standards. The design guide aims at creating a coherent visual system, which carries passengers through the four zones, yet defines clearly the boundaries. Hurst was keen that InterCity had a 'specific feel' from the 'station approach to the interior of carriages'.[24] To achieve this there is a coordination of designs, colours and unified branding. Borrowing from marketing philosophy, Hurst believes that an upmarket company needs an upmarket image, and that good consistent design is an important means by which this is communicated.

As much of the rail network is periodically undergoing upgrading, the report recognizes that the ideal is often hard to achieve. The design guide is an aspiration of concepts and standards that individual designers appointed on separate contracts should seek. Here, the method of procurement and the role of the briefing report are critical to the implementation of these ambitions.

As railways are about linear routes, the role of design guides is to impart a standard upon a corridor. Stations, track and trains are all part of the public's perception of the railway experience. To achieve this, it is important to work across rather than within professional interest boundaries.

Good design for InterCity is a matter of graphics, industrial design, architecture, landscape design, public art, engineering design and interior design. To carry forward the InterCity brand, Hurst appointed an architect and designer to take decisions for each route, irrespective of the nature of the design problem.

The importance of effective briefing

Successful buildings require both an imaginative architect and an enlightened client. The designer can only exploit the full opportunities of station architecture if there exists also a client who recognizes the importance of design to comfort, image and legibility. A good example is the design of the new station at Manchester Airport by architects Austin-Smith: Lord. Here the brief issued by British Rail said that the station should 'clearly demonstrate a railway identity whilst respecting and complementing airport facilities'.[25] The image was to be of a railway station with all the connotations of structure, canopy and presence that this entails. Implicit in the statement was the need for travellers at the airport to recognize the railway station as a station rather than as an airport terminal.

At a detailed level, BR's brief called for a 'sense of arrival and departure' to be indicated 'more by the qualities of the internal environment than by the use of signing alone'.[26] How passengers move through the station and their perception of routes and concourses were matters of fundamental importance. By putting these questions to the fore, the brief presented a challenge at a conceptual level. Some architectural briefs are merely a schedule of accommodation, but others raise issues that, by bridging operational and design philosophy, open up creative opportunities. The brief at Manchester Airport Station also required the architect to exploit the inevitable changes in level in such stations to 'heighten the customer experience of the major spaces'.[27] Spatial drama, combined with clearly defined routes and a celebration of arrival and departure achieved in the design, owes its initial inspiration to an imaginative brief.

In the brief, BR also specified an approach to building services and energy conservation. Services were to be fully integrated into the structural and spatial design with 'complete harmony of all fittings and finishes'.[28] Energy conservation, both the cost of the initial installation and maintenance, was to dictate the overall servicing strategy. At an operational level, the brief also asked the architects to make a contrast between the public areas and staff accommodation, which was to have a more human and intimate scale.

BR's briefing document provided clear and enlightened guidance for the architect. By raising ethical and philosophical questions about the nature of design and the degree to which it should serve passenger needs, the architects were encouraged to break the mould of conventional station design. The receipt of the International Railway Design Brunel Award for the station in 1994 owes a debt to the thought that BR put into the brief.

The example of Waterloo International

With complex stations the task of evolving a brief is often the responsibility of independent consultants. At Waterloo International Station, British Rail appointed Sir Alexander Gibb and Partners to draw up the brief and to ensure that instructions to the architects were consistent with infrastructure support, planning policies for the area, and BR's own corporate ambitions. It was after advice from Gibb that the decision was made to separate departures physically from arrivals; and to ensure that visual clues guided passengers to where to catch trains and the routes to follow when leaving them. The decision by Nicholas Grimshaw and Partners to divide the functions onto different levels and to use structure and light to guide passengers through what was of necessity a complex station stemmed directly from the brief.

The brief at Waterloo also specified departure times of a maximum of 20 minutes (from station arrival to train seat via passport and ticket checks), and a shorter time of 15 minutes for business travellers.[29] As trains were expected to arrive and depart every 10 minutes the capacity of the station had to be able to accommodate a passenger throughput of 6000 people per hour. Gibb also specified as part of the brief that baggage was to accompany passengers throughout their journey and not be separated, as is

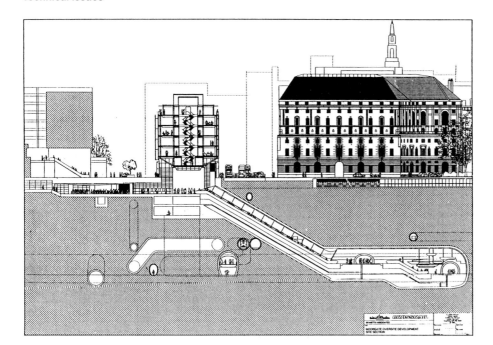

4.35 Relating the interior design of underground stations to that of structures above ground requires particular skill in handling route and changes in level. Notice how the first-floor slab of the office building is profiled to deflect daylight underground. Moorgate Station, CrossRail. Architects: Bennetts Associates.

the practice at airport check-ins. The linear progression, separated for functional reasons onto different levels, which is a characteristic of Waterloo International, follows directly from the brief as formulated by the consultants. The emphasis too upon quality of space and finish, and the guiding role of the station canopy in orientating passengers, also stem from the brief. In this sense, Waterloo's success reflects the partnership between client, briefing engineer and architect at the crucial feasibility stage of the project.

Interior design

Commercial activities and the design of stations

In contrast to the operation of many train services, stations are often highly profitable. Larger stations, especially termini, generate revenue far in excess of the costs of maintenance and staffing. Ticket sales are only part of income creation: as much as 25% of revenue for the railway operator comes from the sale of franchises, advertising and other secondary activities. At stations such as London's Euston, where ticket revenue exceeds £1 million a week, franchising out space to retail and restaurant operators can be nearly as profitable as running the railway service itself.

Stations have yet to assume the commercial status of airports, where 50% of revenue comes from franchising deals with retail operators.[30] They are, however, moving in the same general direction and for similar reasons. Travel is a necessity for many and a recreation for others. Both need to fill the journey with things to read, eat and pass the time. As world economies grow, passenger miles increase and with them a higher expectation of travel amenity. Retail and restaurant outlets at the station feed off these demands in a fashion that is openly parasitic. There was a time when

train catering provided the bulk of journey needs, but now food outlets at the station compete for the travellers' attention.

Increasing numbers of travellers, their higher expectations, longer journeys and business expense accounts all combine to fuel a demand for bookstalls, gift shops, sandwich bars and other services at major stations. Their provision at the station adds to the complexity of designing such buildings, and makes effective briefing and design guidelines essential. For the architect the task is further confounded by the relationship at stations between the owner and tenants. The franchising operators have their own house style, which may not be known in advance, and is likely to be at variance with the aesthetic ambitions of the station architect. Absorbing a collection of competing house styles of architecture and signage of the retail outlets, and perhaps also the operators of different railway services, all within an elegant station design is by no means easy.

If the public spaces in stations are not to become congested and disorientating places under the pressure of commercial exploitation, the responsibilities of architects, engineers and designers need to be clearly defined. Effective design management is crucial in ensuring that duties and relationships are understood by all the parties, no matter what company or interest they represent. In this a distinction needs to be made between design briefing (which spells out specific constraints, opportunities and operating conditions) and design guidelines (which cover generic points applicable across a range of situations).[31] The more complex railway management systems and ownership become, the more crucial is the role of design management and briefing.

Railway stations were initially conceived as essentially a matter of engineering. The nineteenth-century station was

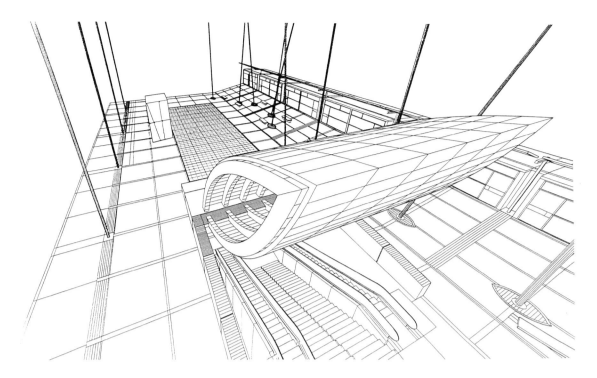

4.36 Suspending elements within concourse spaces can provide interior landmarks, which help with orientation. Proposed Vermont/Santa Monica Station, Los Angeles. Architect: Ellerbe Becket.

a place where engineering, not architecture, prevailed. Today, however, though the strand of structural engineering has not been broken, design has emerged as a major concern, particularly from the point of view of customer satisfaction and image branding. Stations are an expanding market for design at every level – from architectural space to the details of food wrapping and ticket identity. The shift of stations out of the public arena (into private or combined public/private ownership) has opened up the market for fresh design skills. Space planning, safety planning, security planning, shop and ticket office design through to details such as seating and lighting all provide a market for specialist design services.

These wider cultural changes are affecting the design of new stations and the upgrading of existing ones. Changes in the operation of railway services, fresh societal concerns (such as for security and improved disabled access) alter the way stations are designed. As much of our railway infrastructure has already been built, these changes are as much a question of regeneration as of invention. Adapting old stations to new conditions tends to be the norm. Here the changes need to respect the traditions of the past, working with the industrial archaeology of the station rather than against it. Too often the commercial pressure for increased retail outlets or an improved station image has resulted in cosmetic changes, with the emphasis upon cheap finishes and garish graphics. Designers need to balance the conflicting demands, putting the needs of passengers above those of franchising companies.

Architectural skills, which are embedded in the traditions of using structure, light and space to serve public needs, can be undermined by commercial pressure from railway or retail operators.

As stations become more complex, interior design has a crucial role in differentiating the different functions. Distinguishing between companies offering ticketing services from those providing sandwiches is as important as identifying the main routes from secondary ones. Design can help make clear the relationship between public goals and private ones at stations. If such matters are left to signage, stations quickly become visually indigestible. Effective design can make the demarcation between activities clearer: it can define routes and zones, distinguish the major from minor attractions, and suggest the areas of social or private space. Design here is not only a matter of architectural design but of graphic, interior, lighting and product design.

The changes to the perception of what a station is have led to new design consultancy services being offered. Restructuring stations to accommodate greater commercial activity has encouraged an emergence of a fresh understanding of the centrality of design to customer satisfaction. Design at stations was once a matter of engineering with architectural embellishment. New design techniques and facilities management have opened up fresh markets. Greater privatization of railway services around the world and a renaissance in railway investment have created design opportunities at every level of provision.

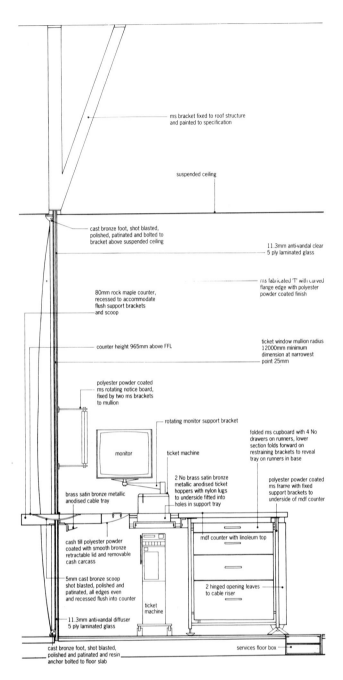

4.37 (left and below, top illustration) Detail of ticket office at Gloucester Station. Architects: Alan Brookes Associates.

ms bracket fixed to roof structure and painted to specification

suspended ceiling

cast bronze foot, shot blasted, polished, patinated and bolted to bracket above suspended ceiling

11.3mm anti-vandal clear 5 ply laminated glass

ms fabricated 'T' with curved flange edge with polyester powder coated finish

80mm rock maple counter, recessed to accommodate flush support brackets and scoop

counter height 965mm above FFL

ticket window mullion radius 12000mm minimum dimension at narrowest point 25mm

polyester powder coated ms rotating notice board, fixed by two ms brackets to mullion

rotating monitor support bracket

folded ms cupboard with 4 No drawers on runners, lower section folds forward on restraining brackets to reveal tray on runners in base

monitor

ticket machine

2 No brass satin bronze metallic anodised ticket hoppers with nylon lugs to underside fitted into holes in support tray

polyester powder coated ms frame with fixed support brackets to underside of mdf counter

brass satin bronze metallic anodised cable tray

cash till polyester powder coated with smooth bronze retractable lid and removable cash carcass

mdf counter with linoleum top

5mm cast bronze scoop shot blasted, polished and patinated, all edges even and recessed flush into counter

ticket machine

2 hinged opening leaves to cable riser

11.3mm anti-vandal diffuser 5 ply laminated glass

cast bronze foot, shot blasted, polished and patinated and resin anchor bolted to floor slab

services floor box

The design of booking halls

The principles in the *Gateway to the Train* design guide lead naturally to the level of consideration and sense of style in the detailing of booking halls by, for example, the architects Alan Brookes Associates. The design guide lists the 'access and ticket zone' as a distinctive part of customer experience, where quality is of particular importance. Queuing for a ticket can be frustrating, with unpredictable delays and the anxiety of trying to buy a ticket with only moments to spare before the train departs. It is also the first point where the traveller stops on the journey to the train. As such, details near at hand matter, and the quality of materials matters most.

4.38 Distinguishing between station canopy, perimeter lighting, structural supports and dwarf walls helps to give travellers a sense of direction. Architects: Jourda and Perraudin.

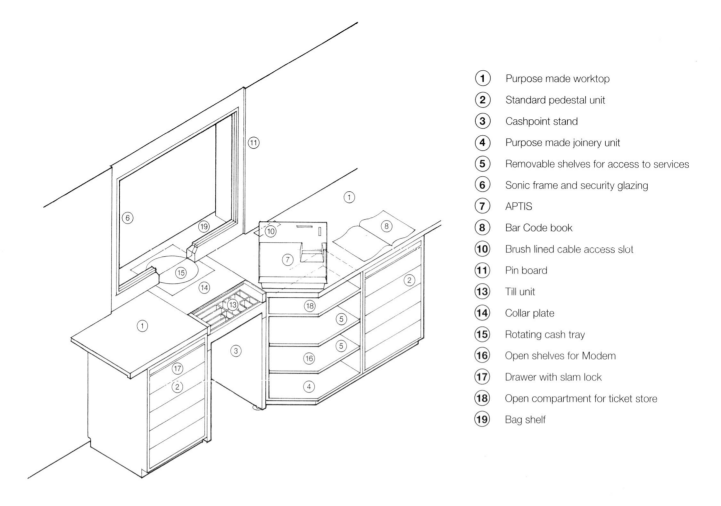

1. Purpose made worktop
2. Standard pedestal unit
3. Cashpoint stand
4. Purpose made joinery unit
5. Removable shelves for access to services
6. Sonic frame and security glazing
7. APTIS
8. Bar Code book
10. Brush lined cable access slot
11. Pin board
13. Till unit
14. Collar plate
15. Rotating cash tray
16. Open shelves for Modem
17. Drawer with slam lock
18. Open compartment for ticket store
19. Bag shelf

4.39 British Rail Network SouthEast's design guide for a ticket office workstation. Notice the many security elements present.

The booking hall and ticket office are clearly defined areas within the station environment. They have an atmosphere determined by materials, colours and textures quite different from other parts. With franchising of railway services (announced under the 1993 Railway Act) the point of customer/staff contact at the ticket office is of fundamental importance to quality control.

Alan Brookes Associates were appointed in 1993 to upgrade three ticket offices in the southwest of England (Truro, Penzance and Gloucester). The brief from Regional Railways (one of four British Rail passenger services) asked for the 'use of indigenous hardwoods, grey granite and a cool range of colours', to create a branding image for the company quite distinct from the stainless steel aesthetic commonplace elsewhere.[32] The look sought was one of high tech, but using materials that were more traditional and reassuring to the passenger. The design evolved by the firm was intended to establish a standard that would, over time, become the norm on Regional Railways. As such, the construction allowed for a large degree of prefabrication, which held the advantage of mass production without jeopardizing quality.

The high-tech appearance of the booking hall makes obvious gestures towards new, finely engineered rolling stock. Hence the experience of ticket purchase and that of travel are united in aesthetic and technological terms. Where Alan Brookes Associates provide cast bronze cash scoops, smooth white beech finishes, stylish inset lights and polyester powder-coated surfaces, the passenger experiences these or similar ones a few minutes later on the train. Image branding is about quality at every point in the experience of travel, but with concentrated effort in particular areas.

With computerized ticket issue and airline-style tickets, the space between ticket windows has had to widen in order to accommodate additional equipment. The effect of the increase in distance between windows has been to enhance the sense of spaciousness in booking halls. This too has practical advantages for the traveller, particularly those with children and trolleys. Expressing the increased sense of space in architectural terms means looking hard at the choice of materials and the image that they project. An earlier generation of booking halls was finished in BR's preference for white ceramic tiles set against black signed fascias and grey rubber floors. The choice of these materials

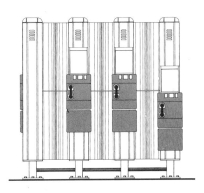

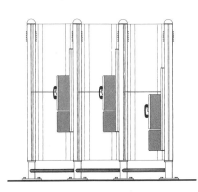

4.40 Lift drum (above, left) and telephones (above, centre and right) designed by Nicholas Grimshaw and Partners for Waterloo International Station.

4.41 Free-standing elements, such as this ticket machine at Roissy Station, need to be designed to the highest standards if the interior environment is not to be sacrificed.

rules. For example, while bronze, granite and timber are used throughout, the percentage of each varies according to the traditions of different locations. At the Cornish stations more granite is used, because it makes up much of the local landscape, while at Gloucester Station timber takes over in deference to the nearby Forest of Dean.[33] Within an aesthetic language it was felt necessary to be sensitive also to changing regional traditions along the length of the railway line.

Station furniture

The quality of station furniture is arguably as important to the passengers' perception of quality as that of the station architecture itself. The design of seats, ticket booths, signs, lighting poles and information boards helps to create an ambience of quality and customer care. Though rarely designed by architects, station furniture tends to be ordered from manufacturers' catalogues, and here it is important that the character of the station and of the piece of furniture in question share the same approach to design. In some more prestigious stations, such as Waterloo International, the architect has adapted manufacturers' standard components to ensure that the design philosophy of the station is reflected directly in the choice of signs, seats etc. used.

A handful of firms dominate the supply of station furniture, especially at the prestigious end of the market. Vitra, a company associated with the supply of seating for offices and airports, has introduced a range for stations. Their Tandem seating, designed by Charles and Ray Eames, with frames of cast polished aluminium and upholstered in vinyl, was used at Waterloo International Station in the departure

gave the booking hall a sense of utility that is now considered poor for customer relations. Today's emphasis upon softer, more natural materials borrows from the philosophy of airports. Stations, however, have to be more robust and able to deal with vandalism, which is commoner than at airports. Consequently, a balance is struck in design between softer, more reassuring materials and resilient, high-tech detailing.

Although the design by Alan Brookes Associates establishes an aesthetic norm for others to follow, it is more a language of materials and principle than a rigid system. The component parts respond to the requirements and characteristics of each station while obeying consistent

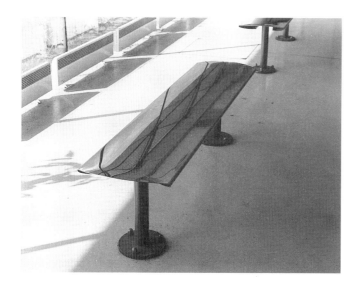

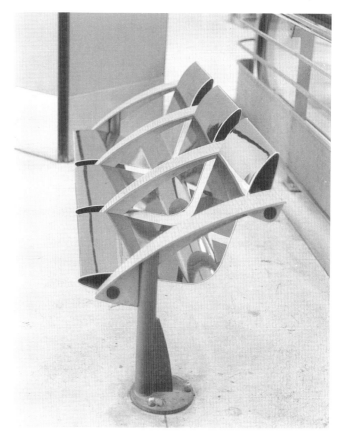

4.42 Lille-Europe Station. The design of seats in particular helps to establish quality in interior design. Elegant lines, robust design and the use of easily cleaned materials help in maintaining good appearance over a long period of time.

lounge. Grimshaw's office also specified Eames' wire chairs (also from Vitra) for cafe areas. The Italian furniture company Tecno provides a range of structures designed particularly for transport termini, and suitable for use in airports, bus stations and railway stations alike. The company provides a standard pattern of ticket booths, control desks and counters, which can readily be used unaltered or adapted (as happened at Waterloo and Bilbao) to suit the conditions at different stations. The platform control kiosk provided by Tecno, based upon a 3 m square, is constructed of steel with rigid steel panels, curved and flat glass in beadless frames, and incorporates its own air-conditioning, lighting and sprinkler system. Amongst its other products the Tecno range includes a circular customer care desk in stainless steel suitable for two members of staff, with leaflet display areas and integral storage.

The design of lifts, stairs and escalators is particularly important as the travelling public comes into immediate contact with them. Along with station furniture, the moving parts (lifts, escalators, travellators) help to create the ambience of quality that station operators increasingly seek. Companies such as Railtrack recognize that quality and comfort expressed through such items helps them to compete with airports and bus stations for customers. Lifts and their enclosing walls are often free-standing structures within the station environment, and need to be designed accordingly. The use of contrasting materials and high-tech finishes allows them to be recognized within the competing world of station interiors. As passengers may need to wait for the lift to arrive, the design should contain interest down to the finest detail.

Escalators and travellators too are part of the moving landscape of stations, and points where passengers engage

directly in the experience of travel. After the King's Cross fire and the subsequent Fennell Report, greater attention has had to be paid to safety in the design of escalators. It is now mandatory to provide heat and smoke detectors and fire sprinklers, and glass where used has to be heat-soaked and toughened. Emergency stops need to be provided at frequent intervals, and skirting lighting adds a further element of safety that in the event of smoke provides obvious guidance to passengers. The new safety requirements add to the difficulty of design, but elegance and style are still attainable.

The design of station furniture is usually a question of selecting an appropriate choice from a manufacturers' catalogue. On more prestigious contracts, the architect may be able to modify a standard platform seat or escalator design to suit the conditions of the station. In either case the choice of product or finish adds greatly to the ambience of the station. The sense of design quality as perceived by station users is not solely a question of structural design or the management of interior space, but extends to furniture, fittings and moving parts.

Commercial and railway integration: Union Station, Washington

Union Station is the finest of several once-grand American railway stations (p. 6, Fig 1.6). Designed in 1902 by Daniel H. Burnham, the station was intended to anchor the end of one of two processional routes through the capital. Its role was as much urban monument as the centre of a web of railway facilities in the city with fingers extending from coast to coast.

Burnham designed Union Station with characteristic regard for celebrating the civic realm. The huge voluminous arrivals hall, the grand facade (inspired by the Arch of Constantine in Rome) and the internal barrel vaults (borrowed from the Basilica Roma) made the station the finest monument to American railways. Like many stations, however, it fell into decline in the 1950s as Americans discovered the motor car and the convenience of air travel. Other less prominent stations were allowed to be demolished in the 1960s, but Union Station, terminating a diagonal axis focused at the other end by the Capitol building, was too visible for that. Instead, in 1981 Congress enacted the Union Station Redevelopment Act, which provided national funds for the station's restoration, and provided the means for a balanced redevelopment of retail and railway interests within the former shell.

The redevelopment of Union Station in 1985 by Benjamin Thompson Associates made it the first major international station to take advantage of the retail and commercial potential of relatively underused internal volumes. Without compromising the character of the station as a grand historic gateway to Washington, the interior was converted to a collection of new transport interchanges (connecting long-haul with suburban and metro lines) with a supporting panoply of bars, shops, cinemas and offices.

In the adaptation, little of the splendour of Burnham's station was lost. Instead, new cultural and commercial life was added, which gives the main concourse (when built in 1902 the largest space in the world under a single roof) much of the social vitality it possessed originally. New shops and restaurants have been added around the perimeter of the space and on galleries overlooking it, with a central island of bars grouped around the original station clock.

Today, Union Station recalls a blend of the American shopping mall and a grand Edwardian railway station. Like most retail malls it is zoned into main and speciality retail, food and conveniences and restaurant areas. Some of these occupy former banqueting spaces (such as the orig-

inal dining room, which now houses speciality shops); others squat in the open spaces; and where background sound is a problem fountains with splashing water have been provided. Space beneath the station has been excavated to form cinemas at the level of local metro services.

Architecturally and commercially the revitalization of Union Station is a success. The scheme had the undoubted benefit of Burnham's dramatic internal volumes and the architect's sense of procession. The station as transport interchange has, however, lost some of its sense of purpose and legibility. Though few trains use the station today, it remains the city's major focus for public transport. Retail and restaurant uses, though they have added vitality to the spaces, have also weakened the identity of Union Station as a great railroad interchange. There is no denying the quality of the restoration of the building or its improved social purpose. What is in doubt is the shift from a railway character to one of a market hall. The meaning of the building as expressed in the grandeur of the facade and the scale of the internal malls seems at odds with the present function.

References

1. *Terry Farrell: Urban Design*, Academy Editions, London, 1993, p. 113.
2. Ibid., p. 109.
3. Dennis Sharp (Ed.), *Santiago Calatrava*, E & FN Spon, London, 1992, p. 65.
4. *Railway Group Safety Plan*, 1995/96, Railtrack plc, London, p. 18.
5. *Ibid.*
6. James Holmes-Siedle, 'Creating universal access', *Architects' Journal*, 9 February 1994, p. 35.
7. *Ibid.*
8. The list is adapted from James Homes-Siedle's article noted above and from InterCity's design manual for disabled access.
9. Helena Russell, 'Double Dutch rail', *New Civil Engineer*, 18/25 August 1994, p. 19.
10. Alan Brookes, 'Structure', *Architects' Journal*, 8 April 1992, p. 41
11. *Ibid.*
12. *Building Design*, 3 February 1995, p. 2.
13. Peter Davey, 'Waterloo International'. *Architectural Review*, September 1993, p. 44.
14. *Ibid.*, p28.

15. Here I am indebted to a personal interview with Roland Paoletti held on 19 April 1995 in London.
16. *Building*, 7 April 1995, pp. 37–77.
17. 'Commercial advertising', in *Gateway to the Train* design guide, InterCity, London, 1992.
18. *Railtrack Property*, brochure dated March 1995, Railtrack, London.
19. *Ibid*.; the points are paraphrased for brevity.
20. Based upon an interview with Ian Hurst on 19 April 1995.
21. *Ibid*.
22. 'Better by design', *InterCity*, September 1993, p. 7.
23. *Ibid*.
24. *Ibid*.
25. *Manchester International Airport Rail Terminus: Detailed Design Report*, Austin-Smith:Lord, Warrington, Cheshire, 1990, para 1.3.

26. *Ibid*.
27. *Ibid*.
28. *Ibid*.
29. Peter Davey, 'Waterloo International', *Architectural Review*, September 1993, p. 28.
30. Andrew Laing, 'Business takes off at the airport', *Architects' Journal,* 30 March 1995, p. 24.
31. This point was made by Ian Hurst, Chief Architect for Railtrack, in an interview with the author on 19 April 1995.
32. Marcus Field, 'Reworking a booking hall', *Architects' Journal*, 22 September 1993, p. 16.
33. *Ibid*.

Part two

Some recent
station projects

International and mainline stations

CHAPTER

5

Lille-Europe

The development of EuroLille, a grandly conceived integration of railway station and commercial development, followed directly from a decision in 1987 to develop the North European Train à Grande Vitesse (TGV) network. The partners in the TGV undertaking (principally France, with support from Belgium, the Netherlands and Germany) decided initially to bypass Lille in the planned line joining Paris and Brussels with a spur northwards to the Channel Tunnel. However, during the planning of the line's route the realization dawned that a new station nearer to the centre of Lille would open up a large tract of derelict inner-city land for redevelopment. Heavily promoted by Pierre Mauroy, Mayor of Lille, the new station became a catalyst for public and private capital investment on a huge scale. Masterplanned by Rem Koolhaas, the TGV station (known as Lille-Europe) is part of a massive urban reconstruction, which also contains, besides shopping and offices, an international exhibition centre (known as Lille Grand Palais) and an auditorium seating up to 6000 spectators.[1]

Had the line not been directed to this area none of these facilities would have been built. The wider advantages to the economy of Lille are obvious, and the secondary uses add greatly to the commercial viability of the TGV station. The mutual benefit of integrating railway, commercial and civic development into one huge undertaking is perceived as enhancing the success of the whole project. It has also enhanced Lille's reputation as a centre for railway-led growth in Northern Europe. It was also in Lille that Margaret Thatcher and President Mitterand signed the agreement to build the Channel Tunnel in 1986. Just as Crewe in central England grew in the nineteenth century because of its position at the hub of railway lines, so too Lille seems set to do the same but for Northern Europe in the twenty-first century.

EuroLille highlights the importance of good rail connections to economic prosperity. Being a pivot on the TGV Nord line, Lille is two hours from London, Amsterdam and Cologne, an hour from Paris and half an hour from Brussels. The geographical asset of Lille has been realized via train links in a fashion that air or road transport cannot rival. Six of Europe's most prosperous capital cities are within two

5.1 View of Channel Tunnel railway terminal at Folkestone, Kent. Architects: Building Design Partnership.

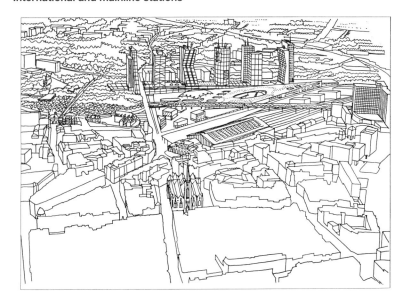

5.2 Rem Koolhaas' sketch of the proposed EuroLille Station, with the commercial development behind a new city park.

5.3 Masterplan of EuroLille, with the new Lille-Europe Station (top), Lille Flanders Station (bottom), and new town square, retail and office area between. Notice how the infrastructure of rail and road determines the layout of buildings and movement patterns for pedestrians. Architect: Rem Koolhaas.

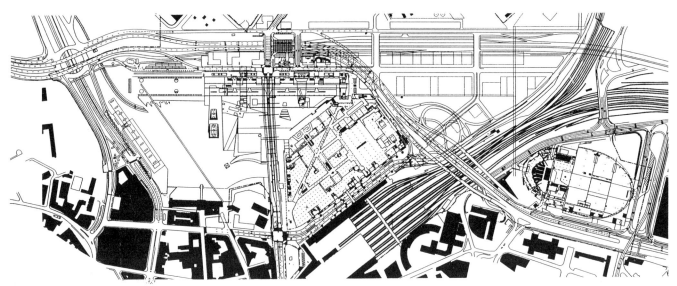

hours' travel time by rail. This potential proved justification for a £650 million development covering 70 ha with a railway station at its centre. With Mayor Mauroy pledging 54% of the funding for the project from city and regional development grants, the private sector had the confidence to find the balance.[2]

The TGV station was undoubtedly the catalyst for one of Europe's largest urban regeneration projects of the late twentieth century. With an estimated 30 million passengers a year passing through the station, there existed a great opportunity to create a new piece of city on its doorstep. The mix of uses accommodated within the mega-structure of the station or immediately nearby makes EuroLille lively and urbane. Besides the conference centre and auditorium, the development contains 45 000 m² of offices, 700 apartments, three hotels, student accommodation, a huge shopping centre and a 10 ha park.[3]

The Koolhaas masterplan involved splitting the new TGV line from the old Lille–Flanders rail route, thereby creating a large triangular site where once derelict industries and fragmented roads offered little welcome or urban cohesion. The re-engineering of roads and existing railways was expensive, but such work was eligible for grants in a town marked by rapidly declining textile industries. Although modern railway construction, urban regeneration and commercial development proved unlikely allies initially, the championing of the project by Mauroy and Europe's inexorable move towards political and transport union has resulted in a project with lessons for other cities.

EuroLille has benefited from the concept of a borderless Europe. It also signifies the importance of cities as against nation states in EU affairs. Though the development is large in scale it contains many elements of sustainable development. EuroLille is rail based, not car orientated; it is pedestrian friendly; it offers attractions of various kinds without the need to travel along hostile inner city streets; it provides a dense mix of activities and services, which can be accessed on foot and at various times of the day and night;

and it exploits daylight, even in the core of the development. Unlike Canary Wharf or Broadgate, the development is not primarily about office accommodation served by railways, but about a section of city, with all the social, cultural and economic factors which that entails.

The Koolhaas masterplan placed the new Lille-Europe station (designed by Jean-Marie Duthilleul) below ground with public entrances from above. This position, essential for sound reduction, provides a grand descending entrance to the station concourse. Above the station sit a series of office towers and alongside, in the point of the triangular site, a 140 unit shopping centre. A large and futuristic roof canopy (designed by the English engineer Peter Rice) extends across the whole, creating unity to the parts and considerable internal drama. The perimeter of the development is largely glazed with clear glass, allowing the activities inside to be clearly seen, especially at night. The visual permeability is greatest at the public elements, such as the station, and least where internal activity is best screened (as at the auditorium).

Various architects were employed to design different parts of the masterplan. Jean Nouvel was responsible for the shopping and leisure element known as Centre EuroLille, and other architects of note have played different parts. This has resulted in complexity and richness, rather than orderly, standardized development. The masterplan rightly gives pride of place to the station, both spatially and functionally. Routes through the development and into the station are defined by structure and light. Scales of engineering vary to reflect the status in public terms of key areas. The masterplan provides order and hierarchy within parameters that allow freedom of expression for other architects. The planning and design of EuroLille reflects the new railway age, with its emphasis upon more sustainable development principles, where the station is a generator of renewal rather than an isolated monument.

The design of the station

By splitting the upper concourse area on either side of a wide elevated road, the architect, Jean-Marie Duthilleul, has effectively created a public space at the station entrance.

Travellers can enter by either building, and once they have descended into the main body of the station can buy tickets and refreshments in a wide and well-lit concourse. Light floods down from the roof through a lacing of arched steel beams or through walls of nearly continuous glazing. As the platforms are a further level down, light here is deflected off interior walls or arrives via angled diffusers. The articulation of the steel structure provides an interior rhythm that, like the columns and vaulting of a cathedral, gives a sense of direction and procession. Walls, in white smooth concrete relieved by segmental arches, provide at platform level a solidity that contrasts with the lightweight structure above.

Connections to the Lille underground railway and the nearby shopping centre are by elegant steel and glass bridges, which project out from the station and lead into paved and terraced public squares, some beneath great glazed lightweight roofs. Detailed in modern fashion with an emphasis upon high-tech materials, the station and public areas round about are united by a common sense of purpose.

As in many French stations, the decision to place the platforms beneath ground (because of the need to contain the noise of high-speed trains) has resulted in clarity of route both horizontally and vertically, thanks largely to the

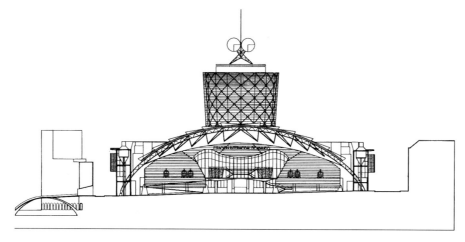

Alzado a la plaza de Abando / Elevation to Abando plaza

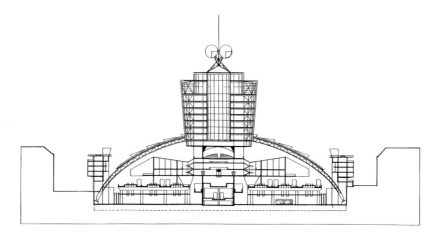

Sección transversal por el WTC / WTC cross section

5.5 Abando Station, Bilbao, as designed by Michael Wilford and Partners.

use of natural light and expressive structure. It is structure that is heavy and monumental in scale below ground and lightweight and delicate above. Architecture gestures towards the earth, on the one hand, and to the sky on the other; to the need to relieve air pressure via great arches and shafts below ground, and to filter sunlight down for the benefit of passengers.

Bilbao Abando Station, Spain

The design by Michael Wilford and Partners for a new railway station in Bilbao highlights the changing nature and growing scale of modern railway architecture. The complex, which is intended to open in 1998 to replace the Abando Station, contains three railway systems (TGV, regional and local rail facilities), a retail concourse, bus station, World Trade Centre, hotel and housing.[4] The bulk of the elements are contained in a huge glazed envelope 160 m wide and 230 m long. As a glazed, arched, steel structure the Bilbao roof will be over twice the size of the typical Victorian station shed.

The railway stations and bus station housed within the transparent, naturally ventilated arch of glass provide the necessary air of permeability and accessibility needed of a massive public transportation facility in the heart of a historic city. Rather than build a potential barrier to movement, Wilford's approach has been to provide a roofed city square, which doubles up as station concourse, shopping mall and public space. The sense of connection to the wider fabric of Bilbao is provided by the use of internal streets that, though constructed beneath the glazed canopy, make direct links to the pattern of streets in the city. Hence it will be possible to move through the station within the protection of the glass roof, rather as one does in cities such as Milan or Leeds, passing periodically under sheltering high-level glazed canopies.

The design is based upon the concept of an enormous galleria contained within a perimeter wall of offices, housing and hotels. The galleria contains three main levels of public transport accommodation (bus station on lower floor, public concourse and ticketing area on ground floor, and trains on first floor), each expressed as solid elements

5.6   Waterloo International Station provides a fine spectacle outside and inside. The design, by Nicholas Grimshaw and Partners, won the prestigious Mies van der Rohe Award for Architecture in 1994.

geometrically arranged beneath the huge membrane of arched glass. The 12 platforms are divided by a central spine of public-type accommodation (bars, restaurants, tourist information, post office etc.), which runs parallel to the linear spine of the station. The two axes, therefore, perform different functions in the perception of station users: the cross axis connects the station to the city, the long axis the station to the trains.

Above the platform level a public viewing promenade is provided to allow non-travelling customers to gaze upon the various activities. Just as modern art galleries contain areas where gallery-goers can watch each other, here Wilford has introduced decks merely for the enjoyment of the spectacle of travel.

Bilbao Station promises to be more than a traditional railway station. The diversity of functions introduced within the glazed station concourse and as part of the perimeter enclosure of the station helps break down the station as a social or physical barrier. The aim of the new transportation interchange is to help revitalize the Abando area of Bilbao by bringing visitors and tourists to the district. These in turn will provide a spur for the regeneration of the wider urban area through the establishment of a new commercial zone in the hinterland of the station. Just as airports have led to the development of a range of different types of building at the edge of cities, major railway stations promise to revive the economic fortunes of more central areas.

Waterloo International Station, London

The Channel Tunnel railway terminal at Waterloo is Britain's biggest manifestation to date of the current renaissance

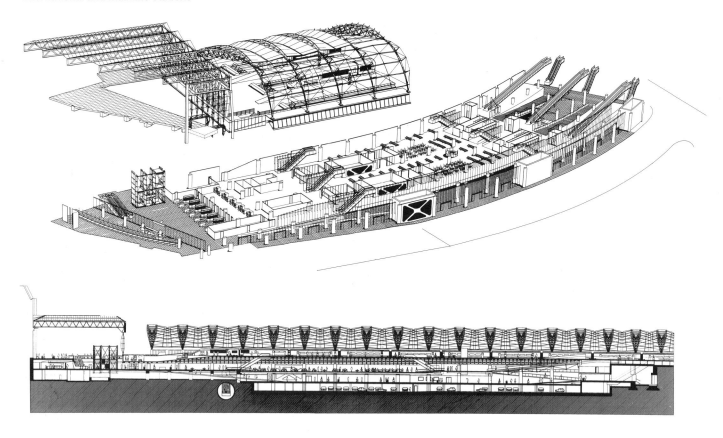

5.7   Perspective and section of Waterloo International Station. Architects: Nicholas Grimshaw and Partners.

in railway architecture. Designed to handle 15 million passengers a year (about the same capacity as Heathrow's Terminal 4), the terminal is only 3 hours away from central Paris by trains, thereby challenging the supremacy of air for medium-distance European transportation.

The Waterloo terminal is a complex transportation interchange designed to handle 3200 passengers at a time. The calculation is based upon four Eurostar trains arriving or departing at about the same time (each has a capacity of nearly 800 passengers). As such, the station facilities have to be able to accommodate this number of passengers without a sense of overcrowding. Such numbers dictate generous dimensions for circulation areas, and encourage a philosophy of quality and robustness in the provision of supporting services (toilets, ticket booths, telephones etc.). Whereas lesser stations are floored in asphalt and lined with ceramic tiles, here at Waterloo International the finishes are carpet, polished granite, glass floors and satin-finished stainless steel. The air of quality and comfort was intended by BR to establish the ambience of modern European rail travel and prepare passengers for Eurostar.

Waterloo International is in the heroic tradition of railway architecture. The station roof is the most conspicuous element, both in the view from the city and in the view from the platform. The roof – a wonderful transparent curved structure – embraces a wide range of station activities beneath. The twist in plan and the use of an asymmetrical

arch (to meet train safety clearances) allow the station to be stitched into the fabric of the city without excessive demolition and still perform its primary role as a civic landmark. The dynamic qualities of the curved canopy stands in marked contrast to the staid architecture of the office buildings in this part of London.

As a building type the station performs many of the functions of an airport. It handles baggage transfer, passport controls and integrated ticketing. In some ways it carries the identity and atmosphere of an airport, yet it is a station right in the heart of the capital. The distinctiveness derives from the client's intention for the international station to be different in character from the domestic railway services on its doorstep and to herald the gateway to European high-speed trains.

The functional objective, according to architects Nicholas Grimshaw and Partners, was to produce a 'streamlined building that would allow the passengers to pass through with the minimum of fuss at maximum speed'.[5] This is achieved by providing generous circulation spaces and by designing the structure of the station canopy to help passengers orientate themselves as they move through the terminal. The grid of the structural columns and the rhythms of the trusses and glazing provide markers for potentially disorientated passengers. To give a sense of direction, and to celebrate the design of the new high-speed trains, the design provides dramatic upward views of the trains for

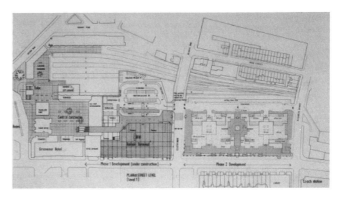

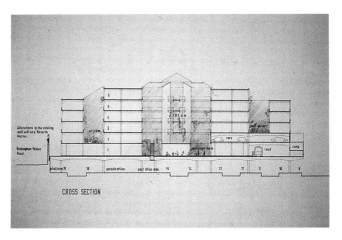

5.8 Office development exploiting the air rights over platforms at Victoria Station, London. View from Buckingham Palace Road. Architects: Arup Associates.

5.9 Plan and section of Victoria Station remodelling.

those waiting in the station concourse. Arrivals are less well handled: whereas departing passengers are taken out to the light of the platforms and rise up to the departure level, those arriving do the reverse. As a consequence, arrival is not a celebration in light and space of concluding a journey, but a movement towards darkness and subterranean passages. This is in many respects a direct consequence of the need to provide immigration control. However, in the use of glass walls and floors the architect has percolated light into much of the lower concourse.

Victoria Station, London

The development of air rights over stations has been a common feature of railway development since the Second World War. Occupying large tracts of city centre land, railways (particularly platform areas) have obvious potential beyond that of merely providing access to trains. At Victoria Station, the developer Greycoat with British Rail Property Board constructed in 1994 new office buildings of 50 000 m^2 above platforms 9 to 19. At street level, facing Buckingham Palace Road, shops, restaurants and a bus station were also provided. The offices consist of two linked blocks focused upon an atrium, the whole sitting behind a

nineteenth-century wall built by the Duke of Westminster to protect his estates from the noise and smoke of the railway.

As in many redevelopments of station land, the exploitation of air rights allowed for the restructuring of public and private facilities. A new bus terminus in the development replaces a number of kerbside bus stops, which formerly faced busy roads, and in the reconstruction of the area by Arup Associates it was integrated with retail spaces and offices. The masterplan connects bus and rail transport to shopping and offices via a system of squares and arcades based upon the pattern elsewhere in London. The existing facade along Buckingham Palace Road provides a screen behind which runs an arcade linked to a series of glazed and open squares. A large central square bounded by shops and cafes provides access to Victoria Station. It is expressed on the outside by a steel glazed roof, which alludes to the traditions of railway architecture.

At a cost of £72 million the development brings benefits to Victoria Station and exploits more effectively under-utilized platform areas. In its integration of activities and pattern of new movements established from station to its hinterland, the development repeats on a smaller scale the precedent (also by Arup Associates) in the Liverpool Street Station and Broadgate area. The main interest of this scheme lies in the new linkages formed between rail and bus transport, and between the station and pedestrian flows. Commercial opportunity has been turned to the advantage of railway passengers, who are able to interchange more effectively and under enhanced environmental conditions with other modes of transport, to use shops and cafes en route, and (for some) to be able to work in new office space above the station itself.

The Channel Tunnel UK terminal, Folkestone, Kent

As a road–rail interchange the Channel Tunnel terminal is an unusual kind of railway station. It handles not passengers arriving on foot but those who come by car, lorry or bus and are transferring with their vehicles onto trains. As such it is not really a terminal building (in spite of its name) but a point of transfer from one transport system to another. Passengers arrive in their vehicles, stop to buy tickets and use various amenities (restaurants, shops, toilets, etc.), and then drive onto double-decker trains for their journey to France via the Channel Tunnel. The railway interchange is not a single building but a collection of structures, each dedicated to an aspect of the transfer. Extending over a site 5 km long, the development, designed by Building Design Partnership, organizes arrival and departure into an orderly sequence of road-to-rail transfer, embracing toll booths, frontier controls and circulation systems that allow vehicles to drive directly onto Eurotunnel's shuttle trains.

The Channel Tunnel terminal is a road–rail interchange duplicated on the other side of the English Channel. As such the concept was to have two terminal buildings, which shared a common philosophy so that passengers had a sense of their functional linkage. Therefore, the visual and functional characteristics of both the English and French terminal buildings (at Sangatte near Calais) share a language of materials (mainly precast concrete, white-painted steelwork, lightweight folded roofs, and textile canopies) and a common vocabulary of primary shapes (cubes, circles, etc.). This unites the stations and, according to the developer Transmanche-Link, gives assurance to passengers, who may be disorientated by the complexity of transfers involved.

Road–rail interchanges of the scale of that at Folkestone are essentially a new type of railway development. They share characteristics with airport terminals, motorway service stations, and traditional railway goods yards. As 25% of the traffic is heavy goods vehicles (nearly 4000 an hour are planned for), the character and scale of the terminal have to balance practical and logistical considerations with the need for the building to be perceived as a national gateway.

The site is organized as a vehicle-based linear progression of ticketing and controls. The planning aim was to provide a swift and efficient transfer system that inspired public confidence by the clarity of layout and sequence of buildings. Engineering, architecture and landscape design are combined within the 140 ha site to provide legible routes, to introduce periodic landmarks, and to define site boundaries. The whole development was conceived by BDP as a 'coherent, low-level and elegant series of structures' set within an informally planted landscape that handled the 'transition from the surrounding native woodlands... to the centre'.[6] Being located in an Area of Outstanding Natural Beauty, the development was subject to an environmental impact assessment, for which the landscape masterplan, CAD modelling and traditional perspectives provided important elements.

The masterplan places a diagonal across the site, which contrasts with the rectangular grids of service roads, bridges, railway tracks and buildings. The main arrival zone is defined by a circular pattern of roads and radiating structures. Near its centre the main terminus building (known as the Amenity Building) is located. The analogy with the railway station is obvious: the Amenity Building reflects the ticketing, toilets and shopping elements of the railway concourse, the car parks represent the platform, and the lightweight canopies of custom points the shelters on traditional railway platforms. Where the railway station embraces all these elements into a single structure, here they are disconnected and expanded as pavilions within a huge car and lorry park bisected by four lanes of railway track.

The Amenity Building is the closest parallel to a railway concourse on the site. It consists of a three-storey cube with an asymmetrical fabric roof over a central, double-height atrium space. The translucent tensile roof, shaped like a mound, makes direct reference to the rounded humps of the North Downs, and the fabric of the roof to the sailing boats on the English Channel not far away. Functionally, the roof brings diffused light into the centre of the terminus without glare. The building is white inside and out, providing a contrast in its lightness and spaciousness to the journey beneath the sea. At night a laser beam projecting through the glazed aperture in the canopy helps to orientate travellers and marks the presence of this, the most important structure on the site.

References

1. Martin Mead, 'EuroLille: the instant city', *Architectural Review*, December 1994, p. 86.
2. Ian Latham, 'The surreal city: Rem Koolhaas at EuroLille', *Architecture Today*, Vol. 55, p. 19.
3. *Ibid.*, p. 22.
4. Paul Finch, 'Bilbao's interchange of heart', *Architects' Journal*, 11 May 1995, p.28.
5. Undated press release from Nicholas Grimshaw and Partners, circa 1994.
6. *The Channel Tunnel UK Terminal*, Building Design Partnership, London, 1994, pp. 10 and 13.

Airport stations

Roissy Station at Charles de Gaulle Airport, Paris

Railway stations are points of transition that facilitate the movement of people across scales of travel. They consist of well-defined sequences of activity, each a distinct psychological experience with ideally a recognizable architectural response. Stations, like airports, are places where perceptions are focused by functional complexity, and where the role of design is to guide, to give reassurance, and to celebrate.

The larger the station the more crucial is the duty of the designer to meet both functional and psychological needs. Big modern stations are complicated, many-layered structures, which seek to connect various types of travel with the tissue of urban life. In this, the grand gesture tc which people can relate provides some of the reassurance and spiritual uplift needed to counteract the tedium of visual and aural

6.1 Public concourse at Roissy Station, Charles de Gaulle Airport. Architect: Paul Andreu.

6.2 View of Roissy Station at Charles de Gaulle Airport: platform level.

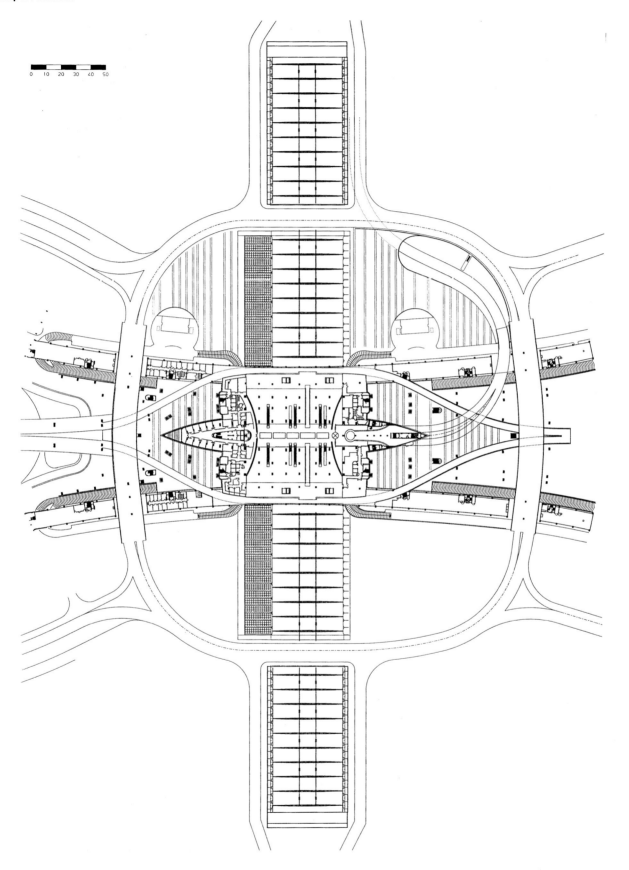

6.3 Plan of Roissy Station. The line of the railway tracks is from top to bottom, with the concourse and hotel in the centre of the interchange.

bombardment. French stations, in particular, have taken the theme of bold architectural statements the furthest, justifying great feats of engineering by the size of many recent stations, particularly those serving new TGV lines. Where these have been to airports, such as Lyon-Satolas Station and Roissy airport rail terminal in Paris, the linking of rail and airport facilities has provided further justification for grand architectural gestures.

A good example of connecting modern rail services to existing airports is at Charles de Gaulle Airport in Paris, where the Roissy Station, designed by Paul Andreu at Aéroports de Paris, takes the TGV and regional railway network to an international airport previously linked to neither. The new station is an enormous, rationally planned interconnection of rail, air, bus, car and pedestrian movement systems with, besides complex ticketing facilities, a large hotel. It consists of five principal levels arranged with a central terminus placed at right angles to the TGV and RER (Réseau Express Régionale) lines, which are constructed below ground. The whole complex is encircled by a high-level perimeter road system arranged as a square with rounded corners. The boldness of the plan and the powerful geometries are typical of recent French architecture and in the tradition of the *grands projets*.

By placing the terminal at right angles to the railway track Andreu has given the relationship between station facilities, platform and train remarkable clarity for a complex of this size. The station acts as a huge bridge, spanning the tracks below on enormous concrete columns. At station level a light glazed canopy held high on angled steel columns, which spread like fingers through the public spaces, creates an airy concourse. The roof itself, which tilts upwards towards the centre, is almost entirely glazed within square-gridded frames.

Natural light is used as a functional and perceptual device. Large areas of roof glazing allow daylight to filter down through the various levels of the concourse. Light and structure together order the spaces and internal decks into a legible sequence of functional parts, each with a clear sense of hierarchy. Even at platform level, constructed for noise and safety reasons below ground, natural light from large areas of roof glazing and strips of clerestory windows gives passengers an immediate sense of direction. The

hotel, which crosses the centre of the station at high level, is a ship-like solid object, which viewed through the glass also aids orientation.

The structure transmits loads to the ground and transmits meaning to the users of the station. There is a layering of the structural language using heavy concrete, lightweight steel to glass canopy from the lowest to highest level, which gestures towards the different internal altitudes. The curved roof and angled columns indicate in their positions the direction of movement. Although the structure is one that gesticulates at almost every point, these are not empty gestures but ones that guide passengers through the terminal.

Bold geometry and expressive structure allow passengers to become 'involved with the materiality of the building as they are drawn up through it by the escalators'.[1] Engagement with the architecture of large stations is one way to relieve the tedium of modern travel. Noticing the structural arrangements and their details allows travellers to get a sense of direction and to appreciate the nature of the space. As light, structural engineering and levels are closely integrated at Roissy, the escalators are the main means by which experiences are gained. They do not criss-cross the internal volumes in a casual fashion but thread their way past columns and through decks with great consideration. Other activities essential to the functioning of the station are subservient to the routes and connections. Hence, if the station's activities were to change, the logic of structure, light and procession would survive to give clarity to new arrangements.

The station is heated only casually. The roofs do not meet, but provide shelter and act like funnels to allow excess heat on sunny days to escape. The split section also provides large smoke vents in the event of fire, thereby eliminating the need for fire compartmentation and mechanical venting. Roissy is a large dramatic glazed tent punctuated by the hotel and bisected by the encircling road. Fritting of the glazing controls solar gain and gives the glass a texture that enhances its 'ethereal insubstantiality'.[2] This allows the glass canopy to glow at night when lit artificially, thereby adding to the station's quality as a public landmark.

do in construction, gives the station functional clarity and considerable psychological reassurance. Roissy exploits design to enhance the travel experience and provide an atmosphere that rivals in glamour the nearby airport.

Lyon-Satolas Station

Santiago Calatrava has done much in our generation to elevate the station to a new level of architectural design, just as Pier Luigi Nervi did after the war in projects such as the Naples Terminus. In a number of examples for different types of station in Europe, Calatrava has developed the language of railway architecture in new expressive directions. Whether in the design of underground stations (such as those based upon a modular kit for London Underground in 1991) or major town stations (such as Stadelhofen Station, Zurich, 1983–90), Calatrava has successfully exploited new forms of plastic structural expression. Being qualified as both architect and engineer he is well equipped to explore the fertile territory between structure and space. His more recent station projects – Basarrale, Bilbao (1987), Alameda, Valencia (1991), Spandau, Berlin (1991) and particularly the airport station at Lyon-Satolas (1994) – add a new spectacular orientation to the design of transportation buildings.

Satolas Station is used by passengers transferring to international flights from the high-speed (TGV) Paris to Marseilles line. The design exploits the dynamic qualities of curved concrete frames, drawing its inspiration from organic forms. The station has the structural clarity of a skeleton, with ribs and vertebrae providing a primary language for bridges, canopies, enclosures and circulation routes. In the open landscape of the airport the ticket concourse beneath a huge double wing-like vault acts as a landmark signalling the presence of the station.

In plan the station is relatively simple: six railway tracks are enclosed by a 500 m long barrel-vaulted roof of criss-cross lattice construction. This is bisected at right angles by an enormous expressive roof, which sails above the booking and ticket area. The two roofs – platform vault and concourse vault – slide into each other, thereby allowing the presence of each to be read within the station. Being tri-

6.4 Four views of Lyon-Satolas Station at Lyon Airport. The platform canopy (opposite, top), concourse roof (opposite, centre) and interior (opposite, bottom), and platform area (above) provide travellers with a clearly differentiated set of station spaces and structural landmarks. Architect: Santiago Calatrava.

Roissy is an assured essay in modern railway architecture, where engineering and building design are fully integrated as structure and experience. The use of clear geometries in plan, boldly cut-away sections, and brava-

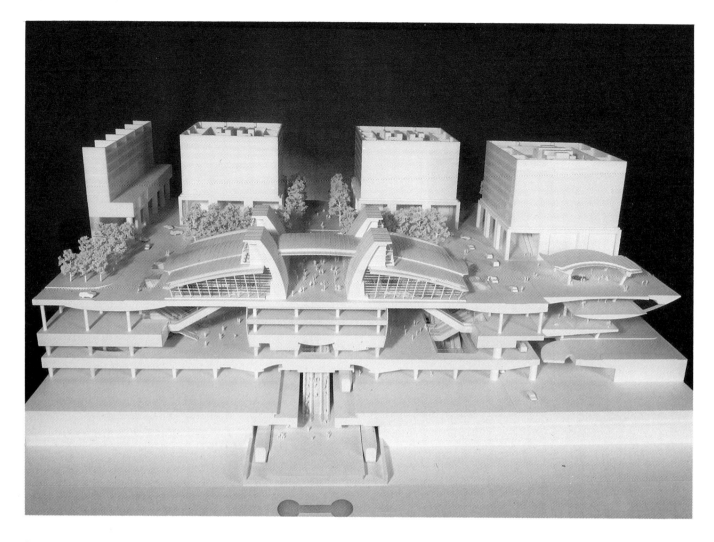

6.5 Kowloon Station, Hong Kong. Architects: Terry Farrell and Partners.

angular in plan the ticket area gestures towards the runway, opening up views of taxiing aircraft. Conceptually it alludes to Eero Saarinen's TWA Terminal at Kennedy Airport, though while the zoomorphic shapes by Saarinen were formed entirely of concrete, Calatrava's sculptural forms are a mixture of concrete, steel and aluminium.

The station is organized on three main levels, with the railway tracks below ground. The station hall takes passengers arriving from the airport via a high-level bridge down on escalators to the two parallel platforms. Each platform serves two tracks, with two further tracks at the centre of the station serving non-stopping trains. The platforms extend symmetrically outwards and are roofed by a diagonally ribbed vault with expressed precast concrete frames and areas of roof glazing. The relatively low ceiling height of the platform vault contrasts with the lofty spread-eagle of the central hall vault. As in all of Calatrava's stations the rhythm of structure, patterns of light, and the geometry of space guide passengers to the various elements. Although his is a gesturing architecture, the different forms employed help in providing legibility to a modern complex

station. An example is the platform roof structure, which becomes more transparent towards the centre where the station hall is provided, thereby using daylight to guide arriving passengers in the right direction.

As Satolas is largely a subterranean station (for safety reasons), much of the experience is one of structure with deflected or shafted light. The triangulated and inclined columns serve to animate space and provide scale. Light is filtered down to the lowest levels via angled walls and borrowed light. Light enters via projecting rooflights, window walls set at an angle, and via clerestoreys. The primary order is a dynamic (and sometimes overblown) relationship between structure, construction, space and light.

In his proposals of 1995 for a station to serve the Lisbon Expo (known as Lisbon Orient) Calatrava takes these elements a stage further by combining them with bisecting avenues, which help to stitch the station into the fabric of the city. The upper avenue is formed by a tree-like grid of columns, which in metallic form alludes to a park, while the lower avenue links the station to bus and metro services and to the streets of Lisbon.

Kowloon Airport Station, Hong Kong

The proposed airport railway station at Kowloon, Hong Kong, seeks to integrate within a single megastructure a railway station, bus station and car parking. Designed by Terry Farrell and Partners, the project also includes the development of air rights over the station to include four hotels, apartments, offices and retail space. The design, planned for construction in 1997, is of value as an illustration of the increasing diversification of land uses at modern stations. Not only is the station itself an array of different functions, but the adjoining land has grown into a mini-city of disparate uses drawn by the magnet of the station.

Kowloon Airport station promises to be a dramatic structure. It is conceived as a huge gateway with doors partly open, gesturing to the sky. A pair of large flat arches on either side of an open central concourse contain the ticketing and transport interchange areas of the station. Below ground, check-in and baggage-handling facilities are provided to the airport, and below that two levels of platforms. In section the arrangement is superficially similar to Roissy, but the use of structure and concourse planning is quite different. Railway and airport links are given equal weight in the planning of the building. Pedestrian movements and urban spaces placed on the upper deck organize the circulation below ground, providing a backcloth of civic values for what is a huge public transport complex.

The emphasis upon the airport station as a small city in its own right is reinforced also by the placing of eight tower blocks, which help to define the central civic space. The effect of the high buildings (containing hotels, offices, apartments, etc.) is to form the limits of a large square, into which the station sits. The sweeping arched structure of the central complex, with its angled glazed walls, landmarks the interchange as forcefully as those by Calatrava.

Light is taken down to the lowest levels of the station by clever manipulation of the building section. The complex programme of functions is contained not within a single rectangular building (as at Stansted) but in an open framework of elements beneath the curved roof. Light is taken into the catacombs of the platforms via diagonal paths of deflected daylight. The arrangement benefits from the use of a central spine of station offices, whose curved glazed walls act as light deflectors.

Kowloon Airport Station promises to be one of the most ambitious stations of the latter decades of the twentieth century. It embodies greater functional complexity than almost any other station, and it does so with an unusual level of density of site occupation. Farrell's office has accepted the argument that modern rail–airport interchanges are cities in their own right and deserve to be made into places rather than buildings.

References

1. Peter Davey, 'French connection', *Architectural Review,* February 1995, p. 35.
2. *Ibid.*

Town stations

Stadelhofen Station, Zurich

Like other stations by Santiago Calatrava, Stadelhofen Station in Zurich combines structural invention with a concern for urban connectiveness. Stations are part of the divisive engineering of urban railways; yet they are also bridges between separated neighbourhoods. It is this latter quality that Calatrava exploits in his skilful manipulation of levels and crossovers. In the process the architect has given the station a distinct sense of place, which distinguishes it from being merely a means of accessing trains.

The site of the station alongside the fortifications of the old city holds the clue for Calatrava's response. The station, located at the bottom of a park-like hillside, forms the boundary between ancient and modern Zurich. The railway tracks are part of this sense of edge, and the station the means by which the edge can be enjoyed, traversed and expressed. The station, following the curve of the hillside, is on three levels, and adopts a common section for its 270 m length.[1] This places a public walkway and viewing deck related to the park and city prospect on the upper level, platforms and booking hall on the middle level, and a parade of shops and a linking tunnel on the lowest level. The angled section, with inclined walls and expressive structure, allows light to enter the centre of the station and passengers to enjoy the views of the old town.

A distinction is made between heavy concrete construction (necessary for the support of trains and track) and lightweight steel and glass canopies (which shelter station users). The dialogue between the two main structural components alludes indirectly to the condition on the hillside, where solid rock contrasts with the delicate foliage of trees and plants. Calatrava takes the vegetation of the park across part of the station roof by way of a pergola connected by wires, along which vines and creepers are encouraged to grow.

As in Calatrava's other stations, structure articulates interior space, providing a dynamic rhythm that relieves the fatigue of travel. The curved rib-like frames and heavy leg-like columns help to establish key routes in the functional organization of the station. Structure and construction are guides to movement rather than empty gestures. At Stadelhofen this is particularly necessary because the curve

7.1 Stadelhofen Station, Zurich. Architect: Santiago Calatrava.

7.2   Woolwich Arsenal Station, London. Architects: Nick Derbyshire Design Associates Ltd. with the Architecture and Design Group of British Rail.

of the station in plan does not readily allow passengers to see along the length of platforms and hence find their way to exits. The pedestrian bridges, which cross at high level the chasm of the station, add to the drama of the station without compromising what Dennis Sharp calls its sense of a 'homogeneous urban whole'.[2]

Like many nineteenth-century stations (such as York) the curve of the railway platforms adds greatly to the experience of structure and light. The radial geometry of the tracks at Zurich and the stepped section adopted by Calatrava combine to produce an exciting station. Although Stadelhofen Station is a contribution to the transport infrastructure of Zurich, it is also an extension to the city park and a place to promenade above the rooftops of the old town. The combination of these elements provides a station that offers civic benefits as well as transport ones.

Woolwich Arsenal Station

Woolwich Station represents a different approach to the layout for the station entrance than is generally found. The

entrance, ticket hall and concourse are united in a largely circular glazed structure, which sits tower-like above the Victorian railway tracks. Where other suburban stations define the main functional zones as separate elements, here they are unified into a dramatic rotunda of stone, steel and glass.

The shape of the station celebrates arrival and departure. Because Woolwich is a remodelling of an existing station, the Architecture and Design Group of British Rail (acting as project architects) chose to concentrate the accommodation into a single beacon-like structure. Limited ground on which to build, because of the railway cutting nearby, led to the exploitation of height, rather than width, in the development of an appropriate form. The tall circular tower that houses the entrance and ticket concourse behind within a ring of stone columns establishes an immediate presence for the station. The transparent circular form addresses both the public realm of Woolwich and the internal world of buying tickets and planning journeys.

From the street the rotunda, projecting marginally into the pavement space at an important road junction, acts as a landmark, effectively signalling the presence of the station from near and far. During the day, the play of shadows from the thin circular canopy and plump columns contrasts pleasantly with the rectangular architecture of the town. At night the rotunda acts as a well-lit beacon, not only beckoning to passengers but, in its illuminated openness, giving them a reassuring sense of safety.

Though the columns are fairly thick there is nowhere to hide in this station of almost total visual permeability. The station entrance evokes that of a theatre, with its sheltering canopy, regular grid of Portland stone columns, granite steps and skilful lighting. Where canopies are used they spread outwards as far as structure and street sightlines allow, providing a delicate balance to the heavier columns. Being on two levels, the rotunda exploits direct and deflected light, which filters down from above to illuminate the train information area.

The detailing alludes to image making. There is the sense of timeless quality in the limestone and granite finishes, but this is attractively counterbalanced by stainless steel and cast aluminium fittings. Metaphorically, the stone materials refer to the architecture of the town and the steel ones to that of the trains. As the station mediates between the two worlds, the contrast in materials carries an air of legitimacy.

Woolwich Arsenal Station breaks with convention, at least in the UK. It celebrates the entrance to the station rather than the platform areas. It compresses the entrance and concourse areas into a tall drum, which casts a luminous veil around travellers. Although glimpses can be obtained of the older platform areas from the booking hall, the station engages, architecturally at least, rather more with the town than with the railway lines. In a town of limited urban assets, the new station does much to raise the image of Network SouthEast (the local railway company). As such it performs an important function in the marketing of a railway company that suffers more than most from poor-quality stations and rolling stock.

Station architecture in the Netherlands

The Dutch are embarked upon an ambitious programme of rail investment, both upgrading existing lines for high-speed services and constructing of new lines and stations to serve new towns formed on reclaimed polders. Dutch stations display a consistency of approach unusual for such a large railway system and increasingly under threat elsewhere as railways are privatized. Under the patronage and design control of the former state railway company's own design team – Holland Railconsult – the new stations have a consistent philosophy and vocabulary of design. This is based primarily upon traveller comfort and safety, expressed in large voluminous public concourse areas at stations, wide elegant escalators and staircases, and generous highly glazed waiting areas at platforms. Shelter from the elements at often elevated stations is a prime concern and has led to conservatory-like platform canopies, which trains enter in almost triumphal fashion via grand portals and archways. As safety and security are parallel concerns, the new stations are highly transparent, with glazed rather than solid walls enclosing different functional areas. Not only do transparency and visibility reduce fear of crime, the lack of solid walls and panels provides little opportunity for those intent upon spraying graffiti. Whereas the tunnels and solid embankments of Amsterdam and Rotterdam Stations are lined with painted slogans, the mainly glazed stations are free of graffiti.

An architecture of glass, steel and lightweight curved panels expressed in bold geometric shapes in plan and section epitomizes Holland Railconsult's approach to design. Colour is used sparingly but with intent. Blue, yellow and red, employed as painted finish or coloured ceramic tile panels, provide legibility for the traveller by highlighting key routes through the station. Against a background of white structure, the introduction of colour provides guidance and sparkle. As Dutch stations are normally elevated, they provide natural landmarks in the open flat landscapes of much of the Netherlands. Holland Railconsult, especially in the stations designed by Harry Reijnders and Peter Kilsdonk, exploit the possibilities of bold superimposed geometry to identify their stations. At Amsterdam Duivendrecht, Kilsdonk places giant red equilateral triangles against smoothly framed rectangles of glazing and interpenetrating cylinders of glass with the assurance of a sculptor. The debt to Dutch modernism, particularly the work of J.J.P. Oud, is self-evident.

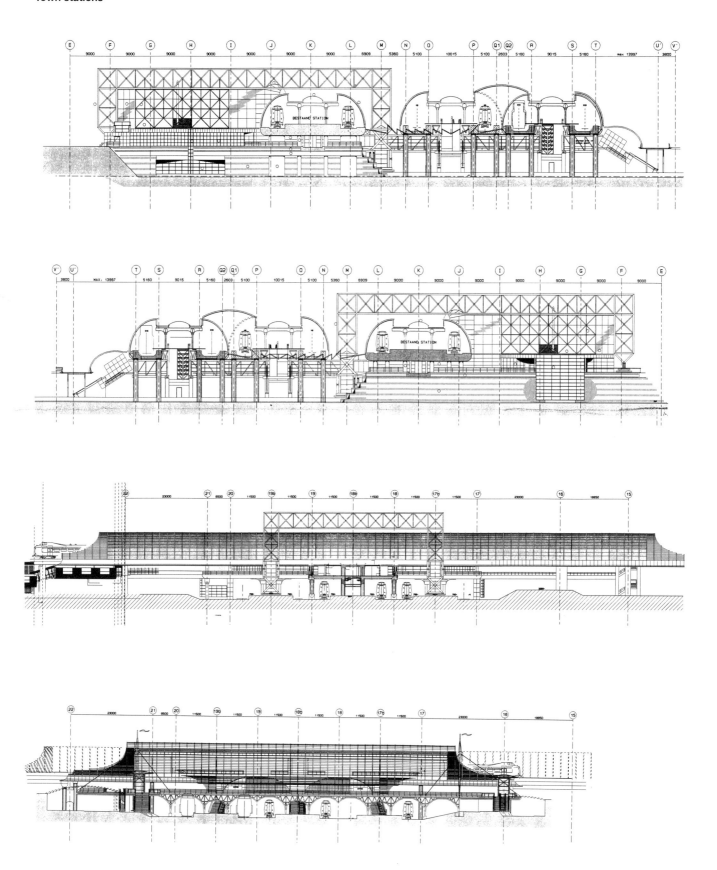

7.3   Sloterdijk Station, Amsterdam: plans. Architect: Harry Reijnders of Holland Railconsult.

At suburban or rural stations such as Amsterdam Leylaan by Rob Steenhuis (Holland Railconsult), a language of elegant simplicity approaching structural minimalism is commonplace. Small country stations are little more than an island platform, glazed shelter and ticket point. The shelter, usually with integral seating, lighting and announcement system, forms the main focus of the station. Framed in steel with jointless glazing and seamless eaves, the shelters carry design thoughtfulness into every detail. Some have areas for prams, others for wheelchairs, while most provide a small electronic panel keeping passengers informed of approaching trains. Platforms are often surfaced in brick with a non-slip concrete strip at the platform edge. The back of platforms is frequently edged with a clipped beech hedge, and where high-speed trains pass, sound baffles in concrete but covered in continuously planted variegated ivy ensure that neighbourhood noise is controlled. Ivy grown on a wire framework is an evidently successful deterrent to graffiti, which dogs concrete sound baffles in urban areas.

Small Dutch stations rarely have a bridge or tunnel to cross the tracks. Normally passengers cross via a controlled barrier system or lights. This not only keeps the costs down but allows the rural station to take on the elegant simplicity of urban tram stops. As most rural stations are unmanned, many have CCTV security systems and are brightly lit to reassure passengers.

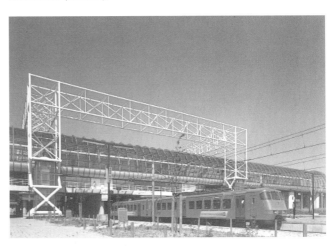

Amsterdam Sloterdijk Station

Sloterdijk Station, designed by Harry Reijnders of Holland Railconsult, is a complex transport interchange contained within an enormous white tubular steel and glazed rectangle. The rectangle is in fact a structural portal, which supports walls and roofs of glass or lightweight panel construction. Within this open, somewhat gesturing framework, sits a large spacious station concourse, which serves all three levels of transportation – high-speed trains to Schiphol Airport on an elevated railway on the top deck, trams and buses on the middle level, and intercity trains at a sub-basement level. As the suburban and mainline tracks cross

at right angles, the white cube of the central concourse is boldly penetrated by the curved diaphanous platform canopy serving the trains to Schiphol Airport. As elsewhere with recent Dutch stations the structural and civil engineering of the station is used to express different speeds and levels of movement, with the architecture of enclosure and space playing a full part.

The station entrance is at mid-floor level. Travellers buy their ticket, or check on the departure of trains, at this central level and either move up or down to their train. The concourse is a cube of space, with escalators, lifts and stairs designed as independent structures fixed by the

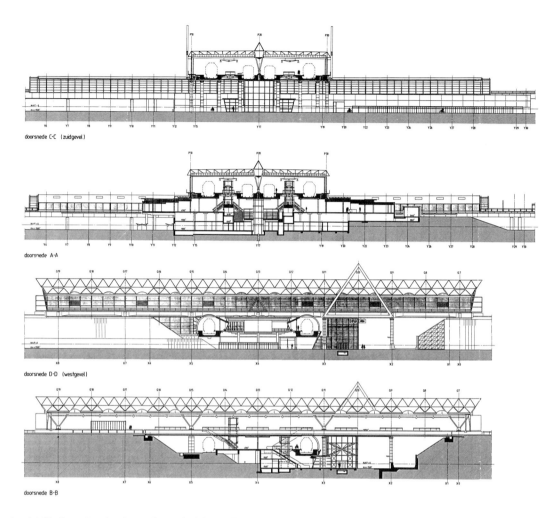

doorsnede C-C (zuidgevel)

doorsnede A-A

doorsnede D-D (westgevel)

doorsnede B-B

7.5   Duivendrecht Station, Amsterdam: plans. Architect: Peter Kilsdonk of Holland Railconsult.

spacing of interior columns. As the station is mainly glazed and open, passengers can see their platform from the main concourse, and hence know in which direction to travel. The design handles transition in scale particularly well: the main steel portal addresses the dimensions of the city, the platform canopies with their carapace-like glazed shell are more in scale with the trains, and the finely detailed stairs and escalators in scale with the travelling public. These three scales of architectural expression are separately articulated, often using their own palette of materials and order of details. The concourse mediates between the three, with all the major elements of the station visible at once.

The gently curving high-level platforms are particularly successful. Just as at Waterloo International, the slight change of angle allows the play of rounded lines of the glazing assembly to enhance the effect. The subtle curve of the sheltering diaphragm of clear glazing, set against the rigid straight lines of the giant tubular framework of the portal, is especially attractive. When the train is at the platform its own curved lines add to the experience of an appropriately engineered station environment. It is design born

of function, for the continuous glazed canopies are needed for shelter and comfort.

The ends of the curved platform canopy are not stopped abruptly but fragment gently with elements of their structure extending beyond the line of glazing. This witty reference to movement explains also how the various constructional elements are put together. Added to this, the platform canopies are mainly coloured blue, the entrance doors red and all other constructional parts are finished in white or pastel yellow. Colour is not abandoned to the natural finish of materials but brightly applied to guide people through the station and hint at the structural or hierarchical logic employed.

Amsterdam Duivendrecht Station

This new station, built at the intersection of the Amsterdam–Utrecht line and the new high-speed link to Schiphol Airport, is another remarkable design by Holland Railconsult. Designed by Peter Kilsdonk, it consists of a high-

7.6 Duivendrecht Station, Amsterdam: platforms (above) and exterior views (right). Architect: Peter Kilsdonk of Holland Railconsult.

level system of platforms enclosed within a great white rectangular container of steel and glass. This is penetrated at lower level by two blue glazed cylinders containing the platforms and lines for the Schiphol express. At ground level the station rises above a series of drainage dikes, lagoons and parking areas for cars, taxis and buses.

Duivendrecht Station is a transport intersection on three levels, with a grand first-floor concourse of ticket hall, shops, restaurants and information services measuring 150 m by 45 m. The concourse is open, drenched in natural light and largely free of columns. There is a feeling of transparency, both outwards to the surrounding Dutch countryside and inwards and upwards to the trains at their different levels.

The station is an engineering as well as architectural feat. The upper level of platforms extend for 115 m on giant precast concrete supports. The platform roof consists of alternate bands of glass and curved steel, not unlike the construction details of the double-decker trains that pass through the station. The low-level platform canopies have the characteristic egg-shaped glazed section found at other recent Dutch stations. Clear glazed to the outside, the platforms afford views out even when wind and driving rain would normally drive passengers into enclosed shelters.

Duivendrecht Station has the ambience of a nineteenth-century palm house. The architectural language of slender steel and concrete columns mixed with almost jointless glazing and delicately folded roof canopies recalls a modern conservatory. The need to create shelter at this busy high-level station and to give passengers a sense of personal safety (particularly important at a station serving an airport, where trains are often at unsociable hours) has combined to produce a transparent cathedral of a station. Although the station is mainly white, colour has been employed to highlight the major routes through the different levels, and via an enormous red equilateral triangle, to identify the station entrance. In his use of the triangle set against a cylindrical entrance tower that leads to the rectangular concourse, Kilsdonk knowingly manipulates the formal sequences to ensure that travellers have a keen sense of direction. The architect has stated that a station does not have to be a 'poorly organized labyrinth or a catacomb';[3] at Duivendrecht structure, light and geometric order provide a complex station with notable clarity of space and directional legibility.

Rotterdam Blaak

Transparency and daringly wide spans are features of modern railway architecture. At Rotterdam Blaak these

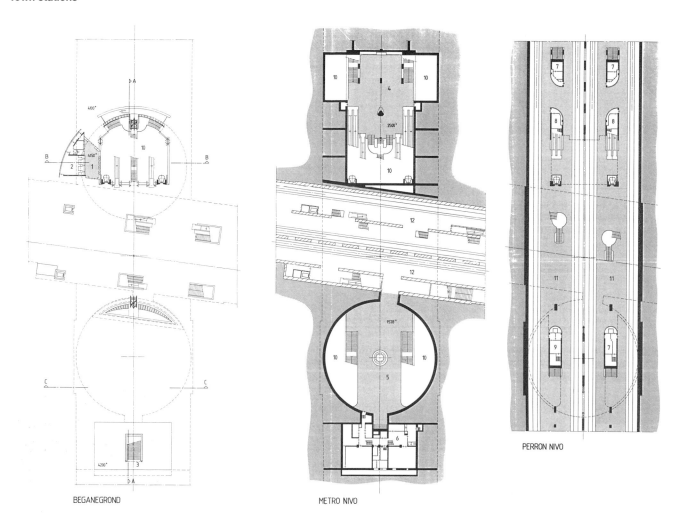

BEGANEGROND   METRO NIVO   PERRON NIVO

7.7   Rotterdam Blaak Station. Architect: Harry Reijnders of Holland Railconsult.

erate contrast with the cubic architecture of this part of Rotterdam. As it is undeniably a public building, Reijnders was keen that the station should also be immediately recognizable as a transport building.

Conceptually the station consists of two circles (metaphors for the wheels of trains) linked by a giant arch, which gestures towards the sky. The first circle is an inclined disc of a roof, which gives access to the mainline trains. The second circle forms an underground station hall, which leads directly to the metro trains. Between the two run at street level a pair of tram lines, whose stops are protected by a wavy lightweight steel roof. Two partly connected concourses exist below ground, one circular and the other square. Each concourse is crossed by banks of escalators and stairs, which are designed as free-standing elements within great underground caverns, and are interconnected via the lower platforms underneath the metro.

The great angled disc suspended from the main arch that marks the mainline station provides a welcoming entrance, sheltered by the overhanging edge of the roof at its upper

elements, true to all great stations, have the addition of tilted discs of roofs and great suspended steel arches, which sweep boldly above concourse areas like an enormous halo. The station is a celebration of movement expressed with the latest engineering techniques combined with an artist's eye for space and proportion. Designed by Harry Reijnders (of Holland Railconsult) the station, with its play of circles, inclined discs and steel arches, is a delib-

7.8   Rotterdam Blaak Station entrance: (above, left) and canopy detail (above, right)

point. Its role is both as landmark for the station within this fragmented corner of Rotterdam and as a means of identifying the main station entrance. At night the glowing of the disc adds to the welcoming and reassuring air, and helps to establish the whereabouts of the mainline station entrance, as against the metro and tram stop.

The platforms are at low level, necessitating a descent from street to train. Because the station is an interchange between rail and metro lines that cross at right angles, Reijnders had the task of forming island platforms for the mainline trains which connected directly to the metro platforms via a huge cylindrical concourse. This concourse, directly below the first of the angled discs, joins the world of streets above ground to that of the platforms below. As it is a circular space, the crossing of the rotunda by stairs and escalators adds to the feeling of spatial penetration.

The use of simple, pure geometric shapes gives Rotterdam Blaak Station a character unlike many new stations in the UK and France. The interpenetration of cube and circle, line and rectangle establishes in plan and section a station of memorable shapes. As the spaces are mainly enclosed by transparent walls there is little physical or visual enclosure – all is open, accessible and safe to use. Noise, a problem in mainly open-plan stations, is reduced by using sound-absorbing plaster and reflecting tiles, which form 'a regular pattern disrupting the sound waves'.[4] Platform

noise is dealt with by placing the railway tracks on rubber mats and by building sound-absorbing chambers beneath the platform lip. Air pressure problems with fast trains entering narrow platform areas are rectified by piercing the station and tunnel walls with large circular openings, and by allowing pressure to be relieved via the open circular concourse areas.

Leiden Station

Leiden Station is undergoing great transformation to cater better for the 40 000 people who use the station daily. Typically of Dutch stations it is at high level, with a passageway underground that provides routes upwards to the platforms. This passageway is (in 1995) being transformed into a great public concourse, with the three island platforms above now placed beneath a giant glazed new roof. Twelve railway tracks pass through Leiden Station, which is the Netherlands' fifth busiest.[5] The new roof, placed on enormous portals spanning along rather than across the tracks, will allow natural light to filter down to the public concourse beneath the platforms. The platforms will in fact become islands punctured by large square holes, which permit the light of the sky to drift down to the subterranean concourse. The angle of the roof, taken along the line of the tracks, allows shafts of sunlight to penetrate downwards via

7.9 Leiden Station, the Netherlands: lift to the mezzanine (left), view from the square (top, right) and canopy over concourse (bottom, right). Architect: Harry Reijnders of Holland Railconsult.

these openings. A central spine of roof glazing sitting directly above the concourse emphasizes the axis of the main public route, and at its outward expression as a triangular truss on the facade of the station helps to identify the main entrance.

As with all large stations the problem is one of both engineering and urban design. The new station roof effectively

landmarks the station and gestures towards the key routes contained within it. The enlarged and mainly naturally lit new concourse is both access to the trains and a means of crossing the barrier of 12 railway lines in the centre of the town. Hence it is a public route lined by shops and cafes, which everybody in Leiden is able to use. The outer edges of the station have also been transformed, with a new square created where a dual carriageway of cars once formed an unfriendly approach to the station. The square is being slightly raised in order to create a vast bicycle store (able to house 3500) beneath a steel glazed roof, which will glow at night. The old road along the front of the station is being relocated below ground, releasing land for a variety of civic uses at the perimeter of the station. Offices, apartments, shops and cafes are being built on the new approaches to the reconstructed station, thereby ensuring that the station is less isolated physically and less alienating socially.

Leiden Station combines civic, commercial and railway company interests in an ambitious programme of urban reconstruction. The integration of rail and bus services at the town square, and the creation of a largely traffic-free station entrance, will make the new station more attractive for passengers. In the reconstruction, the station canopy with its great column-free space, transparency and sweeping roof decks will form an obvious symbol rising above the rectangular frames of the new station entrance.

References

1. Dennis Sharp (Ed), *Santiago Calatrava*, E & FN Spon, London, 1994, p. 33.
2. *Ibid.*
3. Marcus Binney, *Architecture of Rail: The Way Ahead*, Academy Editions, London, 1995, p. 67.
4. *Ibid.*, p. 75.
5. *Ibid.*, p. 72.

Underground stations

Bilbao Underground

Opened in 1995, Bilbao Underground was designed by Sir Norman Foster and Partners. It consists of 18 bored underground stations, four cut-and-cover stations and 14 grade stations. The 36 new stations and 60 km of underground and surface track represent one of Europe's most ambitious underground railway developments in recent times. The 16 m wide and 11 m high underground station tunnels, based upon the New Austrian Tunnelling Method (NATM), follow a flattened egg profile. The engineering and shape of the tunnels is one of the main components of the project, and provides the visual and spatial language at the stations. The large station caverns, which house platforms at either side crossed by elegant lightweight bridges, are contained within tunnels of precast concrete used as a permanent shuttering to the poured concrete tunnel.

Entry to the station caverns is via escalators, which take travellers from shell-like canopies at the ground to the underground station concourses and from there to the platforms. Three flights of parallel escalators are usually employed, the curved canopy of the top flight extending outwards to form the shell-shaped entrance. At the bottom of the flights a ticket concourse (with direct access to the ground via a lift) is provided at the level of the platform bridges. Hence, three main experiential elements occur: the escalator journey, the ticket-level concourse (placed at mezzanine level within the cavern of the station), and the platform decks beneath. Each part of the journey from ground to train is contained within a stainless steel envelope, where the joints of the panels provide scale and rhythm.

The interior surfaces, so important in the design of underground stations, play textures and engineered finishes off against subtle plays of light. The main tunnel finish of precision precast concrete with expressed joints contrasts with the lightweight cast aluminium, stainless steel and glass of the mezzanine structures and access decks. The prefabricated components, which exploit precision factory production, guide passengers to the key parts for access (ticket areas and escalators), while the solid, impervious finishes lead to the platforms. The dialogue between

8.1 Waiting room, Hammersmith Station, London Underground. Architects: EPR with Minale, Tattersfield and Partners Ltd.

8.2 Bilbao Underground; photograph of model. Foster's office was responsible for the whole underground system from concept design to signs and station furniture. Architects: Sir Norman Foster and Partners.

8.3 Genoa Underground: ticket barrier at Dinegro Station. Architects: Renzo Piano Building Workshop.

alludes to the functional divisions of the station.

Natural light filters into the underground system via the projecting shell of the canopy. At night the same surfaces glow with artificial light from beneath the ground. Similarly, light illuminates the inner curved surfaces of the tunnel at station level, allowing the lightweight structures (mezzanine decks, footbridges) to read as separate suspended elements. The approach to materials, especially their sense of weightiness or lightness, added to the attention to lighting, results in a world of underground architecture that is pleasant to use and has functional legibility. The use of contrasts in scale, especially between the tunnel, which is nearly twice the size of comparable undergrounds (as at Genoa) and the promontory-like mezzanine through the centre of the station, adds to the clarity of the interior experience.

Genoa Underground

When in 1983 Renzo Piano was appointed with the Institute of European Design (IED) in Milan to design Genoa's new underground railway he proposed a kit of parts based upon a 'clear discipline of a family of components'.[1] The catalogue of parts added up to a language that embraced the approach to station planning and circulation, structural systems, lighting, direction signs and furniture. As a consequence the 11 stations, which cater for up to 25 000 passenger movements an hour in each direction, share a family likeness whether they are underground or above ground. The use of a standard spatial syntax and recurring components follows in the tradition of the Paris Metro, where around 1900 Hector Guimard employed a common language of decorative and structural elements. The advantages of kits from the point

of view of the railway company are that it gives a corporate look to different stations, it makes replacement easier, and it keeps costs down. From the point of view of the traveller the use of an identifiable language helps to build a sense of identity and brand loyalty, and once the system has been understood and recognized, a passenger at one station can quickly identify the same service or sign at another.

Architects and engineers who develop a language of materials, structural systems and components for a railway system have great influence upon the design of stations, and other structures (such as bridges and tunnels). Where the language also embraces aspects of the design of rolling stock, the influence extends from station concourse to train environment.

In Genoa, Piano and his team worked closely with the Italian curtain walling manufacturer Buiatti SpA to produce a standard shell for the stations based upon a curved steel framework, cross-bracing and glazing.[2] As some of the stations are below ground and others above (this is because Genoa Underground is based partly upon existing railway track, some of which was elevated), the design team sought the same standardizing enclosure for all stations. A curved glass enclosure based upon an elliptical section houses platforms and track, while non-standard ticket and concourse areas join the standard parts to the different site contexts encountered at the various locations. The elliptical tube is therefore a recurring element at each station, with glass that changes colour and tint to suit conditions. For the manufacturer the elliptical tube can be manufactured to a high specification and extended in different bay lengths to suit different station conditions.

The station tube is not a sealed envelope but one that breathes. The different sections of glass overlap each other with an air space between. The glass roof is rather more a rainscreen than a rigid controller of the interior environment. The steel structure, though its main function is to support the glazed roof, provides the means of suspending other services and signs.

The Genoa Underground is an architect-driven (rather than engineer-driven) approach to railway station design. The coherence and clarity of the structural frames, plus the luminosity of the glazed enclosure, give the underground system the disciplined order sought by Piano. Every other component, from station seats to signage, exists within the visual language imposed by the architect. Bearing in mind the mixture of new and existing tunnels that were adapted for the underground, the catalogue of parts effectively marries together the system.

The station tubes, nearly 7 m across, consist of a pair of platforms at the perimeter with two parallel tracks in the centre. Each track sits beneath a line of rooflights, which provide the ventilation and smoke extract system in the event of a fire. Artificial lighting exploits the curve of the enclosure at platform seating level by spreading light along the inner surface of the tunnel from uplighters. Alternate bays of the structural frame are open to views across the city at stations above ground; the other bays are used for signage and commercial advertising. Below ground, the stations use the same structural system but the clear glazing is replaced by stainless steel panels.

Berlin U5 Bahnhof line

In 1992 the Richard Rogers Partnership won a limited competition to design a prototype station for the Berlin U5 Bahnhof line, which is to be upgraded and extended from Alexanderplatz in East Berlin to the greater metropolitan underground network. Subsequently the partnership, working with Berlin architects Collignon Fischotter, has developed the prototype into a detailed design for Rathaus Station, the largest of five new stations planned.

The approach of the Richard Rogers Partnership at the outset was the integration of the underground station into the fabric of the city. This was achieved by seeing the prototype stations as a sequence of spaces or structures

Fig 8.4 Integrating building services into the architecture of internal spaces requires great skill. Here in the Berlin Underground structure, lighting, smoke extraction and mechanical ventilation are well coordinated. Note the glazed pavement lights above to let daylight filter down to the concourse.

above and below ground that linked street life to that of the trains. The stations were not to be entombed in concrete but left as structures below street level, open to the sky and, where roofed, covered in glazed pavements. By placing the station roof at street level the stations were to be perceived as decks, landscaped ramps and sunlit staircases. As a result the platforms are open to natural light, which enters the subterranean areas by a combination of

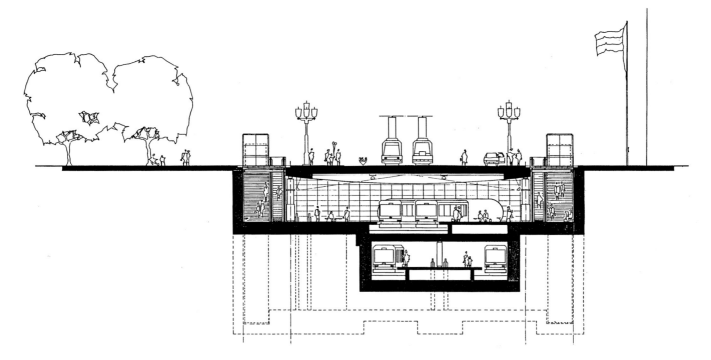

8.5 Section through Rathaus underground station on Berlin U5 Bahnhof Line. Architects: Richard Rogers Partnership.

lighting slots, elliptical skylights, glazed pavements and light bounced off vertical walls.

Daylight is used to associate the world of underground stations with that of the city they serve. The connection with street life is to be achieved by day and night. Where daylight enters the stations during the day, artificial light from the illuminated platforms will animate the city at night. This two-way manipulation of light is a departure from the arrangement at most underground stations.

At the Rathaus Station two lines connect (U5 and U3) at a shallow curve and occupying different levels. In addition, a street-based tram system runs at ground level. The Richard Rogers Partnership has placed the three levels of transport on separate decks with a station roof that floats over the central area surrounded by glazed pavement panels. The section adopted allows daylight to enter the middle level, where ticket offices are located. As the street-level deck supports the double tram lines the structure is of large dimensions, and this gives scale and presence to the station interior. Interior lighting in the form of uplighters highlights the structure, much as the shafts of natural light entering through the glass pavement are used to express the station's perimeter walls.

A large tree-planted square is used to help identify the location of the underground station within the busy cityscape of this part of Berlin. A fan of trees focus upon the station entrances on one side, and a large nineteenth-century warehouse frames the square on the other. These civic elements provide the backcloth for elegant glazed structures and lowered decks, which take the passengers into the station. Signage is relatively understated: instead light and architectural gestures signal the presence of the new station.

Hammersmith Station, London

Masterplanned by EPR architects, the new Hammersmith Station in West London is an example where retail and office development helped fund the construction of a major new underground railway station. Known as Centre West, the site is a tight urban island surrounded by busy roads, including the Hammersmith Flyover with a direct link via the A4 to the M4 motorway. The site beneath which the upgraded and realigned station sits is 1.6 ha in area, and besides being the point where nine roads converge is where 19 London bus routes terminate.[3] Various schemes had in the past been put forward for the redevelopment of the island site (including proposals by Norman Foster and Partners in 1978 and Terry Farrell in 1984), but they foundered either because of cost or because of lack of political support from the local council.

The scheme, costing nearly £90 million for Anglo-Dutch developer Bredero, provides a measure of planning gain in the form of new community facilities and greatly improved quality of access to rail and bus facilities. Like the Foster scheme it consists largely of a perimeter wall of offices enclosing a central raised deck containing bus station and below 40 shops, nursery, fitness centre, council information office and a new Hammersmith Station for London Underground. Both station and shopping arcade are angled so that they cross the block in the form of powerful diagonals. This enhances the sense of drama where the diagonal

8.6 Hammersmith Station. Architects: EPR with Minale, Tattersfield and Partners Ltd.

railway cutting and glazed roofs meet the square edges of the block.

Two aspects of the project are unusual: first, the office element has been used to subsidize the construction of improved public transport facilities; and second, the underground and bus stations are fully integrated. By placing the bus station on the first floor, the underground station has been effectively raised so that it is capable of being lit by natural means. The station is not underground but in a semi-basement open to the sky. This arrangement allows the noise problem to be effectively dealt with without full tunnelling.

Escalators and lifts link the bus station downwards to the main shopping mall, which exists at the level of the new underground station. Hence both station and shops enjoy natural light, which filters through via elegantly glazed canopies. With 100 000 passengers a day expected to use the bus and train station[4] (and hence also the shops), the finishes are of higher quality than usual. The materials of the shopping arcade — marble, terrazzo, stainless steel and painted tubular steelwork — are taken into the station, thereby helping to blend public and private elements. From the surrounding perimeter of 50 000 m^2 of offices (at the time of writing only half of which have been constructed) the view over the station and shops is not one of drab flat roofs but of glazed and planted decks, and courts filled with life.

The shopping mall is arranged so that everybody using the underground or bus station needs to pass through it. Similar in some respects to the arrangement of Canary Wharf, the effect of the redevelopment is to create the appearance of 'instant city' with an air of benevolence on behalf of the developers. Certain of the shop units have been reserved for public service use (such as a post office), and the street facades have been generated to allow public entrances into the block to be readily identified.

CrossRail, London

The development of fresh tunnelling techniques, such as the New Austrian Tunnelling Method, have greatly expanded the opportunities for architectural expression in the design of underground stations. Breakthroughs in the technology of tunnelling have led to larger tunnels becoming more economically viable, and more interesting shapes than the standard circular bore being available. Whereas much of the London Underground is based upon station tunnels 5 or 6 m in diameter, the new tunnels are 9 or 10 m across and in a variety of profiles. Elliptical and egg-shaped tunnels placed horizontally or vertically give greater structural expression than the traditional circular bore. The new shapes also open up fresh possibilities in the deliberate manipulation of light along the inner surfaces of tunnels. These characteristics are exploited particularly in the CrossRail scheme of five new stations in central London planned to link existing rail systems to the east and west of the capital.

Although the Parliamentary Bill to construct CrossRail has yet (in 1995) to be approved, the new stations and connecting track are at an advanced stage of design. Railway systems are particularly prone to political indecision, and rather than delay the project, the promoters of CrossRail (principally British Rail's Network SouthEast and London Underground) have pushed ahead with engineering and station design. David Taylor, coordinating architect for CrossRail, believes that preparation of the project should be undertaken to the level whereby contracts can be let as soon as government approval is given. This saves on the normal two-year or so time delay between project go-ahead and construction beginning on site. Taylor has also departed from precedent by appointing teams of architects three months before engineers were brought in.[5] This was to encourage a fresh approach to station design and to ensure that architectural values rather than engineering priorities were paramount.

Building Design Partnership worked with Ralph Erskine in the development of the concept design, which other teams of architects, including Michael Hopkins and Partners, Allies and Morrison, Terry Farrell and Partners, and Fitzroy Robinson and Partners, have developed in detail at particular locations. BDP has remained as platform architect for all of the CrossRail stations except Paddington (where Alsop and Stormer have designed both ticket halls and platforms), with appointed architects being responsible for concourses and ticket halls. The arrangement, though complex, shares characteristics with the Jubilee Line Extension in the balance between what Taylor calls a 'consistent CrossRail image'[6] and the local identity of individual stations.

The design philosophy overall was based upon 'clarity, ease of orientation and accessibility for all'.[7] BDP was keen to use an 'open spatial form which offset the claustrophobia of being underground'.[8] This is achieved by making where possible direct connection with daylight, by utilizing lofty underground atrium spaces, using reflective walls which direct diffused daylight underground, and exploiting materials whose texture catches the light in interesting ways. Space and light, two qualities all too rare in many underground railway systems, are hence deliberately manipulated to provide the necessary sense of orientation and progressional clarity.

At the materials level, BDP proposed the use in concourse areas of textured ceramic wall tiles, which they contend give a warmer and friendlier atmosphere than traditional finishes. Platform and concourse floors are to be in stone or granite slabs, with timber seating providing a further reference to natural finishes. Ceramic tiles, stone and timber form the main palette of materials, which are to be set against more high-tech finishes used in the moveable parts (lifts, escalators, platform screens, etc.). Steel, glass and cast bronze will thus provide a pleasant contrast and help guide passengers to the circulation routes without the need for excessive signing. As BDP is acting as concept designer, product designer, acoustics and lighting designer (as well as structural engineer), the practice is in a position to coordinate a wide range of elements normally handled by different consultants. The success of the approach depends upon an effective relationship in three directions — between BDP, the appointed architects for each station, and Taylor and his staff at CrossRail. Although only five new stations are planned there promises to be greater consistency than in the Jubilee Line Extension, where the decision was made not to appoint a single design firm to coordinate the stations.

Both CrossRail and JLE introduce to the UK for the first time the separation of platform from train via full-height glazed screens. Health and safety reservations over the toxicity of brake dust and other pollutants from trains are leading to the progressive introduction of physical separation between waiting passenger and train within the confined space of underground railways. The curved glazed screens, which open when a train stops, slide upwards into a space above the platform roof. The effect of the screen is to produce a sense that the platform is a 'room', rather like the waiting lounge at an airport. It will be physically and acoustically sealed, thereby preventing train noise and dust from reaching not just the platform area but also the main concourse and ticket zones. Environmental standards, amenity and a sense of space have been combined in what CrossRail claims is a new generation of underground stations.

Above ground, new station entrances are required, and fresh connections need to be made with existing railway lines both above and below ground. The five new stations (Paddington, Bond Street, Tottenham Court Road, Farringdon and Liverpool Street) have all had to accommodate the geometries and layout of earlier parts of the railway system. The problem of upgrading railways and insinuating new lines and stations into older systems is far more complex than building afresh. This is why the five stations and relatively short length of new subway line are costing about £2 billion. Opportunities have been taken above ground to link new station entrances into existing shopping areas (as at Bond Street Station, designed by Allies and Morrison), or to exploit the air rights over new stations (as in commercial development at Moorgate by Bennetts Associates, with direct links into the new CrossRail Station at Liverpool Street). Identifying and sketching out the potential for site development has allowed those who are funding CrossRail to seek contributions from property developers. The Bennetts scheme, in particular, shows the complexity of site conditions below ground with which the new Moorgate building, proposed as an island development surrounded by streets, has to contend. The role of station architects is to prepare feasibility studies of development potential above ground as well as to design new station entrances to serve CrossRail.

References

1. Alan Brookes, 'Transit systems: Genoa', *Architects' Journal*, 8 April 1992. p. 39.
2. *Ibid*.
3. David Rock, 'Urbanism full circle: EPR's Centre West at Hammersmith', *Architecture Today*, June 1994, pp. 16–18.
4. *Ibid*.
5. Pamela Buxton, 'East–west transfer', *Building Design*, 22 October 1993, p.10.
6. *Ibid*.
7. Building Design Partnership Press Release, *CrossRail, London,* no date, circa 1993.
8. *Ibid*.

Light rail

Bangkok transit system

The elevated, street-based mass transit system currently under construction in Bangkok is typical of the innovative approach to light rail transportation in the Pacific rim. Designed by the UK practice of Building Design Partnership (BDP) for contractors Italian Thai, it consists of 25 stations along a 15 km route. In a country dominated by private transport and the ethics of the market place, the Bangkok authorities opted for a light rail system using the air rights above existing streets. No compulsory purchase powers were used to acquire property in this city of 10 million inhabitants, thereby easing public or private objections to the construction of the railway. The BDP scheme is in fact the most advanced of three new elevated railways proposed for Bangkok to be constructed over a 30-year period.

Wide, main streets were chosen for the route linking suburbs to the city centre. The design consists of a concrete superstructure carrying a steel frame two storeys high, which supports trains and platform canopies on the upper deck, and ticket offices and toilets on the lower. Steel was chosen for the upper levels because it is light, flexible and can be fabricated off site to high standards. Where concrete is used, the material is precast using segmental construction. In a total contract time of 42 months (from design to construction and operation), speed of erection of the basic structural framework was an important consideration.

Stations are positioned at intervals of about 600 m, and being elevated at a height of 8 m they stand out as landmarks in the street. BDP has exploited the structure of stations, particularly the platform canopies, to achieve a distinctive appearance. As each station abides by a similar language of design and uses repeating elements of construction, there is an unusual level of consistency between the stations. The same is true of the elevated track, which adopts a repeating application of shaped concrete columns and cantilevered deck.

Concrete, steel, glass and curved canopies make up the main architectural elements of the stations. Two types of station exist: typical stations along the length of the line and the central station, which connects at different levels both loops of the Bangkok mass transit system. Most

9.1 Sheffield Supertram.

165

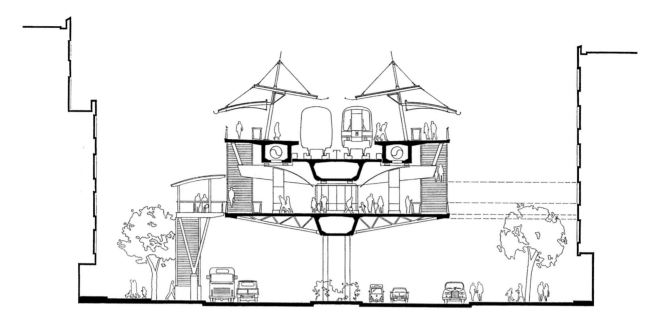

9.2 Bangkok street-based high-level light rail system. Notice the possibility of a direct link into adjoining building. (See also p. 54, Fig. 2.48.) Architects: Building Design Partnership.

stations are supported by a line of single columns placed in the centre of a dual carriageway, thereby avoiding street-based underground services, which tend to be at the edge of the road. The columns support a double cantilever spanning 28 m housing ticket offices on the lower level with a further deck above supporting the trains with platforms on either side. Above the platforms, asymmetrical canopies provide shelter from rain and sun in a fashion that not only animates the design but provides an interesting roofscape for those viewing the station from adjoining high-rise buildings. Passengers reach the stations by external lifts and walkways, which rise up, without doglegs, directly from the pavements. Struts, cables, angled steelwork and smooth concrete provide a simple language of structural systems, which unify a degree of local variation at each station.

The central station is an altogether grander affair, capable of accommodating 90 000 passengers an hour at peak times (this is twice the expected capacity of London's CrossRail). The railway tracks are now on two levels, placed on the periphery of the station with a bank of escalators providing access through the centre. Instead of central columns this station is supported by a large and dramatic concrete portal. Within the arch of the portal a deck of circulation space is provided, housing ticket offices and a wide concourse. Where the lesser stations are two storeys high, the main station is three storeys with a continuous canopy over. Most exciting, at least as far as the experience of travel is concerned, is the placing of the trains to the outside of the structural frame. This allows passengers to view the cityscape as if travelling along the face of a cliff.

Remarkably, all of the engineering and architecture of the system exists within the street space of central Bangkok. Passengers are not placed underground as is usual in new urban railways (such as the Jubilee Line Extension in London) but are allowed to share the experience of city travel with car and bus travellers. Moreover, as the mass transit system is placed high above city streets, passengers will not have to suffer the pollution of those nearer the ground. Also, the exploitation of air rights above the ground by the transit authority opens up the commercial potential of land near the stations in a fashion whereby buildings and station can connect directly at high level.[1] These advantages begin to compensate for the greater cost of elevated rail systems compared with underground systems. There is also one further advantage: the high-level railway structure and its dramatic stations will add to Bangkok's reputation as a city that values good new design, thereby improving its international competitiveness, especially in the field of urban tourism.

Elevated railways are generally more expensive than underground systems, though there may be local conditions that reverse this. Poor ground for construction (waterlogged or unstable) makes tunnelling both hazardous and expensive. Also, earthquake risk favours building above ground to building below. In Bangkok, the initial proposal was to construct the railway beneath the roads, until it was discovered that piles 60 m long were needed.[2] Here the balances, aesthetic as well as practical, favoured street-based elevated railways. The new railway, planned to open in 1998, is seen as an important measure of urban quality, and will help to mesh together the disjointed landscape of buildings above ground.

Docklands Light Railway: Phase 1

Designed in 1984 by Arup Associates as the UK's first light rail project, the Docklands Light Railway (DLR) design

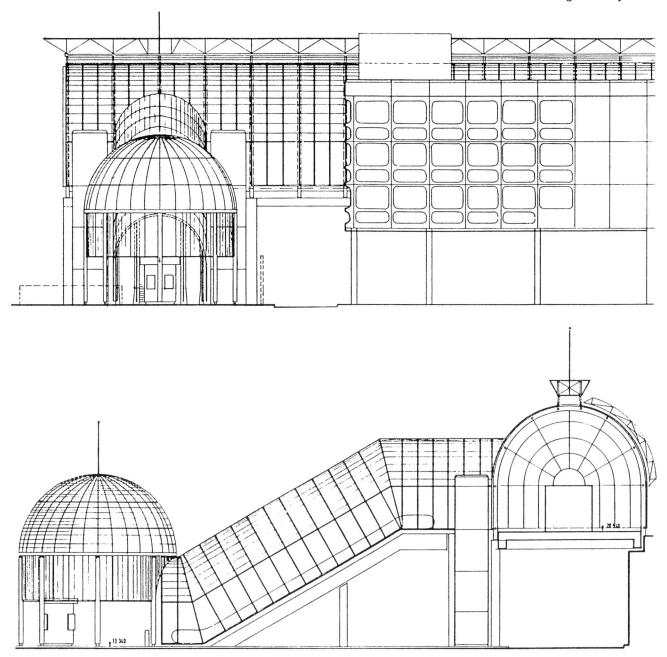

9.3 Docklands Light Railway, Phase 1. Design for Island Gardens Station. Architects: Arup Associates.

consisted initially of visual guidelines and a language of materials for a package dealer to refine and construct.[3] The project marked a shift in UK transport provision, from traditional design, tender and construction, to the involvement of the contractor nearer the beginning of the process. The railway line, utilizing a mixture of redundant British Rail embankments and viaducts and new high-level track built above the old dock basins in this part of East London, was to be 14 km long (Tower Hill to Limehouse and West India Dock) with an extension of 10 km to Beckton (eventually constructed in 1994). Arup Associates with Pentagram Design evolved a concept for the DLR that established aesthetic rules and standards, a specification for materials and assem-

blies, and guidelines for signage, etc. It was a design guide, rather than design drawings, though drawings formed a part of the package.

The principles established in Arup's brief were to design a light railway system within the bounds of known technology, which meant mainly German and French expertise. The UK's experience of light rail was negligible, as British governments after the Second World War had invested very little in innovative transport industries. Arup Associates were instructed to put reliability and value for money before experimentation,[4] and sadly it shows in the finished product. Within these constraints the architects' design guide proposed:

9.4 Docklands Light Railway, Phase 2. Architects: Ahrends, Burton and Koralek.

- a high-quality image with a consistent theme;
- robust construction, which would resist vandalism and reduce maintenance costs;
- consistency between the design of stations and that of rolling stock and graphics.

As the DLR was to be mainly elevated above water and rooftops its impact upon the perception of regeneration in London Docklands was rightly considered important. The design teams wanted a high-quality image, and one that was consistently relayed across the open and disjointed townscape of this part of London. To achieve this, Arup Associates proposed a 'kit of parts', which guaranteed the standard of the basic installation and provided the means for subsequent upgrading. The main elements were to be painted steel, simple curved glass canopies and blue engineering brick walls. Stations were to be unmanned, with tickets bought at ground level and platforms accessed via external steps and a lift for disabled travellers. Platforms were to be 30 m long but capable of being extended to twice this length later. Simple shelters were provided at platform level but no other passenger facilities except a voice announcement system and folding seats. It was not inten-

ded to make a feature of special stations (such as Canary Wharf), as Arup believed that the concept for the whole should override the needs of specific locations. The principle was revised under pressure from developers.

The signage, colour scheme for stations and graphics were evolved by Pentagram, who adopted London Transport's tradition of strong yet simple colours and lettering style. The strident blue, red, black and white of DLR livery was the result of merging the imagery of London Underground with blue, which was intended to represent the water of London Docklands.[5] Pentagram was responsible also for ensuring that the motifs of the station graphics appeared on tickets and in the trains as well.

DLR represents a search for unity, strong image and design consistency. It was an ideal subsequently compromised by the powerful interest of developers, who saw the stations serving their landholdings as part of their estate, with the connotations of image that this entails. The free-market aesthetics of the LDDC also led to the abandonment of most of Arup's principles when the DLR was expanded to Beckton nearly a decade later. One of the problems with the first phase of the DLR is that the planning freedoms exercised by developers (mainly as a consequence of the Enterprise Zone) have allowed them to obscure the location of stations by massive buildings, some of which (as at Tower Hill) almost bridge over the station.

Docklands Light Railway: Phase 2

The extension of the Docklands Light Railway (DLR) was opened in March 1994 at a cost of £280 million. Designed by Ahrends, Burton and Koralek (ABK), it consists of ten new stations from Canary Wharf to Beckton, a distance of 8 km. As in the earlier phase designed by Arup Associates, ABK evolved a kit of parts to accommodate different station types and different context conditions. Like Phase 1, the extension also preserves a high degree of station transparency, a sense of being engineered rather than built, and the feeling of being a light not a heavy railway.

The design revolves around what Peter Ahrends calls 'flexible standardization'.[6] By this he means a standard capable of a variety of applications at different locations, and based upon a set of components able to be readily reproduced. Each station applies the same design language (openness, visibility, structural expression) and a similar kit of parts (cantilevered station canopies, elegant steel structural members based upon tubular sections, vitreous enamelled steel panels). The design also separates primary and secondary elements (structure from cladding, enclosed elements from open ones), thereby giving the stations architectural interest.

Each station consists of three main elements: the platform areas, the lightweight canopies, and the means of vertical circulation (staircases, lifts and escalators). Each is distinguished architecturally rather than combined into a single unified building. The separation guides passengers to the main parts and provides an element of design panache lacking from much of Phase 1.

Different station types from island to viaduct and ground-level stations are accommodated within this functional and aesthetic language. It gives the DLR a pleasant air of consistency in contrast to the disjointed landscapes of East London it serves. Part of ABK's brief was also to form urban connections with surrounding development by identifying possible links. The stitching of the stations into areas presenting undergoing physical reconstruction has allowed the architects to propose squares, walkways and building development at the perimeter of the stations.

Sheffield Supertram

Costing £250 million the Sheffield Supertram was, in 1994, the UK's largest investment in the current renaissance of mainly street-based tram systems. Built entirely from scratch (unlike the Docklands Light Railway, which utilized extensive lengths of existing British Rail lines), the Supertram consists of a 25 km route served by 50 tram stops. It runs from the Sheffield city centre, where the tracks are laid within existing streets, to Mosborough to the south and Hillsborough to the north. Away from the centre the new tram lines are segregated from street traffic and utilize much redundant inner-city land around former industrial areas. Promoted in the mid 1980s by South Yorkshire Passenger Transport Authority (SYPTA) as a means of easing city-

centre traffic congestion and as a catalyst for urban regeneration, it is based upon linked tramcars, each capable of carrying 250 people.

Funded mainly by the UK central government (which provided £200 million under section 56 of the Transport Act 1968) and with contributions from the private sector (such as the owner of the large shopping centre at Meadowhall) and Sheffield City Council, the work was undertaken via a design-and-build contract by Balfour Beatty. The specification provided by SYPTA sought a high-tech look for the stations, rolling stock, bridges and track; ready access for people with impaired mobility; user friendliness for the elderly and parents with small children; vandal-free materials; and design for safety. As such the tram and tram stops share a common livery of materials (mainly steel, glass and brick paviors) and colours (grey, silver, blue and white).

The tram-stops are designed so that platform level and tram-sill level are at the same height. This has obvious advantages for wheelchair and pushchair users. The platforms themselves are 355 mm (14 in) above rail height, and this means that tram-stops are generally this height above surrounding ground level. The difference in height is negotiated by short ramps.

Most tram-stops have curved steel and glass (or polycarbonate) shelters, bright lighting, visible station signing, and ticket facilities. In the town centre they stand in the street space as lightweight pavilions contrasting pleasantly with the sandstone architecture of Sheffield. In the inner suburbs the tram-stops are beacons of hope and modernity in areas often derelict and degraded. The trams themselves, provided by Siemens of Germany, are nearly 35 m long and 2650 mm wide. They consist of two parts: the central section is raised and seated for longer-distance travellers, while the end sections at sill level are more open for those taking shorter journeys. To reduce noise and vibration the trams run on track that is fixed in slots with flexible grout rather than mechanical fastenings.[7]

The design parameters of the track permit gradients of up to 10%, horizontal curve radii down to 25 m and vertical curve radii of 165 m. These dimensions allow the hilliness of Sheffield to be accommodated, and permit existing streets to be utilized without the demolition of buildings. As the trams are powered by overhead wires, the poles and cantilever supports are an important element in the visual impact of the system. Outside the central areas, single poles between the two tram tracks support the overhead lines, which provide power to the trams via a typical trolley bus system. In the city centre, for amenity reasons, the overhead power supply is suspended from buildings or more widely spaced poles. Where listed buildings occur, the policy was one of avoiding the obstruction of views by placing poles further along the street.

It remains to be seen whether Sheffield's investment in Supertram relieves traffic congestion, reduces city centre pollution and aids the regeneration of derelict areas as its promoters contended. Putting aside the environmental and planning arguments, the system brings to the UK a conti-nental air of sophisticated street-based travel in an age dominated elsewhere by the squalor of deregulated bus services.

References

1. *Bangkok Transit System*, Building Design Partnership, London, brochure dated April 1995.
2. Personal communication with Tony McGuirk of BDP, 1 May 1995.
3. Patrick Hannay, 'Docklands' guiding light', *Architects' Journal*, 8 August 1984, p. 23.
4. *Ibid.*
5. *Ibid.*, p. 24.
6. Ruth Slavid, 'ABK's kit of parts', *Architects' Journal*, 27 April 1994, p. 13.
7. Michael Harris, 'Sheffield Supertram', *Modern Railways*, May 1994, p. 282.

Part three

Reflections

The station of the future: ideas and perspectives

CHAPTER 10

What is a station?

It is clear that the function of the station as a distinctive building type is changing. The station is no longer dedicated to travel alone: it is a place in its own right, with retail, social and cultural facilities enclosed within its shell. As the function of the station is broadened, so too are the collection of spaces and structures that constitute its parts. Where once the station was entirely a transitional space through which travellers passed en route to the train, now it has become another urban venue worthy of a visit in its own right. The station is where city dwellers can buy groceries, use a bank, get a haircut or change money. It is a civic gathering space, where music can be heard, where transit information is dispensed, and where the drama of urban life can be witnessed in full flow.

As the clarity of the function of the station is blurred, its form has become more complex. With hotels, shops and social facilities constructed as loosely attached elements, the station has evolved into a small version of the city. Like airports, larger stations are satellites within the gravitational pull of the city but independent and self-contained structures. While this has always been the case for mainline termini, now medium-sized stations are evolving into a cross between shopping malls, bridges, squares and traditional stations. The hybrid animal that results from these fusions of function represents a new invigorated breed of transport architecture.

Where stations were once open to ticket holders only, today they are public structures where all are free to pass, often right up to the point of the train seat. Being sheltered and animated by human life and that of the trains, they attract people who have no ambition towards travel. Like art galleries, stations have become places to watch people and to be seen. The cross-flows of different types of people and the islands of life around shops and cafes make stations places to visit. Where a station bridge is involved, this can become a focus for non-travelling urban tourists. The spectacle of travel, expressed both in the mechanical forms of trains and in the human drama of rushing people, is an entertainment to many. Stations are part of the world of leisure: a resort for the urban tourist, the shopper and the

10.1 The renaissance of the railway has led to a new generation of stations and station types. This building, at Manchester Airport Station, provides a worthy landmark at a busy airport, based upon elegant roof canopies. Architects: Austin-Smith: Lord.

173

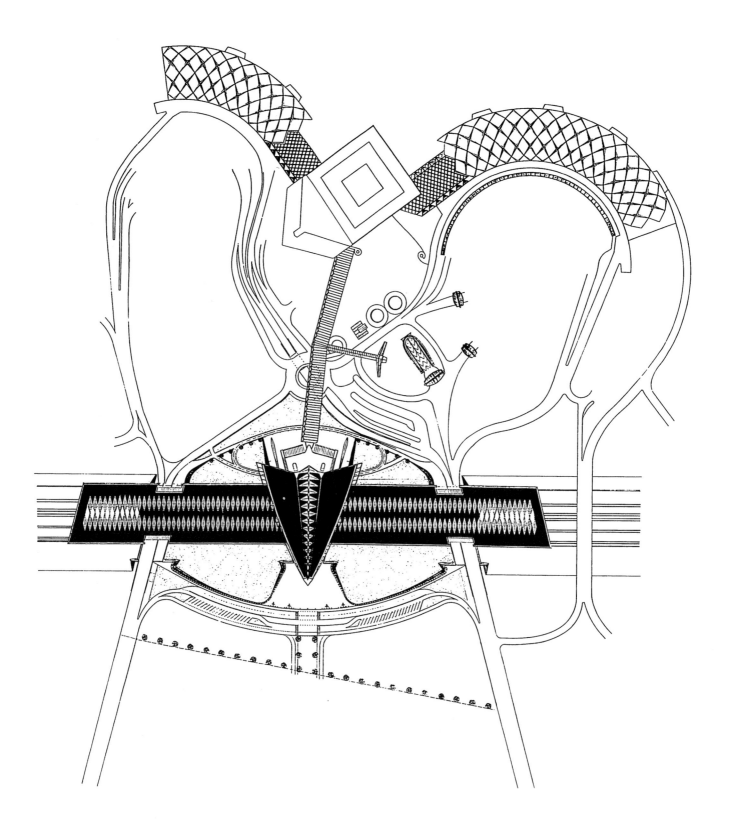

10.2 More than most designers, Santiago Calatrava has made a spectacle out of modern railway stations. His buildings, as here at Lyon-Satolas Station, are visited by those with no intention of travelling.

10.3 Canary Wharf Station on the Jubilee Line Extension. Architects: Sir Norman Foster and Partners.

unemployed. As long as stations remain free enclosures containing the tension and excitement of movement they will draw people excluded from other areas of the city. As access to modern urban land becomes increasingly restricted, the public role of stations takes on greater social meaning. In spite of the privatization of railways the real estate of railway companies expressed in the stations has remained within the public arena.

Railway stations are fast following in the footsteps of airports. Revenue at some stations is now greater from non-railway activities, such as shops and cafes, than from the sale of floorspace to train operators. Stations too, having converted their older hotels to offices, are now building new ones over the tracks or on land nearby. As travel becomes more complex, involving often greater distances, the need for support of various kinds increases. This has traditionally involved convenience goods, but the trend is towards integrated travel, hotel and entertainment facilities. In the new travel matrix the station is the hub of a system, not an end in itself.

The station as urban element

Railway lines and stations have traditionally divided towns. The large discrete neighbourhoods separated by the tracks of railways have been crossed only by bridges, tunnels and the stations themselves. The station is, therefore, a form of bridge – a connection between parcels of cityscape. Many modern railway architects have designed the station as an urban link; the station as 'bridge' is a common modern interpretation of the type.

If the role of the station is to stitch together the city divided by the railway tracks, the main elements of the station can be seen in different ways. The roof of the station can, for instance, be seen as a square – a public deck that people can use to cross a physically divided city. Similarly, a footbridge crossing the railway lines to facilitate movement from one platform to another can be seen as a public bridge crossing not just individual tracks but all of the railway lines and their embankments. Hence the bridge becomes a civic element rather than merely part of the railway station. This

10.3 Canary Wharf Station on the Jubilee Line Extension. Architects: Sir Norman Foster and Partners.

extra function of the bridge could be used to justify its bigger dimensions or the greater prowess employed in its engineering.

The station is both a place of transition and a destination in its own right. Stations are points of departure, urban bridges and town squares. The best-designed stations are those that accept the ambiguity of function, seeking in the distribution and layout of parts to relay the message that stations are different things to different people. Meeting

10.4 Platform canopy at Sloterdijk Station, Amsterdam by Holland Railconsult.

10.5 Good design helps to ease the frustration of missing a train. Amsterdam Leylaan Station, designed by Holland Railconsult.

primary and secondary parameters of programme within tight cost budgets is often the greatest challenge.

The station as structure

Of all modern building types, stations engage more than most in questions of movement and structure. Unlike airports, where the movement of aircraft is often some way removed, at stations trains pass through the centre of the building. This gives them great immediacy and drama. As trains are also moving through at speed and stopping, there are different realities of movement. In parallel with the speed of trains is the slower pace of movement by people. Train and people movement within the same overall structure establish two complementary rhythms. Designers have to accommodate both at a practical and perceptual level. One way in which this can be achieved is by the use of architectural structure that allows the rhythms and pace of movement to be readily understood.

The role of columns, beams and panels is to help travellers read the travel in which they are engaged. The pace of platform columns passing by outside the train window helps to establish the speed of the train in the mind of the passenger. The engineer may see the column as merely a means of supporting the station canopy, but the designer exploits the same column as a mobility guide-post. Where the column is placed in space, its proportions and angle are all part of the communication of the drama of movement. Likewise, the pace of shadow lines and the patterns of light and shade are part of the aesthetic experience of speed. The architecture of stations accepts that the main structural elements define routes, axes and speed.

10.6 Modern stations are a fusion of architectural, engineering and industrial design; their creation requires considerable inter-professional cooperation. Lille-Europe Station. Architect: Rem Koolhaas with Jean-Marie Duthilleul.

10.7 New train design and new stations go hand in hand. Waterloo International.

Expressing the sensual possibilities of structure rather than the loadbearing ones has been a feature of recent railway architecture, particularly in the hands of Renzo Piano and Santiago Calatrava. Curved and angled structural members, often employed with cable-held ties, give richness and complexity to station architecture. There is usually a clear distinction between members held in tension and members held in compression. Expressing how structure works, how the laws of gravity operate when subject to wind loads or asymmetrical column layouts (which often follow from the essential asymmetry of station design), leads to more interesting stations than if the engineering design is more understated. Expressing rather than suppressing the structural engineering aspects of station design provides visual richness, even excitement, which can only benefit jaded travellers. The sources of complexity and parti-

cularity (rather than standardization and orthodoxy) are more likely to be found in new solutions to the structural engineering and construction of stations than in other fields of station design.

Stations are plays of structural forces held in tension and compression. Usually the tensional members are lost to view, buried within the details of suspended ceilings or panel construction. The delicacy of the lines of tension (expressed as slender ties) contrasted with the great heavy weights of compression (expressed as plump columns) allows the laws of physics to be understood by the public. Waterloo International and Rotterdam Blaak are prime examples. As stations are public places, it seems reasonable to engage in public issues, even at the level of engineering design.

The structure of stations – train sheds, platform canopies and concourses – provides opportunities for expression at both broad and detailed levels. Whereas much of the perception of movement is gained from the view out of the train window, the perception of being stationary is gained waiting on the platform. Structure has therefore to address two scales – the motionary and motionless. Each scale has specific conditions: in movement, rhythmic patterns are important; when still, the detail and assembly of parts has our attention. Designers have to evolve station structures that entertain the eye and challenge the curiosity at two levels of movement. The frustration of waiting for a train means that details normally overlooked need to capture our attention as a means of allaying boredom. This may simply consist of specifying a material such as a metallic sheet that changes its appearance in the sun. Using light, particularly sunlight, to help define the passage of time, mixed with structural solutions that exploit the two main movement levels, can help to make stations special places.

The structure and construction of stations is part of their essential texture. The systems of movement in stations, the dynamics of vertical and lateral loading, and the sequences of function, give stations their distinctive character and strength. The prime task of station architects is to express these features as boldly as possible, thereby ensuring that stations are immediately recognizable structures in spite of the blurring of the functional distinctiveness of the station as a building type.

The station as a fusion of design skills

Stations are places where the worlds of architecture, engineering and industrial design coalesce. From building to train design, a wide range of professional skills cooperate to make the station a unique place. Although the various disciplines of design exist throughout the modern world, at railway stations they display particular focus. Much has been made already of the pivotal role of the structural engineer in the evolution of stations of distinctive form; but the mechanical and civil engineer play important parts at the macro-level, and the graphic, product and textile designers at the micro-level.

Stations are the hub of design skills within the railway system. Whereas much design effort goes into the development of trains, at the station the railway carriages and locomotive exist as just another element within a totally designed and engineered world. Design – used here to embrace a broad spectrum of engineering, product and building design elements – needs to reflect the values and image aspirations of the modern railway age. There is often a correspondence between the precisely engineered environment of the trains and that of the station. The interior of carriages is a precision world of high-tech assemblies, modern fabric designs, finely tuned lighting and acoustics, and good functional layout. Increasingly, these values and often the materials themselves find their way from trains to stations. In the work of designers such as Alan Brookes Associates the details of booking halls allude directly to those inside the trains or even on the locomotives. In some underground railway stations, such as Norman Foster's designs in Bilbao, the precision engineering of trains and their lighting finds a direct parallel in the shaping, finishes and illumination of the platform areas.

If train and stations are increasingly united as part of an overall designed environment, the same is true at the level of many details. The colours of trains and of platforms shares a common livery (as at the Docklands Light Railway); the uniforms of staff and the visual styling of stations and trains is deliberately coordinated (as on the French TGV system and Japanese Railways); and maps, ticket and station signs employ a common currency of graphics through the estate of a single railway company. In parts of the Swedish railway system, the colour of tickets and that of seat upholstery on the trains is unified. Such coordination is to project a single image for the company, and one based upon the value attached to good design. Although design standardization through such complex activities as the operation of trains and stations is not easily achieved, it remains an aspiration for most companies. In this the station architect has a key role to play. As the orchestrator of other professional inputs, the architect sets the overall tenor of taste and language. The example set by the approach to building design needs to influence that of station engineering on the one hand, and interior details on the other. Recent stations in the Netherlands, such as Amsterdam Sloterdijk, aspire to this goal, with every part adhering to the same set of rigorous design principles.

The task of design coordination is a complex one. Various forms of design manual or design guide are employed to ensure that technical and aesthetic standards are met. However, it is easier to prescribe a performance standard for, say, a lighting system than to establish the aesthetic aspirations that should be accommodated. It remains a problem that most design guides for stations deal not with aesthetic issues but with technical ones. A common fault of station design is that of mismatch between the designed parts. Often good station architecture is let down by the poor engineering of track, tunnels and bridges, or attractive station interiors by shoddy shopfronts and graphics installed by retail franchisers. Equally common is the sight of a well-designed platform compromised by poorly selected seats and litter bins.

Much of the problem of lack of design coordination is the result of the processes of time. The lifespan of the different elements that make up stations varies greatly. Stations themselves have a design life of 60 years, yet the interior design will probably be periodically upgraded on a 15-year time scale, the seats every 10 years, and the lighting, graphics and uniforms perhaps more frequently. The different timescales of change mean that what starts as an integrated system quickly breaks down into a mismatch of parts. Nowhere is this more evident than on the London Underground, where the brilliantly coordinated landscape of trains and stations of the 1930s by Pick and Holden has degenerated into the current collage of misfitting elements.

Railway architects come in two kinds: those who work permanently for a railway company and those who are employed to undertake the design of specific stations. Frank Pick was the former and Charles Holden the latter, just as David Taylor of CrossRail and Will Alsop (designing the new Paddington Station) represent their contemporary equivalents. The company architect has the task of establishing the visual and technical standards involved; the appointed architect works within these constraints to evolve a station design. The creative tension between the two is important: it determines the aesthetic balances. Often independent architects working to the same general brief can produce quite startlingly different designs (as on the 15 stations on the Jubilee Line Extension), and this can enhance the experience of travel as long as an overall language is employed. Alternatively, a single architect can directly shape a whole new railway system by designing all the stations to a single recipe (as on the Bangkok Elevated Railway by BDP).

Where design coordination is strong, the correspondence between stations and between stations and trains adds to the pleasure of travel. Unlike airports, where a number of airline companies operate from a single building, the station is usually a place where a single railway company provides all the trains. Larger stations, however, such as London Waterloo or Lille-Europe, have begun to mirror the operational complexity of airports with the variety of trains run by different regional and national operators. Design coordination here is less straightforward, and the best the company architect can achieve is the employment of a similar palette of materials and the avoidance of design competitiveness between the different companies.

The station as architecture and engineering

If stations represent one of the great concentrations of design talent in the modern world, one should not forget the breadth of disciplines involved. One cannot stand at the station without being surrounded by designed goods or engineered members. Not a single surface, detail, colour or texture has not been selected by a designer of one kind or another or shaped by an engineer. Even the computer-generated station audio announcement has been formed by an engineer with an ear to design. Design and engineering are the two principal interactions at stations, yet each is not a sealed activity but one that impinges upon its neighbours. Textile design for instance may shape the visual landscape of a seating area, but the choice of textiles influences the acoustics of the room, and this has repercussions for the placing of announcement speakers. Dialogue between the designers is as important as between the worlds of design and engineering. If stations are the focus of design, they are also a point where traditional views of design and engineering become blurred. Much of the engineering of stations is a question of design just as much as the design of stations is a matter of engineering. The two disciplines (represented traditionally in the clash between the architect-designed station front and the engineer-designed station shed behind) collide more forcibly at stations than in most other building types. It is a collision at different scales: between the large-scale engineering and design of stations at one level, and between the small details of engineering and product design at the other. Within the resolution of these cultural and aesthetic differences lies the essence of good station design. Many of the best stations are ones that have an engineering design

The station of the future

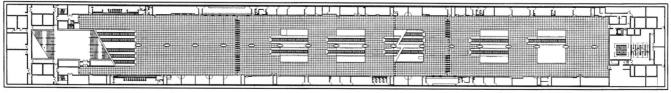

Ticket Hall Plan

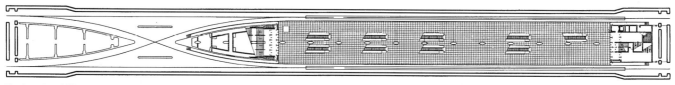

Platform Level Plan

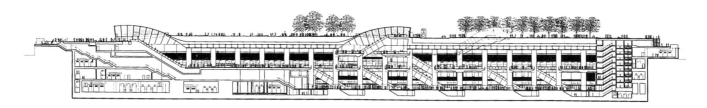

10.8 Plan and section of Canary Wharf Station on the Jubilee Line extension. Many of the world's most prestigious architects are currently engaged upon the design of railway stations. Architects: Sir Norman Foster and Partners.

10.9 As the function of what a station is has become blurred, so too the distinction between inside and outside, and between public and private, has lost its distinctiveness. The increasing complexity of modern stations opens up new architectural opportunities. Rotterdam Blaak. Architect: Harry Reijnders of Holland Railconsult.

edge: where technology is not suppressed but leads to new approaches to railway architecture.

The station as a bridge across the millennia

In presenting stations as a new and invigorated building type it is important that the reasons for the change in status of the railway station are given. Stations have contemporary relevance because they represent the post-industrial phenomenon of buildings with fluid functions and complex meanings. They are part of the transportation web, but they serve equally well as places to shop for leisure items, meet people and buy food. Stations are also bridges that connect neighbourhoods, thereby enhancing their social and cultural value. In addition, stations serve as urban gateways and help to define town centres. Of growing importance is the sense that the station is an expression of sustainability – of shared transport and reduced emissions. For these reasons the modern railway station has emerged

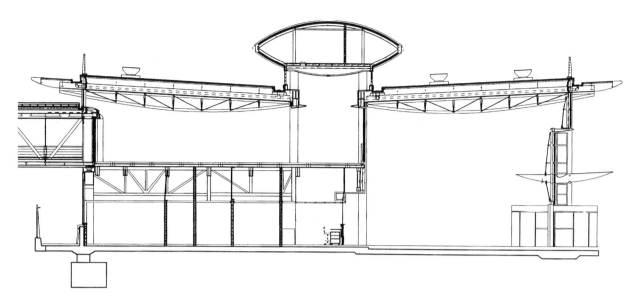

10.10   Ashford International Station concourse. Architect: Nick Derbyshire Design Associates.

as a revitalized and distinctive new building type with particular significance for the twenty-first century.

The modern station, whether expressed in the form of Waterloo International or that of Bilbao Underground, has a distinct typological identity. Stations share characteristics with airports and bus stations, yet they have an individuality and character of their own. This derives from their sense of structure: the rhythmic play of columns and beams that are their anatomy. It derives also from the dynamic relationship between track, trains and people. The station is the point where architecture and engineering interface; the sharpness of this conjuncture is an aesthetic as well as a practical ingredient.

If the station is entering a new age it is partly because some of the best architects in the world are engaged in their design. Calatrava, Piano, Foster, Rogers and Grimshaw have all produced stations that extend the aesthetic and structural possibilities of railway architecture. In the process the new railway age has ushered in the epoch of the universal designer – architects able to create memorable stations anywhere in the world. The station is an important building type within the classless, nationless, global village of the future, and their designers are celebrated in increasingly ubiquitous professional journals.

The internationalism of railways has led to an internationalism of railway architecture. Just as airports have broken down cultural and ethnic barriers so too do railways, and just as airports have become mini-cities in their own right, so too have the larger stations. But where airports depend upon high fossil fuel use, and exploit growth at the perimeter of cities, railways are relatively benign in their effects upon global warming, and act as magnets to help in the renewal of city centres. Stations are an essential element of sustainable development, and combine environmental considerations with social and cultural ones. Their significance for the decades beyond the millennium is partly a result of this confluence of postmodern imperatives. In the new urbanity of the post-industrial age the station, with its democratic open structure, its public spaces inside and out, and its corridors of movement etched upon the face of the city, represents an important civilizing element.

Selected bibliography

Books

Binney, Marcus and Pearce, David (Eds) (1979) *Railway Architecture,* Orbis, London.

Binney, Marcus (1995) *Architecture of Rail: The Way Ahead*, Academy Editions, London.

British Rail (1977) *Railway Architecture: A Glance Back and a Look Forward*, British Railways Board, London.

Cockman, F.G. (1976) *Railway Architecture*, Shire Publications, Aylesbury.

Green, Oliver and Rewse-Davies, Jeremy (1995) *Designing for London: 150 Years of Transport Design*, Lawrence King.

Lawrence, David (1994) *Underground Architecture*, Capital Transport.

Lloyd, David and Insall, Donald (1978) *Railway Station Architecture*, David & Charles, Newton Abbot.

Pevsner, Nikolaus (1976) *A History of Building Types*, Thames & Hudson, London.

Technical manuals

British Rail (1991) *Network SouthEast Design and Briefing Guide.*

British Rail (1993) *InterCity Design Guide.*

Jubilee Line Extension (1993–94) Various design guides and technical manuals.

Journals

Current practice and examples are to be found in various journals, notably the *Architectural Review*, the *Architects' Journal, Building, New Civil Engineer* and *Modern Railways*.

Illustration acknowledgements

The author and publishers would like to thank the following individuals and organizations for permission to reproduce material. We have made every effort to contact and acknowledge copyright holders, but if any errors have been made we would be happy to correct them at a later printing.

Photographers

Crispin Boyle 5.8
Geoffrey Calderbank 1.4, 3.10, 3.13, 4.23, 6.4
Paul Childs 1.7
Peter Cook 5.6
Richard Davies 1, 1.2, 1.3
Michele Denancé 4.28
Peter Durant 4.37
Hans Ekestang 4.31
Paul Mauren 6.1
Tom Miller 1.19, 10.3
Emanuela Minetti 1.11
James Morris 3.23
QA Photos Ltd 5.1
Nigel Young 1.8
Sybolt Voeten 7.4, 7.9 (left)

All other photographs by Brian Edwards

Individuals and organizations

Ahrends Burton & Koralek 2.46, 2.50, 3.14, 4.20, 9.4
Allies and Morrison 4.5
Paul Andreu 2.24, 6.3
Arup Associates 1.21, 5.8, 5.9, 9.3
Austin-Smith:Lord 1.12, 2.21, 2.22, 3.11, 3.15, 3.22, 4.7, 4.13, 4.15, 10.1
Bennetts Associates 4.35
British Rail, Network SouthEast 2.35, 4.39
Brookes Stacey Randall Fursdon 1.17, 2.30, 2.31, 4.19, 4.37
Building Design Partnership 1.5, 2.23, 2.48, 4.2, 4.11, 9.2
Santiago Calatrava 1.14, 2.18, 2.25, 2.26, 4.22, 7.1, 10.2
Nick Derbyshire Design Associates Ltd 7.2, 10.10
Docklands Light Railway 2.51
Ellerbe Becket 4.36
Terry Farrell & Partners 1.9, 2.4, 2.9, 2.19, 3.4, 4.9, 6.5
Foster and Partners 2.10, 2.36, 4.6, 4.24, 4.25, 4.29, 8.2, 10.3, 10.8
GMPTE 1.4, 1.22, 2.47
Philippe Guignard/Paul Andreu 1.13
Nicholas Grimshaw & Partners 1.15, 4.21, 4.40, 5.7
Arne Henriksen 2.33
Hilmer and Sattler with Hermann and Ottl 3.26
Holland Railconsult 2.7, 7.3, 7.5, 7.7
Michael Hopkins & Partners 2.38, 3.6
Jourda & Perraudin 2.6, 2.13, 2.40, 2.43, 4.10, 4.38
Rem Koolhaas 5.2, 5.3
Minale Tattersfield & Partners Ltd 8.1, 8.6
RCAHMS 2.11, 2.17, 4.17
Reich & Hall 4.1
Renzo Piano Building Workshop 1.3, 1.5, 1.6, 1.16, 2.37, 3.12, 3.17, 4.4, 4.12, 4.16, 4.18, 8.3
Richard Rogers Partnership 8.4, 8.5
South Yorkshire Supertram Ltd 2.53, 9.1
Benjamin Thompson Associates 1.6
Troughton McAslan 1.7, 2.32, 2.45, 3.9, 4.14, 4.34
Michael Wilford and Partners 1.1, 2.2, 2.12, 2.15, 3.3, 4.3, 5.5
Weston Williamson 2.16, 2.27, 2.28, 2.29, 2.44, 2.52, 3.16, 4.27

Index

Page numbers appearing in **bold** refer to illustrations, and those in *italics* refer to Tables.